THE SEARCH FOR LEADERSHIP

An Organisational Perspective

William Tate

Published in this first edition in 2009 by:
Triarchy Press
Station Offices
Axminster
Devon. EX13 5PF
United Kingdom

+44 (0)1297 631456
info@triarchypress.com
www.triarchypress.com

A catalogue record for this book is available from the British Library.

Cover photograph by Max Smith.

ISBN: 978-0-9557681-7-0

Contents

Contents

LIST OF FIGURES

List of Tables

List of Tables

ACKNOWLEDGEMENTS

To Nick Georgiades for setting me off down the road marked 'organisation development' (OD). To W. Warner Burke for providing the inspirational spark for this book. To Ian Robson, John Seddon and Eirian Lewis for their work and insights on systems. To Trevor Bentley and Gerard Egan for their work on the organisation's shadow. To Robin Field-Smith for his helpful advice. To Richard Cullen, Barbara Geary, Linda Holbeche, Jon Lamonte, Kate Lye, Karen McKenzie-Irvine, Alison Macfadyen and Chris Talbot for their friendship, interest and support, some over many years. And to my publisher Triarchy Press, notably Imogen Fallows, my patient and expert editor, and Andrew Carey for his judgement and support throughout this latest book project, and earlier in *The Organisational Leadership Audit* in 2003 to which *The Search for Leadership* owes its origins.

A Personal Story

This is a personal story. It changed my professional life in the mid-1980s. At the time I was working inside British Airways, part of the turnaround team that was learning how to put the passenger first, how to privatise a state-owned business, how to make a profit.

I was fortunate to be working alongside W. Warner Burke, the world-renowned American organisation development (OD) consultant. One day Warner addressed a small group of internal HR professionals. He drew four circles in the form of a square at the corners of a large sheet of paper. The circles represented top executives: let's say the chief executive, chief operating officer, HR director and finance director – I cannot remember their titles precisely and it doesn't actually matter. He asked those assembled 'Where is your client?'. His audience responded with a variety of views – some the CEO, some the HR director, etc. 'You are all wrong', Warner said, adding, 'The client is to be found between the executives', and he marked a series of random crosses in the open space.

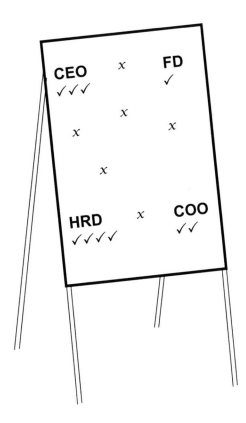

We were puzzled. What did Warner mean? He went on to explain (I paraphrase): 'Think of one's client in terms of where you add most value. You add most value in the spaces'. I don't recall his saying expressly that he was referring to brokering and working on the relationships between key executives, though I took him to mean that. I also think he was referring specifically to the practice of OD consulting, his area of expertise and the new role for HR being developed in the company at that time.

Years later, recalling Warner's lesson, and with much practice and reflection in the intervening years, my own conclusion now goes further. Personal lessons include: 'performance escapes down all manner of gaps' (identify, bridge and fill them). 'What happens at the edge of a job matters more to organisational effectiveness and performance than what happens at the heart of the job' (therefore concentrate on the periphery, interfaces and interactions). 'The competence of individuals isn't the prime factor that determines the *organisation's* performance' (improve the system).

With these wider messages in mind, I now overlay the spaces with a hue that covers the whole sheet. That hue represents the organisation's milieu in which everyone is swimming (and often struggling): its climate, culture, protocols, injunctions, rules and so on.

That's both the starting point and the meaning of this book. When improving leadership in an organisation, don't focus primarily on individual managers, and certainly don't begin your journey there. Instead, put your energy into the spaces and the gaps. Notice the effect of the haze that envelops everyone and everything. And consider the organisation's own leadership agenda and journey as a crucial and positive element of what the organisation surrounds its managers with.

This radical conclusion presents a challenge, as does convincing colleagues that this is where you should devote your energy. It's a controversial message. It's counter-culture: western society is invested in the primacy of the individual. Many don't 'get it', don't want to, or cannot afford to, especially where the skills and fate of identifiable individual leaders are their life's work. There are commercial, reputational and mental barriers to overcome. But be in no doubt: the holy grail of leadership improvement is to be found in what surrounds people in the 'system'. Improve that and you will set leadership free to serve the business.

Thank you, Warner!

William Tate
Prometheus Consulting
United Kingdom
2009

About this Book

I had been feeling frustrated and limited by obsessive discussion about what makes a good leader and how to best develop leaders and leadership. The approach to leadership that lay behind such discussion didn't seem to have much impact on organisations facing deep-seated systemic issues in a complex world. It seemed that a different relationship between leadership and organisations was needed. So at the 2003 annual Windsor Leadership Dialogue I put forward the idea that leadership could more usefully be thought of as a resource to be managed. That way, organisations could get their hands more directly on leadership and consider how to make better use of that resource to meet their needs. Some people 'got' the idea and ran with it. Others didn't and still don't. For many, the shift of thinking about leadership from individual to organisation is troubling. James Krantz (1990) highlights one of these concerns:

> 'Shifting the focus for understanding leadership capacity from the person of the leader alone to the context of leadership is likely to stir up massive anxiety. … This sort of reorientation calls established modes of thinking and relating into question. When responsibility for leadership is distributed around the system, people have to relinquish some of the shared notions they have developed with respect to more hierarchical authority systems.'

At the time I was working on *The Organisational Leadership Audit*, published that same year by Cambridge Strategy Publications. *The Search for Leadership* is its natural successor and is a substantial enhancement of the earlier audit, but the book's foundations are to be found in those shared principles. The mantra used to be 'If you want leadership, look for a leader'. My response is: 'Look inside the organisation first and see what is happening'.

At the book's core is a rationale based on strengthening the connection between leadership, the organisation and their mutually dependent improvement. Leadership journeys are no longer simply for individuals; the organisation is on a leadership journey too. There is a leadership 'industry' out there, one built on rather shaky foundations. But in an increasingly complex world, 'leadership' as currently conceived (and – surprisingly and shockingly – largely left to manage itself) is not delivering the future that customers, employees and other stakeholders need. The time is ripe for a new paradigm for leadership and its improvement, and I attempt to provide that as a contribution to discussion and practice.

With that aim the book offers a journey in organisational literacy – helping readers think deeply about a seriously deep matter. In that respect, I have taken my cue from Kurt Lewin, the founder of modern social psychology. While highly practical in its ideas and explanations, the book's advice on leadership practice is grounded in theory, accepting his dictum (1951):

> *'There is nothing so practical as a good theory.'*
> (Kurt Lewin)

A founding father of the discipline of 'systems thinking', W. Edwards Deming, would no doubt agree with Lewin. Deming's guiding light has helped me to see and think more clearly during the process of writing this book:

> *'Without theory, experience has no meaning.*
> *Without theory, one has no questions to ask.*
> *Hence without theory there is no learning.'*
> (in Seddon, 2003)

The Search for Leadership is a practical book that answers the question 'how?'. How can we improve leadership in, of, by and for organisations – organisations in all sectors of business, economic, and political and public life? It is as much about those organisations and why they need to find better leadership as it is about the nature of leadership and methods for its improvement. The book's ultimate purpose is to increase organisations' effectiveness and success through better leadership. It challenges conventional wisdom and some long-established development norms. Its ideas overturn deep-rooted beliefs about how best to release, promote, improve and apply leadership.

To help readers, leaders, managers and developers think their way through tough questions and take up the challenges presented by the book, I have supported the conceptual input with numerous real stories and topical examples. The book is highly practical in suggesting things you can do to improve leadership in your own organisation.

Leadership preoccupations, troubles, needs and development vary according to position. Chief executives' views on leadership will differ considerably from those at succeeding levels. I have done my best to embrace all managerial functions and levels in how I approach the subject, not least because all levels have a role to play in using leadership to improve their organisation.

The book is in two parts. Part One provides a conceptual foundation and a *thinking challenge*. It explores theories, models, assumptions, mindsets and definitions. Part Two addresses the *intervention challenge*, demonstrating how the new model can be applied practically in familiar and unfamiliar territory: culture change, competency, performance management, and so on.

The opening chapter builds a foundation by challenging commonly held assumptions and defines some important terminology for talking and thinking about leadership in organisations. Subsequent chapters examine:

- the difference between managing and leading
- what is working and what's not
- why the process of leadership needs to be managed and how to do it
- ways of improving leadership, besides development
- how to balance supply of leadership talent with the organisation's demand

- gaps down which leadership escapes
- how to stop wasting leadership
- the importance of the context in development, but why this is not enough
- differences between management and organisation development in building leadership
- the contribution of leadership competencies
- how to develop a leadership culture
- how to arrest the natural processes of decline and decay
- how the learning of leadership is affected
- how to talk the language of systems and how to think systemically
- what is below the surface in the organisation's parallel shadow leadership system
- a range of processes by which leadership can be properly held to account
- how to diagnose organisations to discover where the potential lies for releasing leadership and how to achieve that.

The book's messages are then pulled together in a Conclusion. I have ended the book with two appendices. The first summarises the new model for leadership improvement on which this book is based. The second provides some information about the *Systemic Leadership Toolkit*, which I have developed to guide practitioners through the improvement process – from diagnosis to implementing the practical applications of the systemic leadership model.

Finally, the book will have failed if there is no trouble tomorrow. In this sentiment I have taken inspiration from the indefatigable, and sadly late, Anita Roddick. For her, causing trouble was what leadership was for:

> *'If we come here today and there's no trouble tomorrow, we haven't done our jobs.'* [1] (Anita Roddick)

William Tate

---

1   Roddick, A. (2000) 'Taking it personally'. *Geographical magazine*. London: Royal Geographical Society, 1 November.

PART ONE

THE NEED FOR A NEW APPROACH –
THE THINKING CHALLENGE

This first part, consisting of five chapters, provides the necessary conceptual foundation upon which the book's practical applications and advice is built.

Part One shows how the present model of leadership development fails to meet today's complex needs. It builds the case for why we need a complete overhaul of the popular approach and replaces it with one that better connects with host organisations and their needs separately from those of individual managers. Here you will find an exploration of the numerous assumptions behind conventional practice in this field, many of which are unsound and long overdue a challenge. We explore needs and opportunities for new mindsets focused on the organisation as a system. Part One proposes and defines a new model based on principles of systems thinking; many readers will already be familiar with this management discipline, though not as applied to leadership.

CHAPTER 1:

PREPARING THE GROUND

- ☐ *Leadership and leaders*
- ☐ *Leadership apart from people*
- ☐ *Leadership apart from development*
- ☐ *Development versus improvement*
- ☐ *The organisation versus its people*
- ☐ *The organisation's persona*

It used to be so simple, or so we told ourselves. For a long time the assumption was: 'If you want leadership, look for a leader' (Krantz, 1990). An industry was (and still largely is) built on that hypothesis. HR's response has been to 'develop' leaders. But that seemingly obvious connection between leadership and leaders is now recognised as inadequate and simplistic: it is a circular argument, confusing leadership with authority, and leaders with 'who is in charge'. Furthermore, leaders – in companies, society and politics – are failing to deliver the leadership that employees, customers, investors, businesses, societies, economies, nations, and the planet need. Leader development doesn't seem to work. A new model and a new approach is called for.

To think afresh about leadership and how best to obtain it, improve it and apply it means challenging a number of common but misplaced assumptions:

- that leaders and leadership are inseparable
- that leadership is a property only of individuals
- that talk about leadership is necessarily talk about development
- that development is the only means of improvement
- that the business and the organisation are one
- that the organisation is its people

In this opening chapter I will prepare the ground for this book's new approach to leadership and its improvement by highlighting some of these misapprehensions that can both result from and perpetuate conventional approaches to leadership. In making these distinctions and separations, I am advocating a mental shift in the way leaders, leadership and organisations are perceived, which I believe will hasten the journey towards improved leadership and better-led organisations.

The approach that I am advocating links two disciplines. The first is organisation development (OD) – a term that refers to ways of intervening that focus on the 'soft' internal aspects and dynamics of organisations in order to improve the organisation's effectiveness, efficiency, culture, climate and wellbeing. The second is that of systems thinking – based on the belief that the component parts of a system (especially including leadership) can best be understood in the context of relationships with other parts of the system and other systems, rather than in isolation.

Separating leadership from leaders

It is generally accepted these days that leadership is not tied to elites or authority. Leadership is not mainly about position. Leadership is not confined to top management. Even those who are formally designated as leaders spend only a little of their time leading. Leadership, however fleeting, can be a vital aspect of people's jobs anywhere in the organisation.

While not claiming that everyone can be or wants to be a leader, this basic proposition of mentally separating leadership from particular senior executives is attractive and empowering. It releases leadership from the preserve of leaders and distributes it more widely.

Before going further, I need to get a small linguistic nicety out of the way. When using the words 'management' and 'leadership', I am referring to the *process* and *activity* of managing and leading, not to the top managers in an organisation who some people also refer to as management and leadership. I am applying improvement activity to the leadership process and not to leaders. Referring to development activity, Paul Iles and David Preece (2006) capture the distinction this way:

> '*Leader development* refers to developing individual-level intrapersonal
> competencies and human capital (cognitive, emotional, and self-awareness skills,
> for example), while *leadership development* refers to the development processes
> and social capital in the organization and beyond, involving relationships,
> networking, trust, and commitments, as well as an application of the social and
> political context and its implications for leadership styles and actions.'

That way of distinguishing *leadership* from *leaders* helps to reach into the organisation to see what is happening there. However, this book goes far beyond social relationships, trust and commitments and instead treats the organisation as a system. It looks back at leadership from the organisation's end of the telescope to observe and magnify how that system itself shapes leadership.

The financial crisis beginning in 2008, and today's international banking sector leadership as understood by an acutely interested public, is a dramatic case in point. A long-term shift away from traditional banking to a more aggressive business model and associated culture has led to a leadership model that is now in tatters. The old model based on retail markets has been replaced with one dependent on wholesale ones. Computers have replaced branches and personal contact and service. Global markets have replaced local ones, not least for recruiting talent. A trusted guardian role has been replaced with an aggressive selling one. A 'shareholder primacy' view has replaced responsibility to and for public customers, enabling excessive rewards for those at the top and those who take risks. A drive for short-term profits (sought by institutional investors) has led to under-supervised and labyrinthine investments, enabling traders to earn vast sums for their employers, and justifying their claims for large bonuses, of which their bosses want a share. A takeover culture means that a bank will be hunted if it is not a hunter. The upshot: a macho culture of gamblers, who bet their investments and their companies to satisfy their instinctive competitiveness, greed, risk-taking and ambition, and who are careless with the public stakeholder. For a number of years, that leadership has been complicit in the design and prosecution of that system. Curiously, it is now expected to reform it; for example, one of the dismissed chief executives is now advising his bank as a consultant.

This complex cause-and-effect compact reflects what happens to leadership in mainstream organisations. Leadership is often falsely portrayed as a one-way activity: leadership gives and the organisation and its stakeholders receive and gain. But this is not how leadership comes about. The reverse effect is just as crucial: the system impacts leadership as much as leadership impacts the system.

At the heart of any attempt to improve leadership lies this challenging question:

> How does leadership need to apply itself to the organisation, and how does the organisation need to apply itself to leadership?

In years of consulting, I have rarely encountered an organisation seriously considering that fundamental issue.

Separating leadership from people

On its own, the above way of thinking still leaves the focus of leadership on people – managers who lead. I am going to ask you to put that deeply ingrained approach to one side, and think in a radically different way about what a more organisational approach to leadership could mean.

Leadership activity that is grounded not in the individual but in the organisation is called *systemic leadership*. It captures two important ideas: (1) leadership of an organisation conceived of and understood by managers as a system, and (2) the application of the discipline of *systems thinking* to the subject of leadership. From an improvement perspective, I define systemic leadership as:

> *Improving the way an organisation is led, based on an understanding of the organisation as a system, focused on the interdependency between leadership and the organisation, concerning how leadership is applied, managed and developed.*

Systemic leadership is concerned with the *activity* of leadership more than with its *personification*. To adapt a quotation: systemic leadership 'votes for the painting more than for the artist'.

To take the artistic metaphor a step further, think of leadership development as drama school, while leadership itself is the live performance – including what happens on and off stage. The whole performance is what people most look for and what they value. Performance depends on having good relationships between the individual actors as well as with the audience, good props, good front-of-house and back-of-house support, and – crucially – a compelling script or plot. Star actors alone are not enough. The wider system and its overall performance is what matters. The system makes or breaks the show.

Expressed like this, leadership can be thought of in terms of a *leadership system*. There are many components in the system that need to work together. An individual's leadership within it is but one interdependent element, with other components being colleagues and others being *things* (such as a feedback process).

While individual leaders are an invaluable resource, this mental separation between leadership and people allows us to value *leadership* in the organisation as a distinctive and strategic asset of the company. Table 1 presents the two contrasting paradigms:

	POPULAR PARADIGM	COMPLEMENTARY PARADIGM
	INDIVIDUAL LEADERSHIP AND ITS DEVELOPMENT	SYSTEMIC LEADERSHIP AND ITS IMPROVEMENT
OUTPUT	Leaders	Leadership in, of, by and for the organisation
WHOSE AGENDA	Individual leaders	The organisation
PERCEPTION OF LEADERSHIP	Heroic leaders	Organisation well led
MEASURE OF SUCCESS	Individual managers' leadership potential	Expanded organisational leadership capability/capacity
METAPHORS	The artist The actor	The painting The performance
INTERVENTION STRATEGY	Development Management development (MD)	Improvement Management development plus organisation development (OD)
PROCESS	Developing individual leaders (either generically or in their organisational context)	Developing individual leaders in their organisational context Developing team leadership Improving systems that affect leadership Improving the leadership culture Removing obstacles to leadership Cutting out waste of leadership

DRIVER	Request for better leadership skills	Need for better-led organisations that serve stakeholders
BENEFICIARIES	Individuals and their organisation	The organisation and its stakeholders
SUPPLY AND DEMAND	Increasing the supply of leadership talent	More demand-side pull, blended with supply-side push
SOURCE OF SUPERVISION	Inside the HR function	Top line management
FORM OF NEEDS ANALYSIS	Learner's training needs analysis	The organisation's needs analysis
THINGS RIGHT/ RIGHT THINGS	Doing things right	Doing the right things as well as doing things right
ACCESS BY DEVELOPERS	To individual learners	To the organisation's agenda (aims, problems and opportunities, etc.)
ENVIRONMENT	The leader's environment in the organisation	The leader's environment in the organisation, plus The organisation's business environment and society
MOST SIGNIFICANT INPUTS	Developers Leadership theory	Line management Business context
TIME HORIZON	Timeless truths	Emergent issues
HR ACTIVITIES	Leadership talent development	Leadership talent definition, recruitment, assessment, appraisal, promotion, succession, utilisation, reward, tenure, exiting
HR SPECIALISMS	Management training and development function	All HR functions/ specialisms
PROFESSIONAL EXPERTISE	Occupational psychology	Organisational psychology

Table 1: Comparison of individual and systemic leadership paradigms

Separating leadership from development

When an organisation identifies a need for 'stronger leadership', the first thing to emerge is always a development agenda. The discussion bypasses any consideration of how leadership is applied and how the organisation performs. Instead, the agenda heads straight to development of people (managers). The discussion typically starts with 'Let's have a leadership development programme', rather than starting with a questioning process that begins with the organisation's needs and goals.

Such defective thinking often carries through to jobs. It is common to find job advertisements for a Head of Organisational Capability and People Development. On closer examination the description makes no further reference to the organisation. Sometimes this is an instance of simply trying to sex up the title by using OD-sounding language. But, giving the benefit of the doubt, it is more likely that such advertisements reflect the popular misconception that the two parts of the job title amount to the same thing – that the route to organisational capability is through people development.

Many senior executives do not even realise that there is scope for a discussion about the organisation's leadership that is separate and different from discussing managers' personal leadership and their development. If they do realise that the organisation's needs are not (simply) those of its people, they may not know what the differences are.

> 'There is a tendency to treat 'leadership' as a catch-all and a panacea. It is made to stand for all the qualities that are desirable in a top team or responsible post-holder – for example 'clarity of vision', 'a performance focus', 'flexibility' and 'innovation', 'HR capability' and 'winning commitment'. In reality, most reports make little detailed examination of the concept of leadership. Its value is simply asserted and its nature assumed. Attention then typically switches to what are commonly seen as the apparent training and development 'needs' in order to attain these desirable ends.' (Storey, 2004)

This proposed mental separation (of leadership from development) is not saying that leaders (and leadership) won't benefit from development. But it *is* saying that the mental separation helps us think more clearly and imaginatively in two key respects:

First, it allows us to focus on organisationally strategic, non-development related questions; for example, what the organisation needs leadership for, how leadership is currently being used and applied, and how leadership is held to account.

Secondly, it opens the door to a wide range of improvement options besides development; for example, how the organisation can stop wasting leadership, and how to join up the various related HR levers to improve leadership.

Separating development from improvement

The familiar practice of equating the wider leadership agenda with development closes down exploration about the *application* and the *management* of leadership in the organisation. The organisation gets away with needing to do very little itself and very little *to* itself. Leadership can safely be left to individual managers to sort out and HR to develop, at least so the thinking goes. It can't – a point long recognised by James Krantz (1990):

> '… the leader's personality has been vastly over-rated in attempts to understand leadership. Furthermore, by clinging to the hope that leaders will solve our leadership crisis, we prevent ourselves from addressing the underlying problems that disable even enormously capable leaders.'

Acquiescing in collapsing the leadership agenda into personal development is where the quest for improved leadership in organisations starts to go wrong and why so much development fails to make an impact.

Shifting from a 'development' to an 'improvement' perspective is fundamental to systemic leadership. When people talk and think about 'development' most of them instinctively think about individuals and programmes. But asking the question 'How can we *improve* leadership in this organisation?' brings other ideas to mind. This linguistic trick opens the door to a wider variety of interventions and a wider range of targets for improvement action that reach well beyond people into the systems that enable leadership to happen, including removal of the kind of obstacles that Krantz hints at.

There is a saying that prevention is better than cure. Development programmes are analogous to an attempted cure without having first identified, halted and treated the ills in the organisation's culture, policies and practices. Improvement, on the other hand, deals with both prevention and cure. Improvement of the organisation's leadership-related systems can therefore be thought of as a more upstream activity than development.

Separating the organisation from the business

The word 'organisation' is commonly used as a substitute for company, firm, corporation, enterprise, partnership and institution, as well as being used as a synonym for 'the business'. This umbrella term 'organisation' conveniently spans the public, private and not-for-profit sectors, and for this reason I use 'organisation' in this way in this book. Yet this popular usage glosses over an important distinction between the business and the organisation.

The *business* is essentially outwardly focused and profit driven. Business factors are concerned with why the company exists and how it survives. A company's *business model* answers the question 'How will this company make money out of what it is doing?'. By contrast, the *organisation* is the set of internal arrangements at the service of the business. These internal organisational arrangements enable a soundly conceived business to succeed. The *organisation model* answers the question 'What is the best way of organising ourselves to serve the business objectives?'.

> 'We needed ... an initiative to define the kind of organisation Boston Borough Council needs to be in the future to deliver its community plan objectives ... it defines the shape, style and values ...'[2] (Martin Rayson, Director of Resources, Boston Borough Council.)

---

2   Rayson, M. (2008) quoted in *Making Successful Change Happen* (report). London: Improvement & Development Agency.

Organisation models sometimes convey a strong financial message and contain objectives for managers that risk blurring the boundary with the business model. Few managers may have any practical control over them.

> A large American-owned publishing house has an organisation model based on the principle that the only customer is the shareholder. Managers are frequently reminded of this. Managers have very low sign-off authority and the hierarchy is applied rigorously to all spending decisions and to impose strict financial discipline. Budgets are set centrally without managerial input and bids. Bonuses are generous but are dependent upon hitting these financial targets. Cost cutting is frequent. Managers' annual objectives are imposed without discussion and consist entirely of financial targets (e.g. 'Achieve calendar year revenue and contribution to profit targets for your publications').

The table below lists some of the factors that comprise the two halves of the company or institution: the business and the organisation.

THE BUSINESS (external, 'what' focus)	THE ORGANISATION' (internal, 'how' focus)
Mission	Leadership
Markets	Philosophy
Core business competence	Structure
Customers	Values
Products	Ethics
Services	Culture
Brands	Climate
Reputation	Funding
Prices	Skills
Margins	Management and supervision
Channels	Staff competencies
Outlets	Relationships
Competition	Communication
Availability of raw material	Training
Regulators, etc.	Rules and procedures
	Budgets
	Targets
	Remuneration, etc.

Table 2: The business contrasted with the organisation (Tate, 1999)

In conducting the annual *Global Leadership Forecast for 2008-09 (UK Highlights)*[3] leaders were asked 'to identify the most important *business* priorities for their *organisations*'. At the top came *growth* (indeed, a business item), then improving

---

3   CIPD (2008) *UK highlights, Global leadership forecast 2008-09*, research by Development Dimensions International, published by the Chartered Institute of Personnel and Development, London.

customer relationships/service (also a business item), then *improving/leveraging talent* (an organisation item). The leaders surveyed had been asked to choose from a list that conflated business and organisation factors, with the risk of confusing the means (internal/organisation/how) with the end (external/business/what).

The distinction between 'organisation' and 'business' is helpful here. When there is a problem with the company or institution, thinking separately about the business and the organisation helps to pinpoint issues and opportunities, and helps decide where to direct effort. Without this distinction you may pull on internal organisation levers when you should be asking fundamental questions about the business itself.

But should one think about the business ahead of the organisation that is there to serve and support it, or the other way round? The answer is that there is no fixed rule that always favours one over the other. A case can be made for both these sequences depending on the context. The key point is to recognise the difference between the business and the organisation and understand how a systems perspective and an improvement agenda are affected by that simple division.

■ Putting the business first

Once the journey for the business is clear (e.g. planning to move into new markets or out of old ones), the internal organisation can be designed and run in the best way to serve the needs of the future business. Gerard Egan (1988) argues against prioritising the organisation at the expense of the business:

> 'Some companies and institutions become too preoccupied with inner concerns.
> The organisation becomes an end in itself to the detriment of the business,
> that is, to the detriment of markets and the satisfaction of needs and wants of
> customers and clients in those markets through products and services.'

Egan points out that it is quite common to find the internal organisation structure being re-jigged when the real problem lies with the business structure, such as wrong products, markets, prices, etc. Training (an organisational intervention) is often mistakenly invoked to solve a more fundamental problem with the business.

'At the beginning of this year, we brought in a new managing director to run our business, because we felt that we didn't have the requisite skills between us to do it. Our business had morphed from a website for young people into a large educational publishing company over a six-year period, and Kirsty and I thought we were out of our depth. It soon transpired though that it wasn't us that were the problem, it was the business itself.

'The new MD didn't work out. We had to look again at the business and lost lots of staff. We appreciated those people who stuck with us. We re-thought the whole thing. Now we are running a more manageable, more profitable and more enjoyable business.

cont. overleaf

> '... It's worth remembering that often it isn't the leadership at fault – it's the business model itself, and sometimes you need a revamp to make things work again. This goes for large organisations or small businesses.' [4]

If the leaders in the global survey had exclusively identified organisational factors, we would have cause to be worried about their leadership of the *business*.

■ Putting the organisation first

There is a counter argument that runs like this. The future shape of the business is uncertain. The future shape of an ideal organisation is also uncertain, but less so. Arguably, more can be said about the organisation than can be said about the business in terms of how it can best be arranged to serve the needs of an evolving business. Therefore, it is suggested, developing the organisation's *adaptive capacity* is what is most crucial. The organisation can be set up to enable appropriate leadership to flourish, without needing to know in advance quite what the business will need that leadership for. The HR director below held that view.

> The director of human resources in a large corporation decided to cease attending the chief executive's regular business meetings. They were very time-consuming, and the purpose for his attending was mainly to hear what was happening in the business. The HR director took the view that he had worked out how the organisation culture needed to change in a way that would give it the capacity to serve the general direction of the business. He would concentrate his time on changing the organisation instead. His decision was controversial because his fellow directors expected him to want to be present as a member of the executive management team and to hear about the business details.

Separating the organisation from its people

If the business is to receive the leadership it needs, the organisation has to provide more than a context. It needs to be directly engaged in the journey. More than back-seat driver, the organisation is at once our vehicle, companion, route and destination.

So the organisation is not a passive vessel waiting to have leadership poured into it. The organisation is an active player that has to contribute to leadership appropriately if it is to receive its due from managers. This explains why this book is as much about organisations (their needs, challenges and dynamics, and their infuriating flaws and neuroses), and the part they must play, as it is about leadership itself. The connection between leadership and its host is symbiotic, with the organisation proving a vital partner both to leadership and improvement, and to making use of leadership action delivered by managers.

---

4   Jordan, R. (2006) 'On being the boss'. London: *The Guardian*, 7 October.

You may be thinking that an organisation is inanimate, merely a legal creation, a social construct. How can an organisation be a companion or partner? How can an organisation have a view or decide? Surely, it is only *individuals* who can do such things. Critics of the use of 'organisation' as an actor make a valid point. In its leadership development programme, the BBC appears to agree:

> 'You are the organisation; if it needs changing, it's up to you to change it.' (Tate, 2006)

There is a paradox here: the BBC is itself an organisation; how can it hold this view? The answer is, of course, that the view expressed was uttered by some person, perhaps the director general Mark Thompson. And can the BBC be changed, or – if the BBC is only its people ('*you* are the organisation') – is it only the behaviour of the people in it that can be changed? There is some confusion in the BBC's statement, and possibly some naivety.

> *'I don't like the administrative side of the BBC, it's enough to drive you crazy, but the bosses are by and large extremely good people.'*[5]
> (John Simpson)

In the BBC leadership programme it is unclear whether 'you' is singular or plural. Does the BBC believe individuals have magical powers to change the BBC, or does it expect managers will organise together to bring about change – perhaps during its leadership development programme? In a moment I explore that second option during my discussion of The Critical Mass Argument.

There is a wider question: When planning an intervention, should one begin with the organisation or with the people? Disciples of organisation development are divided. Is the organisation responsible for people's behaviour?, in which case we should work to change the organisation (its systems, structures, rules, culture, etc.). Or can people be said to be responsible for the way the organisation 'behaves'?, in which case we should examine their selective perceptions and actions. The latter is the standpoint of the late Iain Mangham (1975), then Director of Bath University's Centre for the Study of Organisational Change and Development:

> 'We must address the question as to how far and to what extent, in what manner, being a member of this or that group or organisation, influences the kind of perception and response of particular persons in specific situations. ... We must start with them and try to discover how they see their organisational world and what consequences their world-pictures have for their actions.'

> *'Organisational behaviour may be seen as a number of responses in search of a stimulus rather than the product of a complex of factors such as structure, technology and environment.' [Paraphrasing Pirandello]*
> (Mangham, 1975.)

---

5   Armstrong, J. (2008) 'The British press has no sense of irony'. *The Guardian*, 20 October.

Mangham arrived at a sceptical view of OD concentrating its attention on the system, while being supportive of the view that people's perceptions of the organisation, among other things, is largely responsible for how they behave. The irony here is that Mangham has, of course, arrived at his view of OD ('put the people first, not the system') as a consequence of his own selective perceptions. A giveaway is his being a devotee of Bertolt Brecht (1965):

> 'I have an insatiable curiosity about people ... the way they get along with each other ... the way they cheat, favour, teach, exploit, respect, mutilate, and support one another: the way they hold meetings, form societies, conduct intrigues. I want to know why they embark on their undertakings ...'

The answer to Brecht's question, of course, has something to do with those people's perceptions of the organisation from what it surrounds them with. This makes the argument circular and brings us back to the other OD school of thought: diagnose the system (drawing out people's perceptions) and work on the data. This is the OD school to which I belong, of which Mangham (1975) appears dismissive: He claims:

> 'Organisations do not behave, they do not do anything. Systems do not make decisions. ... To claim that organisations or systems engage in any form of behaviour makes sense only if we can specify some person or sets of persons who perceive, think, move and have being.'

Yet, speaking of organisations as separate entities is at the very least a convenient shorthand for writers, readers and employees. It refers to a position that key parties (who may be just a few top managers) are happy to represent as the official view to be put forward in the name of the organisation (as in 'The organisation has decided that ...'). It may also represent the externally perceived collective attributes of the mass of people plus artefacts (as in 'the organisational system, culture or personality') that people feel accurately sums up the place. The convenient practice avoids long-windedness and unwanted and unnecessary personalisation.

Readers with a philosophical disposition will be aware of the risk of straying into the contentious practice of reification (the fallacy of misplaced concreteness – the process of regarding an abstract construct as a material entity). This misgiving may lead some people to agree with Mangham in concluding that one can only develop something tangible; hence a possible explanation for the dominance of people development over organisational development.

The BBC's view of the organisation (i.e. 'it's just its people') is commonly held and carries much appeal, not to say political convenience. It evokes memories of Margaret Thatcher's 'There's no such thing as society'. But just think about what happens when managers act on the BBC's advice. Despite what Professor Mangham thought, managers are up against the system and its bias for the status quo.

At times the organisational system really does seem to have a life and mind of its own. The same is true of other systems, including the economic system and the financial system. Following the collapse of investor support for the bank HBOS (Halifax Bank of Scotland) and its proposed takeover by Lloyds TSB in September 2008, it was said 'you could observe the market trying to identify the next victim'. [6]

But was it the market, was it individuals, was anyone trying to identify the next victim? To answer that, and to comprehend organisational behaviour that seems to have a mind of its own, we need to factor in Chaos Theory. (For more on this explanation, see Chapter 13, *Leadership and the Shadow*.)

This book's anthropomorphic way of talking about organisations having their own independent personality is also stretching a point, but it has more going for it than just useful shorthand. After all, most managers acknowledge that they can 'feel' an organisation's culture.

But how far should we accept that an organisation has human-like attributes of its own, such as a psyche, mind and morality, that can be considered separately from the people who work in it? Where does this leave the notion of the organisation having its own systemic leadership capability that is apart from that of its managers, both individually and even collectively?

> 'It is not just a question of having up-to-date equipment, like the celebrated 12 miles of computer-driven baggage belts at Terminal 5. It is having the *organisational capability* [my italics] to run them continuously, a question of skill, employee engagement, management dexterity and punctilious observation of the right process'. [7]

The systemic approach to improving leadership in organisations is based on the key assumption that not only does the company have its own organisational capability as a system, but also its own organisational *leadership* capability. This claim rests on its having several key system variables, as explained below.

What gives the organisation a distinctive character?

Just what is unique about the organisation that differentiates it from merely being its people? There are some workplace characteristics that are incontrovertibly and clearly organisational, not merely linguistically convenient. Many of these directly affect leadership; for example, there is the hierarchical structure, appraisal policies and promotion systems. There are succession plans. There are norms and standards in the culture that determine how failed leaders are removed (or allowed to remain in post). And there is a leadership culture that shapes how acceptable are displays of power, bullying and ambition.

6   Pratley, N. (2008) 'Suddenly it's a good time to be ripping up the rulebooks'. London: *The Guardian*, 18 September.

7   Hutton, W. (2008) 'Terminal 5, another British cock-up that had to happen'. London: *The Observer*, 30 March.

It cannot be argued that such system variables are really properties or characteristics of individuals (although, of course, individuals are ultimately accountable for the design and maintenance of systems such as succession planning). It is these independent variables that together give an organisation an identity and its own standing. It is also what turns the organisation into a system and not merely an employer.

So, if leadership isn't working in the way the organisation requires, we do need to reach beyond individual performers and examine the organisation *as a system* to find explanations and seek solutions. There is a need to pull on levers beyond those of individual managers in order to develop the *organisation's* leadership capability. And the organisation itself needs to have its own leadership agenda and a strategy for achieving it.

You wouldn't think like this if you looked at the way most organisations sub-contract leadership to individual managers, and then further subcontract individual development to providers. Many top managers make the dubious and risky assumption that trained leaders will know to what aspect they need to apply their newfound skills and energies. More importantly, they assume that they will not experience obstacles when they try: obstacles that organisation cultures, hierarchies and bureaucracies (or other managers) typically put in people's way. Tell that to the BBC managers.

The 'critical mass' argument

Organisations often claim to have an answer to the problems posed above. They call it 'critical mass'. It is rather as though the number of managers trained over time would somehow reach a point where those in favour of change would comprise a simple majority and could outvote those who preferred the status quo and they would then get on with it. But can enough trained managers comprise a *meaningful* critical mass that can achieve something by sheer weight of numbers alone?

The answer to the above question is No. Even a numerical majority of managers is not a solution: they don't meet formally, don't know each other, don't share the same aims, they normally compete against each other, lack a unifying structure, have no collective authority, lack a practical means of having their collective behaviour performance managed, and have no means of being held to account. In short, the mass of managers don't comprise a group. Added to this, over the duration of a major leadership programme – many programmes last for several years – the organisation that managers are being invited to change will have continued to change anyway, with new bosses, new structures, managers changing jobs. It is a moving target for those seeking change.

A critical mass of managers is no doubt preferable to a few managers attempting to act alone. The numbers resisting change may be fewer, and that might be a positive factor. But the managers are unlikely to be able to get their act together sufficiently to achieve change – without considerable help from the system.

To return to the question posed on page 13: Can the managers be sufficiently organised as a group to combine their power to affect change? The answer is Yes, using the principles of distributed leadership explained on page 60. This enables managers' action to be 'concertive', so that they combine their energies and contribute their various perceptions and expertise. In the presence, and with the active participation, of more senior levels – including the chief executive – large numbers of managers collectively identify, discuss, agree and plan changes to the way the organisation works. Structured in such a way, a critical mass can have meaning.

What next for leadership?

This book's subtitle *An Organisational Perspective* makes clear that my interest in leadership is in its organisational setting and mission. This context is fundamental for leadership development, improvement and delivery if the ultimate goal is improved business performance. But, while awareness and consideration of the organisational context is necessary, it is nowhere near sufficient.

Leadership continually needs to adapt to changes taking place in the world, in each organisation's environment, and in the demands placed upon it. Leadership needs to improve and renew both itself and the organisation, to remedy dysfunction and to counter the decaying effects of entropy. These natural forces ensure gradual degeneration, decline and disorder, necessitating the countervailing force of never-ending reinvigoration. That calls for leadership rather than management, a distinction explained in Chapter 3, *Leading Versus Managing*.

Leadership is needed to realign the organisation with its customers and the business, and to overcome the tendency to become inwardly obsessed and self-serving. Leadership is needed to dismantle power bases, empires, personal fiefdoms and 'silos' as rapidly as managers build them. The status quo is not tenable; those who hope to remain in their organisational comfort zone will find the status quo shifting under their feet. Leadership is needed to make change and itself needs to change, in response to its changing environment.

To the extent that the above is at least partially accepted and understood, some organisations map the externally changing scenarios. They attempt to use these drivers to inform their leadership agenda. Typically, they divine appropriate leadership skills and prescribe content for the development agenda for individual managers. Sadly, many organisations are then content to leave it at that.

Besides offering a new perspective for thinking and talking about leadership in organisations, the book presents a practical way of intervening in the nexus between leadership and the organisation by:

> *seeing what is happening in and to an organisation, and what needs to be happening, to bring about improvement both to leadership and to the organisation.*

The practical toolkit outlined in Appendix 1 (the *Systemic Leadership Toolkit*) is designed to enable that insight. It includes a diagnostic instrument and contains detailed advice on how to make interventions successful and the proper roles of the various parties.

The two aspects of leadership – the organisational and the individual – are, of course, both important and related. While I focus on the organisation as the vehicle for leadership, I also argue that the organisation is the key player in enabling the individual to lead.

The book brings both the organisational and the individual arms of leadership improvement together, as managers learn and act as leaders and display leadership in conducting the organisational diagnosis and carrying out improvements. This linkage mechanism fulfils a key managerial responsibility: that of connecting people, and hence leadership, to the organisation.

SUMMARY OF CHAPTER KEY POINTS

1. Leadership is not confined to elites or authority. It can be an aspect of people's jobs anywhere.

2. Leadership is a subject that can be looked at, its capability and capacity expanded and its delivery enhanced separately from development focused on managers.

3. Talking about leadership 'improvement' opens the door to a wider range of interventions than 'development'.

4. The organisation is not the same as the business. The organisation is the set of internal arrangements at the service of the business.

5. Solve problems with the business before assuming that changing the organisation will solve them. But developing the organisation's adaptive capacity will benefit any business.

6. The organisation is more than simply its people.

7. When studying organisation behaviour, expert views differ as to whether to begin and concentrate on the system, or on the people and the selective perceptions that lie behind their behaviour.

8. The notion that a meaningful critical mass of managers can be built up over a series of development events and can then be relied upon to make collective change is a seductive idea but is largely fallacious.

CHAPTER 2:

FROM INDIVIDUAL TO ORGANISATIONAL

☐ *Why leadership isn't improving*
☐ *The organisation's power – to help or hinder*
☐ *No organisational leadership agenda*
☐ *Matching leadership to the organisation's needs*
☐ *Leadership's many challenges*

Leadership and its development, and its observable failure to transform organisational life, business performance, the economy and society, might justifiably lead to a claim that the current paradigm is 'broken'.

Stakeholders from across the globe, spanning public and private sectors, confirm the stark appraisal. Customers, employees, investors, the public, communities, suppliers and the media perceive too many organisations as fumbling, unhealthy, inefficient, murky, and self-serving. Such organisations often lack quality relationships and a lived realisation of whom they exist to serve. Few are lauded without equivocation. But many hold substantial scope for improvement and would benefit from better leadership. Take one example: Speaking of the Civil Service, Zenna Atkins, a director of the Royal Navy Executive Board, makes this trenchant criticism:

> 'I have never met such bright people who really care about what they are doing, but they are working in a machine with a set of customs, cultures, values and practices that are utterly antiquated. A lot of the time the process is more important than the outcome. …. Nowhere is worse than the Ministry of Defence. It is impenetrable.' [8]

WHY ISN'T LEADERSHIP IMPROVING?

Leadership development activities abound – fun, professional, stimulating, stretching and invigorating. But they don't seem to make much of a difference to how well an organisation is led – the acid test.

---

8   Atkins, Z. (2008) 'Civil Service damned as 'utterly antiquated'. London: *The Observer*, 15 June.

Why is this the case? Building on the new, systemic way of thinking about leadership introduced in Chapter 1, we might ask: are developers setting their sights too low? Could they be aiming their efforts at the wrong target? Are they neglecting the organisation? Are they so close to it that they cannot see it sideways on, so to speak – both part of the problem as well as part of the solution? Do they view the organisation simply as client and recipient, rather than as an active player that needs to be drawn into the argument?

However it is portrayed, development activity rarely engages seriously and directly with an organisation's identified need to change or even to improve. Yet this is what any organisation actually requires – continual change, adaptation, renewal and improvement, whether it wants and acknowledges it or not. Without improvement and change, the organisation will be bypassed by changes happening in its environment, including what competitors are doing.

Despite substantial investment in leadership development, real improvement _for business_ is slow to come. Whatever gains there might be for managers in their individual jobs, it isn't obvious that the organisation as a whole improves and benefits. Some organisations' undoing is self-inflicted.

> 'Although leadership development courses may assist individuals in their self-development, their impact upon organisations is, at best, inconclusive, and may indeed be negative if they result in an increase in cynicism towards the organisation.' (Alimo-Metcalfe *et al*, 2000)

Heroic individual leaders

Barack Obama has evidenced the public's need for, and the appeal of, a heroic leader. He will no doubt be used as a role model for managers' development. Much will be written of his presidency. The bookshelves are full of stories of strong personal leaders. We are regaled with tales of these heroes' successes, strategies, character, personality traits, competencies, style, behaviour, methods and advice. Their authors seductively hint that 'you too can be a leader' on the basis that 'leaders are developed, not born'. Role models are paraded: a captain of industry (say Jack Welch), wartime leader (Winston Churchill), military commander (Viscount Slim), Arctic explorer (Ernest Shackleton) or Shakespearean character (Henry V). And now Barack Obama. Just listen to those speeches! Listen – learn – do!

One corner of the market perhaps, but the stories reflect managers' hopes and organisations' assumed needs for strong individual leadership. But there are voices of doubt.

> 'The vast majority of studies into, and books on, leadership are of limited help. They concentrate on the activities of charismatic and maverick chief executives or famous explorers whose situations are so far removed from those of most managers and supervisors as to be of minimal value.' (CIPD Terry Gillen, 2008)

In the modern business context, BP's ex-CEO Lord Browne used to get a frequent and favourable mention. But such reputations may be built on sand and quickly evaporate:

> 'Lord Browne was the UK's most respected businessman. All that changed overnight with an explosion at a US oil refinery. BP wasn't a great company, after all: in fact, it was a very bad one. Browne's achievement likewise went up in the smoke of the accident. ... Tony Hayward, Browne's successor, said in an interview that (in effect) the company was a bloated, over-complicated mess in need of a root-and-branch makeover that would take years.' [9]

While leadership may be viewed less heroically and charismatically these days, the expectation and the norm remains, in spite of the evidence, individual-centred. The thought pattern runs: 'Leadership means leaders means individuals means individuals' development means providers of individuals' leadership development means provider-led ...' The logical conclusion here is that, while individual managers may benefit, the host organisations themselves as business entities will probably see little or no improvement.

The 'heroic deeds' approach caricatured above may be stimulating and harmless fun, but it offers cause for scepticism and worry. It seems remote from the real world of any one business and requires a leap of imagination and goodwill to make the connection stick.

Today's complexity doesn't work well for heroes; there are too many traps. Coordination, cooperation, partnership and a stakeholder's perspective is required for appropriate things to happen. That said, individual leadership – whatever it is, distributed to all levels, and however it comes about – is still deeply important to organisations, their employees and other stakeholders, as well as to the wider economy and society.

Though I am scornful of the flood of commercial opportunism that attends the subject of leaders and leadership, I readily acknowledge individual leaders' importance. The new way of thinking and the action advocated in this book – and made practically applicable in the diagnostic toolkit – will mean that acts of individual leadership by managers are more, not less, likely. The organisation-led approach provides a strategic platform that helps to make individual development more robust and rooted firmly in the organisation's future.

Without such a base, leadership and its potential will choose to remain loose, tentative, infrequent, hazardous, and hidden below the parapet. In the absence of direction, challenge and security, many managers will continue to believe that their best personal strategy is to keep their heads down; this represents leadership *waste* – an important theme that I shall return to in Chapter 7, *Leadership and Organisation Development*.

> *'If I keep my head down I might be able to get right through to retirement age.'* (Manager)

---

9   Caulkin, S. (2007) 'Strong leadership? That's the last thing we need'. London: *The Observer*, 21 October.

In espousing systemic leadership, the book is not a cloak for communitarian or collective leadership styles. Fully recognising individual leadership, the book offers a complementary and reinforcing perspective, especially for *improving* leadership at an organisational level by revealing and pulling on a wider choice of levers than is usual in most companies' development portfolios.

But how do we make the leap from an individual-centric model to one that is more organisational and strategic? Something is missing from current practice. Something big.

The elephant in the room

It's there, but no one sees it. No one mentions it. Is it invisible, taboo, or taken for granted? When we look at it, do we simply see ourselves?

The problem of understanding, developing and improving leadership is not so much that the standard of leadership described is out of reach. Nor is it that depictions of some of the leaders are controversial, questionable and contested. Nor is it the dubious claims that the skills required for leadership can be acquired through personal development. These are problems that need addressing, but they miss the main point about leaders and leadership in organisations. It's obvious when you think about it: the main player – the ubiquitous, powerful and ever-present 'elephant in the room' that nobody wants to acknowledge – is, of course, the organisation itself.

The new model presented in this book is about recognising that elephant. It points out the beast to those who haven't noticed it. It puts the elephant in front of those who don't want to admit to it. It respects the elephant's enormous power – both for good and harm. And it wants to ensure that the elephant, aka the organisation, doesn't trample on its people.

The mislaid agenda

Top executives are interested in leadership. Yet many who are responsible for heading up organisations have lost sight of, and lost control of, their company's leadership agenda. Under pressure from many directions – the relentless need to deliver results against targets and deadlines, the absence of time to read and reflect, being sold universal best-practice, generic leadership competencies where you can't see the wood for the trees, and national schemes, being urged to delegate, outsource HR, let go and trust – many top executives have ceased to think clearly about what they currently and specifically need leadership for in their organisations, and just what are the priorities for leadership action.

Many senior executives fail to appreciate how the organisation and its leadership *acting together* can change things for the better and need to change. Instead of thinking about leadership and the organisation in the same breath, they think about them separately, with leadership hived off as an HR interest and activity: semi-detached from the business.

Executives may know (or think they know) where to take the business and possibly where to take the organisation that is designed to support the business, but they often don't know where to take leadership or where leadership is taking them. The problem is that, to the extent that they think about leadership, they think of it in terms of leadership development programmes for individual managers. If the subject of leadership finds a place on the executive board meeting agenda at all, it will take the form of such a programme.

■ Unhealthy dependency and detachment

This tendency to view leadership development programmes as the default answer to all leadership problems has led to a situation where top executives are frequently over-dependent on HR and on development providers – internal and external – who have their own professional, and in many cases, commercial agenda. The executives have relinquished the organisation's leadership to individual managers. Either these managers are left to work out for themselves what is in the organisation's mind or, if the organisation has spelt out where the business is going and what it requires, the managers are expected to be able to achieve this once they have received their dose of leadership development.

The indirect route into the organisation's needs

Development in response to individual learning and skill needs alone won't deliver against the organisation's own needs. In the absence of a strategic and imaginative alternative, most organisations continue a vain attempt to get their own needs met via the indirect and uncertain route of developing individual managers, then hoping that some good will come of it.

The case of the bank cited below and its 'corporate university' illustrates the familiar problem of disconnected talent.

> One of the UK's main high-street banks, Lloyds TSB, invests heavily in its in-house corporate university. The stated aim is to:
>> *deliver business performance by developing individual capability'.*
>
> This is an example of the consciously indirect approach. This route contains risks since it entails delegating responsibility for the organisation's future leadership to developers and individual managers. Does the bank have its own organisational capability strategy? What does the bank want leadership for? What are the big issues and major changes required that the 'university' should feed? Do the manager/ graduates know? Do the university's staff know? Is graduates' leadership part of that?

The above problems are inherent in the assumptions that underpin a quasi-university model; that is, that managers' talent can be developed independently of future jobs, and of the demands they face in their managerial jobs. A case can be made for it. But there is far more that employers can do to mitigate the downside of a lack of connectivity and to make development more strategic for the business.

Individual-focused development has an important place. It helps managers in their jobs and careers. It helps where people are not in employment, or where they simply want to improve their marketability. But most leadership development is sponsored by organisations, not by those individuals, so its prime purpose should be to benefit the organisation. Even if the organisation's intention is to improve individuals' performance and thereby benefit the organisation *indirectly*, the gain will only be realised if there is organisational input to the planning, design, conduct and support of the learning process.

The chief problem arises when the organisation has a clearly spelt out context, has clear needs, and is the sponsor of the development, but has no strategy for addressing its needs other than to settle for individually focused development. If this is an organisation's only strategy for getting to where it needs to be, then it's in trouble. The risks are apparent in the case below.

> 'The challenge is to ensure that the police service engages effectively with all communities however diverse and complex. These community engagement issues highlight the skills of partnership working, communication and influencing skills, understanding others, and equality and diversity as key areas for leadership development.
>
> 'The challenge is to close the gap between perceptions and reality. This is about stakeholder management and building trust and understanding with the public and comes from personal leadership styles and the skills of marketing and reputation management, which need to be part of the leadership development framework.' [10]

The above example comes from the National Policing Improvement Agency (NPIA). The agency has wisely injected organisational context into personal development programmes. And, encouragingly, it has not put all its eggs into the leadership development basket, but has other improvement strands to its bow. Yet, in common with most large organisations, the agency may be pinning unrealistically high hopes onto individual development. And that may divert ideas and energy away from higher-leverage interventions pitched directly at the organisation, rather than at its members.

What is missing in most companies is a route to addressing the organisation's needs that doesn't rely on the improbable sum of individuals achieving these changes for the organisation. Worse than this is where there is no awareness or openness to the possibility of the organisation needing to do some work on itself, as in the case of this publisher:

> 'I work as a production editor for a large publishing house that took over my previous smaller, independent publisher. I have been nominated to attend a management development programme, which I am very pleased about. But it is my company that needs to change – a lot. I have little respect for it. I get upset every day thinking about how much we have lost from my previous company.' [11]

---

10 NPIA (2008) *Leading policing: A strategy for the 21st century* (report). London: National Policing Improvement Agency.

11 Anonymous employee (2008) Confidential email, September.

Leadership in managers' own jobs

A successful outcome for individual managers is important, of course – if it can be achieved. Improvement in individuals' leadership is difficult and cannot be taken for granted; it has to be developed, then hung onto, translated to real work situations, combined with the efforts of colleagues, and not blocked by bosses or the system. Much of the new skill and energy evaporates; such experience and negative feelings are not uncommon.

> 'We tend to be fairly poor on the implementation end. If we could actually ever implement what we created we would be setting the world alight.' (Manager quoted in Alimo-Metcalfe et al, 2000)

Two conclusions flow from that:

First, in spite of the reservations I have identified above, attempts to improve individual managers' leadership remain important because those managers encounter unpredictable needs every day that call for leadership. It is impractical for the organisation to tell them how to respond; individuals are paid to use their initiative.

Secondly, when it is so patently obvious that organisations have a lot to answer for in how effective and how efficient individual managers' development is enabled to be, why isn't a stronger spotlight turned on the organisation to find out what is going on there?

SYSTEMIC LEADERSHIP:
THE INDIVIDUAL-ORGANISATION BOND

This book attempts to redress the present imbalance between the focus on the individual and on the organisation by presenting a systemic model for improving leadership. It enables the organisation to get its hands onto the vital lever of leadership. This new approach offers a fresh way of opening minds, exploring options, and achieving improvement in what leadership means and can mean for an organisation. My purpose is to foster and bring about better leadership in, of, by and for organisations, by applying – and promoting the understanding, developing, improving, expanding and releasing of – organisational leadership capabilities.

More specifically, the new approach helps to:

1. develop the organisation's systemic leadership capability;
2. expand the organisation's leadership capacity;
3. link leadership development with business aims and objectives;

4. align leadership with where the organisation is going;
5. unite and build corporate leadership cohesion and spirit;
6. address conflicting perceptions of leadership in the organisation;
7. join up disconnected 'levers' at the service of improved leadership;
8. cement leaders' individual and collective accountability;
9. solve thorny leadership problems (e.g. shortage of leaders);
10. stop the waste of leadership.

The organisation as a system

Unlike the range of issues concerning *individual* leadership, this book concentrates on quite different matters. For example, what are the *organisational* forces, political dynamics, enablers and blocks? *Where* and *how* does action need to be taken in and on the organisation to improve leadership with a view to the enterprise as a whole being better led? A simple way of capturing the essence of the systemic focus is to ask:

> *How can the organisation, <u>working as a system</u>, enable appropriate leadership to flourish?*

Note that word *system*. We are interested in the organisation not as an employer but as a system. A system with power. The 'elephant in the room' is an elephantine system – always bigger and more powerful than you think – power to make the earth (or at least the organisation) move, and power to get in the way. The beast needs taming and acknowledging. The more you look for it, the more you find it, notice it and respect it. And the more you realise that the system is here, not out there – you are part of it. Change the system – don't blame it.

Working with and within the system calls for an understanding of how the organisation's many elements work together to facilitate and deliver a desired leadership outcome? These system elements include not only departmental functions such as marketing and operations, but also components such as resources, customers, purpose and mission, policies, rules, protocol, hierarchy, roles, culture, climate, competencies, rewards, communication and accountability. And even leadership itself.

This view of the system as *the way it works together* has to be qualified by interjecting the phrases 'is designed to', 'actually does' and, most importantly, 'needs to be improved to'. Added to this is the official system's obverse: its unofficial, hidden, informal, dark, shadow side, which helps explain the gap between intention and reality.

My particular focus in this book centres on the question 'How does the system work to deliver leadership for the organisation and in return take advantage of leadership, the system itself being understood by and shaped by leadership?'.

THE CHALLENGES

To be able to intervene appropriately to improve leadership, you will first need to be able to think, observe and talk.

The thinking challenge

Rarely does an organisation have a leadership strategy that expressly captures the organisation's own needs and the direct systemic contribution it plans to make; usually there is a strategy only for individual leadership. Neglected questions of interest to the organisation about leadership remain:

- What does leadership mean *to* the organisation? (How different would it be if it was better led? How would that affect its reputation?)
- What does leadership mean *for* the organisation? (What would leadership be doing?)
- What does the organisation think it wants leadership for?
- What does leadership need to change?
- How does leadership itself need to change?
- What has to be happening in the organisation that has a bearing on the application of leadership, and what is being done about it?
- What is the organisation's leadership strategy and agenda?
- When the organisation sponsors a major leadership development programme, what does it really want, at what levels, and does it come with strings attached?

The observational challenge

We also need to be able to notice and consider what is happening:

- What is happening outside the organisation that has a bearing on the application of leadership?
- What is happening inside the organisation that has a bearing on the application of leadership?
- What are the internal dynamics of this organisation that are helping or hindering the conduct of successful leadership, and what is getting in the way of improvement?

> 'The range of what we think and do
> is limited by what we fail to notice.
> And because we fail to notice
> that we fail to notice
> there is little that we can do
> to change, until we notice
> how failing to notice
> shapes our thoughts and deeds.'
> (Poem by the psychiatrist R. D. Laing)

It can often help to get groups to take time out from their daily work pressures and surroundings, to stand to one side and be faced with questions that are not part of everyday discourse.

The conversational challenge

In practice, most organisations will not have answers to all these questions. The questions are challenging. But in a sense this misses the point: it isn't always getting the completely right answer that matters.

There is value alone in recognising that the questions are deeply relevant and then engaging in thought-provoking conversations with colleagues. The conversation itself is half the point, more than simply the need to obtain information. The conversation is the intervention that prompts learning, change and growth for those who engage in it. Conversations open minds and begin to shift people's thinking and perceptions about the means of improving leadership and how to make it more strategic.

The outcome will help anchor leadership development in the organisation's needs. It may also reveal that much current development activity may at best be tactical – only loosely connected to the company's journey and desired future.

■ Business-related questions

There are also fundamental *business-related* issues that it is important for developers to engage in conversations about:

- Where is the business going?
- How does the organisation need to change if it is to enable the business to go there?
- Where is the organisation failing to deliver what the business requires of it?
- Where is the organisation holding the business back?

The goal of becoming better led

Capturing the *purpose* from the company's perspective (i.e. to become better led) serves as a reminder of the driver and client behind development activity. It expresses the goal as an *outcome* for the enterprise, one that must necessarily take account of the 'system' (what it does, its business model, its ethos, how the organisation works and how it feels) and improving that, as well as developing individual managers.

Compare the goal of 'becoming better led' with the goal 'to improve the overall leadership of the organisation'. They sound very similar, but the latter wording risks being interpreted as an *input*; i.e. a development activity (a means); whereas a goal of 'becoming better led' prompts wider questioning around 'what are the range of things we can do to become a better-led company?' (an end).

Rarely in the mind of sponsors or developers does there appear to be a high-level aspiration that directly drives development to serve the enterprise. Mainly, employers are content to settle for something more tactical: managers being better leaders in their own jobs.

Searching for something better

Reflecting this conventional way of thinking about leadership improvement, attempts to analyse the leadership shortfall – quantity or quality – are usually written from a development perspective. Such analyses rarely delve into what goes on inside organisations, instead choosing to focus on what goes on in classrooms and programmes. Developers' work and talk are dominated by *supply* rather than *demand* considerations; that is, the supply of talent and methods of developing it, rather than the organisation's demands.[12] The people whose views are sought are usually developers, and, if not, they are asked their views about development. But development is the wrong place to start.

What are people not consulted about? They are not asked for their opinions on the organisation's use of leadership, the leadership culture, and leadership-related systems. They are not asked what leadership is like round here, what goes wrong with leadership, what happens when people show leadership? These are all issues on the organisation's demand side. It is unlikely that people lower down the organisation who have insights to offer on these points will be asked for their views on leadership at all; it is simply deemed their job to receive it.[13]

Yet it is in the heart of organisations, and in people's experience of and in organisations, that we find the vital clues to making the leadership effort cohesive and pointed in the right direction.

REFRAMING THE
LEADERSHIP MODEL

As I identify in Chapter 1, the systemic leadership model challenges the conventional, individual-centric model. In reframing the model more firmly in favour of what is directly going on in the organisation itself, and what needs to be going on, this book may seem to be swimming against the popular tide. But there are signs of a welcome shift in a number of areas, including the public sector and executive coaching.

---

12   Understanding supply- and demand-side issues is fundamental to the systemic leadership model. The subject is fully considered in Chapter 5, *Switching the Leadership Mindset to the System.*

13   In systems thinking terms, this is a classic example of change by planning without knowledge: there is no proper understanding of the demand side.

In the public sector

Public-sector organisations are particularly drawn to the systemic model. Local authorities are attracted by the focus on the organisation as the springboard for making improvements in leadership practice, rather than the more familiar and near total reliance on individuals. The sector's ethos appears wary of approaches that suggest high-profile individual leadership. They may fear credit being given to a few leaders at the expense of the organisation as a whole, and at the expense of the service they provide to the public. They may be anxious about creating short-term personal reputations against long-term stewardship.

What convinced one local authority to go down the systemic leadership route was demographic realism. Cheshire County Council's succession planning process concluded that the council was simply running out of talented young individuals who could be earmarked for future top jobs and who could be sent on development programmes. So they needed to look more imaginatively at means by which the council's needs for leadership could be met. The answer: an organisation that is run in a way that allows leadership to flourish – where talent for leadership is recognised, valued, liberated and used for the right things. And where leadership is not wasted. This cannot be achieved without organisation development (OD) methods.

> *'You can't deliver OD unless you've got strong leadership and one of the main requirements of today's leadership is to deliver OD. One is very dependent on the other.'* [14] (Richard Crouch, Head of Human Resources and Organisational Development, Somerset County Council.)

Local government is in the forefront of recognising the importance of OD and building expertise 'to achieve significant business improvements'. Besides Somerset County Council, other examples include Gateshead Metropolitan Borough Council, Cheshire County Council (since split into two authorities) and Norfolk County Council. These councils are leaders in building OD capability and using it with large numbers of managers to tackle corporate issues.

> 'Gatehead's programme *'Working together to explore our corporate roles'* uses an assessment process to establish whether there is the right balance between control and flexibility, innovation and risk in the work that people do.' [15]

Cheshire and Norfolk are two councils that have used the systemic leadership methodology and practical toolkit directly to expand their organisation's leadership capability.

---

14   Crouch, R. (2008) quoted in *Making Successful Change Happen* (report). London: Improvement & Development Agency.

15   Gateshead Metropolitan Borough Council (2008) *Organisation development in Gateshead* (report). London: Improvement & Development Agency, 8 January, www.idea.gov.uk/idk/core/page.do?pageId=7820465 [accessed 11 March 2009].

In executive coaching

Executive coaching provides another good example of the mood change. Coaching is now embracing OD. Sam Humphrey, writing in 2006 as Unilever's coach, claimed that the company's set of competencies included one called 'organisation awareness' (though further changes have since occurred).[16] A workshop on this subject run by the Corporate Research Forum in 2006 advises: 'Coaches must learn to unpack the box marked *context* and find other levers to pull on alongside the one labelled *coaching*'.

The popular mistake made by executives and their coaches is to assume or pretend that leaders have more control than they really do. Anne Scoular, Director of Meyler Campbell, talking about the 'fundamental attribution error' in relation to coaching, says:

> 'The tendency [is] for people to over-emphasize personality-based explanations for behaviours, while under-emphasizing the role and power of situational influences. In other words, people assume that what a person does is based more on what kind of person he or she is, rather than the social and environmental forces at work on that person.' [17]

It is what *surrounds* managers that has such a powerful influence – internal social and environmental forces in the organisation's culture, systems, policies, climate and protocol. An overbearing boss's instructions and injunctions can be particularly tyrannical and ludicrous:

> *'Never discuss ideas with the Director of Marketing! Never!' (*Executive in a Dilbert cartoon reprimanding a cowering junior*)

Many of these features and pressures that are part of someone's environment are not rational; many are crazed and crazy, as the Dilbert example shows. The point is that one cannot isolate any one system variable (including leadership) as though it can exist independently from its surroundings. Facilitators neglect what Gestalt psychologists call the field. The field perspective acknowledges the indivisibility of the individual and the environment, and the constant interdependence of the two. The ability to be a transformational leader is dependent on many other contextual factors. These include the followers, their willingness, people's reputation, the reputation of previous leaders, those in an advising capacity such as HR, the culture, particular current challenges, the wish and readiness to be transformed, etc.

> 'Traditional 360 degree feedback methods, alongside many other quasi-scientific people management processes, imply that we can lift an objective, expert opinion from the messiness of human experience. Many consultants are repositories of these fantasies, and plenty collude with them.' (Fiona Coffey and Simon Cavicchia, 2005)

---

16   CRF. (2006) *Managing Coaching in Organisations.* London: Corporate Research Forum.

17   CRF. (2006) Notes based on Scoular, A., *ibid.*

The fishtank at work

The employees (including managers and leaders) in the organisation are like fish in a fishtank. People outside are adept at seeing the fish, but most fail to recognise that it's the water that sustains them and gives them organisational life. And the water is dirty! If you will pardon the expression, people, including leaders (Dilbert's boss character in the previous section is a good example) – in the same way as the fish – are constantly shitting in it, making it fearful, stressful, murky, confusing and insecure. The water – the occupants' environment – needs inspecting and cleaning often. Take this real example from the newspaper industry:

> In a letter to the executive chairman David Montgomery, seven editors working in Wegener (the Dutch arm of Mecom, a European newspaper group with over 300 titles) wrote:
> 'Confidence in the company names of Mecom and Wegener is fading away on the shop floors ... Although people work very hard, stimulus from the company management is often negative and seldom encouraging.' [18]

As the Wegener editors are themselves management, who do you think they were really aiming their criticism at, while being obfuscating about their target to protect themselves? It is obvious who beyond the shop floor had reason to feel fearful.

This example raises a number of leadership issues about executive behaviour and communication: 'what is the *company management*, beyond its executive chairman?', 'What is the role of executives who find themselves in a position like the editors? 'What can they do practically?' The position is not dissimilar to those living unhappily under a political dictatorship in many countries. There are no easy answers if you are to escape with your career (or life).

But if there is a genuine wish for managers to become and behave as leaders, then organisations need to improve what managers have to wade through. There is a big problem – the managers themselves have to make those improvements, and they need permission to do so.

> *'We are the ones we have been waiting for.'*
> (June Jordan, 1980)

Such a task isn't easy and calls for those managers to exercise leadership in order to liberate leadership. You can begin to see why it's difficult and entails breaking norms and taking risks. (I discuss managers' role as fishtank cleaners in Chapter 7, *Leadership and Organisation Development.*)

---

18   Tryhorn, C. (2008) 'Montgomery paper group to cut Dutch jobs'. London: *The Guardian*, 27 June.

Rise and fall

There are natural forces at work, which means that organisations cannot forever continue to improve, or stay at the top, or even stay the same. It's the same for people, products, campaigns, structures, reputation, health, leaders and culture. Even an organisation's leadership culture – *the way leadership is round here* – is not immune.

Everything about organisational and leadership health follows a life cycle, rising and then falling. The decay of leadership affects the organisation's decay, and vice versa. Think of the history of Enron: voted America's 'Most Innovative Company' for six consecutive years before hideous scandal and bankruptcy in 2001. Think of the history of Robert Mugabe, democratic saviour of Zimbabwe in 1980 to power-obsessed tyrant in 2008.

A dynamic that shapes the downward path in organisational health is the principle of entropy (briefly touched on in Chapter 1 and discussed fully in Chapter 11, *Leadership and Decline*). Based on natural scientific laws, entropy ensures that everything decays as it declines from a state of order towards a state of increasing disorder. Organisations can counter the natural process by taking timely injections and refreshments ('interventions'). As we shall later discover, recognising the need and rejuvenating the system calls for leadership. A vivid example in this book is the cycle of decline and rejuvenation of a staff college (see page 127).

Looking ahead

Most organisations are confused about leadership. They are unclear about what they want it for, how to plan for it, how to handle it, how to release it, how to supervise it, how to hold it to account, and how to improve it. They variously sponsor, license, support, thwart, and squander their managers' attempts at leadership. Not knowing what they want, what they are doing, or what to do, they dump the leadership agenda at HR Development's door.

This book demonstrates that the key player in the process of *improving* leadership is the organisation itself. It elevates the organisation to the role of responsible and informed partner, indeed driver, in the provision and delivery of leadership to the business, firm, enterprise or institution, as well as the many stakeholders that the business is there to serve.

SUMMARY OF CHAPTER KEY POINTS

1. Individual leadership – whatever it is, at all levels, and however it comes about – is deeply important to organisations, their employees and other stakeholders, as well as to the wider economy and society.

2. An organisation-led approach offers a strategic platform that helps to make individual development more robust and rooted firmly in the organisation's reality and future.

3. Without a firm organisational base, leadership and its potential will choose to remain loose, tentative, infrequent, hazardous, and hidden below the parapet.

4. The essence of the systemic dimension of leadership development and improvement is found in the question: 'How can the organisation, working as a system, enable appropriate leadership to flourish?'.

5. Leadership coaches tend to assume that what an executive does is based more on what kind of person he or she is, rather than the social and environmental forces at work on that person. What surrounds managers/ leaders has a powerful influence on their behaviour and what they can achieve.

6. Organisations need to improve what managers have to wade through if the latter are to become and behave as leaders. But it is managers who have to make those improvements to their surroundings.

7. Organisations are unclear about what they want leadership for, how to plan for it, how to handle it, how to release it, how to supervise it, how to hold it to account, and how to improve it. They variously sponsor, license, support, thwart, and squander managers' attempts at leadership.

8. Leadership needs to be applied to the organisation, and the organisation needs to apply itself to leadership.

9. Organisations have a habit of unwisely and unthinkingly dumping the whole of the leadership agenda at HR Development's door.

CHAPTER 3:

FROM MANAGING TO LEADING

- ☐ *Making a distinction*
- ☐ *Why the distinction matters*
- ☐ *Focusing on the system or the people*
- ☐ *Turning managers into leaders*

Leadership. Most people say that leadership is important. But what is it? Leadership resists all attempts at definition. People recognise leadership when they experience it. They know when leadership is missing and when it is most needed. Can there be any subject more important to business and organisations, to the wellbeing of the economy and society, and to safeguarding our future and that of our children, a subject that has attracted so much study and so may books, yet which still eludes understanding and definition, let alone agreement? One thing is for sure: experts will continue to disagree about what leadership is.

> 'Like beauty, leadership is in the eye of the beholder and therefore cannot be defined.'
> (Interviewee during research study)

It is possible to feel some sympathy with this interviewee. Like the question often asked of art, is it essential to have a formal and agreed definition? Can one simply not appreciate leadership for what it is? Yet, without agreement, or at least some form of consensus, how can firms claim to be able to develop it?

But there is a problem. Even national bodies and institutes which claim that success depends on high-quality leadership cannot distinguish leading from managing. Some don't try. Some go so far as to claim that trying to define leadership is unimportant. So what is going on? Welcome to the paradox of leadership.

This chapter proposes its own view of leadership. It makes a clear distinction between leading and managing; based on this it then draws conclusions for how leadership can be developed and improved. Some of the territory may sound familiar; some will be new, especially how firmly leadership is placed in its organisational setting, and the importance of an organisational context that takes account of the future.

Note: when speaking of 'leadership', I am talking about acts, activities, processes and functions, not the job positions of people who describe themselves as leadership or management. Although the words 'leadership' and 'management' are commonly used, where there is a possible risk of confusing the process with people's positions, this book talks about *leading* and *managing*.

DOES THE DISTINCTION BETWEEN
LEADING AND MANAGING MATTER?

Every day we encounter the terms 'managing/management' on the one hand, and 'leading/leadership' on the other, used loosely, almost interchangeably. It's understandable. Many people's job titles contain the word 'manager'; fewer contain the word 'leader'. Managers have both roles: they are expected to display leadership at times as well as manage. And, confusingly, senior executives and directors need to be good at managing too, not just at leading. Some people think of leadership as the focus of a manager's particular behaviour to suit a given context. Does any of this matter?

The widespread lack of any consensus on what leading means, and how it differs from managing, invites the question as to whether this discussion concerning the difference is about nothing more than linguistic niceties, labelling, upmarket fashion and management-speak. Or is it about something real that has important ramifications? Essex University finds the distinction helpful:

> 'Management and leadership are two distinct functions. The first is about the achievement of today's requirements; the second [concerned] with the creation of the dynamic that realises tomorrow's.' [19]

In *A Manager's Guide to Leadership*, Mike Pedler, John Burgoyne and Tom Boydell (2004) make an important distinction:

> 'Leadership is concerned with finding direction and purpose in the face of critical challenges, whereas managing is about organising to achieve desired purposes – efficiently, effectively and creatively. … Without challenging tasks there is no call for leadership.'

In *A Force for Change: How Leadership Differs from Management*, John Kotter (1990) argues that strong managers produce predictability and order, but leaders create, communicate and implement visions of the future which enable companies to change themselves in a changing competitive marketplace.

In *Leadership in Organizations*, John Storey (2004) echoes the point that 'leaders' seek to 'challenge and change systems', whereas managers 'seek to operate and maintain current systems'. He also argues that the focus of leaders is longer term and more 'strategic big picture'.

Based on the above, there are two points to make:

First, these views may be of their time. They convey an image of a small number of leaders who are in commanding positions of authority. There is no hint here of leadership being widely distributed among managers. (As evidence of implied exclusivity, just consider: How frequently are large numbers of managers expected to have visions, think long term and 'big picture'?)

---

19   University of Essex (2008) *Summary of management development strategy 2003/4 – 2006/7*, www.essex.ac.uk/staffdev/ [accessed 11 March 2009].

Secondly, two of the authors imply that the managers are different people from the leaders; a person is one or the other. Compare this with the current view that managing and leading are different roles/acts of a manager, both coming and going according to need, and sometimes only fleetingly. They are not separate people based on different personality types (Mitch McCrimmon, 2006).

In any case, not everyone wholly agrees that it is important to distinguish between managing and leading. Britain's Chartered Management Institute (CMI) – the representative institute for the occupation of managers – chooses not to make the distinction. Their view appears to be that the Institute's members practise both, switching seamlessly between them, in which case the decision not to define each term against the other makes practical sense. Managers don't come to work saying 'I'm going to do some managing this morning, and this afternoon I'll do some leading. Managing and leading aren't compartmentalised as easily as, say, reading and writing. Here is CMI's combined definition:

> 'The key purpose of management and leadership is to provide direction, gain commitment, facilitate change and achieve results through the efficient, creative and responsible use of resources.' [20]

Given the Institute's role and market, the lack of a distinctive focus for the activity of leading, however pragmatic it may be, nevertheless hinders those who wish to increase, develop, assess, recruit, performance manage, or reward managers' distinctive capability at leading, separately from managing.

Take another example, this one from the *Leadership Strategy for Policing*:

> 'The debate that focuses on the difference between management and leadership is unhelpful. It is recognised that although good managers may not become good leaders, it is not possible to be a good leader without an extensive understanding and skills base in the facets of management, including the management of people, finance and technology.' [21]

At first glance a stance that says the difference is unhelpful seems rather shocking in a formal leadership strategy document. Is it possible to publish a leadership strategy and then state that it not worth defining the subject? But context is paramount. Given that the NPIA's context for its view is 'development content', you can begin to see their point. Their courses are, they claim, *for leaders*, who need to learn many things, including leadership, management, business skills, and so on. Their leadership courses are not about *leading* and *leadership per se*. So the question arises: while officers and managers need to learn professional skills, executive skills and business skills, is the underpinning taxonomy – what skill fits under which label – important? Actually, I would argue that the answer is Yes, though not so much for the officers and managers themselves as it is for the organisation.

---

20   MSC. (2008) *National Occupational Standards for Management and Leadership*. London: Management Standards Centre (part of the Chartered Management Institute).

21   NPIA (2008) *ibid*.

Why a definition of leadership *does* matter <u>to the organisation</u>

McCrimmon (2006) argues that there may have been a time when the difference didn't matter very much. That view began to change in the 20th century with the inroads made by Japanese business in the United States. American managers, researchers, academics and commentators woke up and realised that something different was needed, including a need to differentiate managers and leaders in organisations according to their primary function. This approach defines leadership in terms of *what it is for*, not personal behaviours, qualities or personality. The point of leadership is that it can produce useful change, while management can create orderly results. Change is the function of leadership, claims John Kotter (1990). This viewpoint is summarised as:

> **Management** – To execute today's business in line with agreed goals.

> **Leadership** – To create the future, to reinvent themselves, to adapt to new demands.

In the 21st century that search for differentiation and a modern understanding continues apace. Differentiation by primary function appears fairly set (although some are still battling with outdated notions of personality and behavioural differences). But whereas once the differentiation was between managers and leaders, now it is between managing and leading. The point is that these roles are more likely now to be needed and found in the same person: sometimes a manager leads and sometimes a manager manages. The real debate has moved on to the question of who in organisations needs these roles, and how far are they distributed.

One area where it is most difficult to separate managing and leading is that of people management, which leads some to conclude that trying to find the distinction is not worth the effort. If a manager has both a managing role and a leading role, and if both managing and leading call for people skills, then the two roles don't appear to look very different. But what about an area where the act of leading concerns non-people activity, such as the way managers think and plan for the future or steer change? It may then become more obvious where leading is noticeably different from managing; i.e. in their fundamental *purpose*.

To further clarify the distinction, we can ask 'What does leadership mean <u>to whom</u>?' It can mean one thing for the individual manager, something else for those being managed, and something else for the organisation.

The feel of leadership is also affected by whether you are on the giving or receiving end. Recipients – all manner of stakeholders and staff – view leadership from their own perspective. People may readily accept that they are being managed – even if badly – but deny that they are receiving leadership; poor leadership may be interpreted as an absence of leadership. It seems a more subjective and loaded term than does management.

■ Confining leadership to its social context

Most definitions of leadership stress its social role, arguing that leadership primarily concerns a person's ability to conduct relationships successfully (Goffee and Jones, 2000). The National Policing Improvement Agency supports this line in suggesting that leadership means how the individual officer manages people relationships, adding that since leading is akin to managing and that people need to learn both, it is not worth teasing out the difference; what matters ultimately is that officers' behaviour is appropriate.

The Royal Air Force takes this a step further.

> *'Leadership is what you do in a front-line combat situation when you have to get men to risk their lives.'* (High-ranking RAF officer)

No doubt getting men to place their lives at risk includes special qualities, which many people would call leadership. This fits with the view that leadership lies in the domain of relationships between managers and those who report to them. Some senior RAF officers go on to conclude that 'Everything else is management'. The quoted officer's wing commanders, who manage a large RAF base station, hold this view, asking why they need to study leadership in their management roles.

So the question arises: Does running the RAF entail leadership? If it does, then perhaps such behaviour is simply not thought of as leadership and is not called that. But does how we think of leadership behaviour and how we label it prevent the exercise of appropriate leadership behaviour? Let's look at an example from the British Army:

In 2005 the deep-seated culture problems of Deepcut Army Barracks were denied by senior Ministry of Defence personnel and politicians until the House of Commons Defence Committee published its scathing *Duty of Care* report on 14 March 2005. It concluded that the Army's leadership had been failing in its duty of care towards young and vulnerable recruits – whether the bullying has been from officers, NCOs or fellow recruits.

The Deepcut scandal is an example of what I mean by the 'context' that should be built into the leadership improvement process. It answers the question: When developing leadership capability, what does the Army want it for? Does the Army accept that leadership is relevant for both combat and non-combat situations? Does it accept that the role includes leadership *of* the organisation and not just *in* it? (See Chapter 4, *New Conceptions of Leadership*, for a full discussion of this distinction). This confusion about where leadership is needed, who needs it and what it is for, goes right up to the top, as the Commons report makes clear.

■ **The naming of parts**

Much comes down to language. Can language – in this case the difference between 'management' and 'leadership' – be dismissed so lightly? It's as though the *naming of parts* was unimportant militarily, provided that the rifle could be dismantled, properly cleaned, and put back together. Where does that leave the philosophical point that a different word triggers a different mindset and a different way of thinking? As the Austrian philosopher Ludwig Wittgenstein put it: 'Different words create different worlds'. If the wing commanders thought of their home base roles as entailing leadership, would that open their minds to different learning, different behaviour, and a different focus for their work and time? And might it lead to a different way of viewing the management of the leadership aspect of their performance?

■ **A sphere of leadership beyond leaders**

If we assume that leadership is different from management, that we need a way of talking about leadership that makes the distinction clear, and that this is important for running an organisation successfully, then that takes us to the next question: Is there scope for a sphere of leadership beyond individual leaders? The key test is this: if the leading is done well and is well-received (i.e. people respond as you need them to), does this entirely satisfy the organisation's need for leadership? Put another way, will managers' leadership behaviour alone ensure that the organisation is well led?

The policing example helps us with this test. Compared with today's policing mission and role, the NPIA portrays a very different future: policing with consent, harnessing the energies of communities and partners, globalisation, a child protection role, new technology and science, etc. Given this changing context, presumably leadership *does* have an impact and a meaning that includes, but importantly reaches beyond, each individual officer's relationships, whether they are inside the organisation with peers and their teams (the usual assumption) or outside with 'customers' and increasingly with partners and other stakeholders. That sphere of leadership concerns change and improvement to secure a better future:

> 'An inspiring leader induces us to change direction while an inspiring manager motivates us to work harder to get a tough job done.' (McCrimmon, 2007)

The same applies to the RAF, Army and indeed all organisations. Ergo, the definition of leadership cannot be confined to individual relationships or individual leaders; it has an organisational dimension, a system carrier and company ownership. It is in this setting that we must search for what is at the heart of the organisation's own interest in leadership.

Choosing leaders and leadership

If you don't know whether your organisation needs leadership, and you don't know what leadership is needed for, then you are likely to end up making poor choices when selecting candidates for senior positions. Take this example.

A friend was interviewed for a high-powered OD job in a public utility. She was invited to discuss how well she mapped against the list of competencies drawn up for that job. This presented my friend with a dilemma: she could either try to be convincing and play the interviewers' game, or she could be bold, take a risk and say:

'You're asking the wrong questions! You are checking how well I can fit in with an organisation that sees itself as a bureaucracy. Your competencies perpetuate the status quo. But your organisation needs to change, because your future is changing. You need to appoint someone with leadership qualities not just management competencies. You need (but may not realise it or even relish it) someone who has ideas, energy and courage to challenge things as they are. If OD is about anything, it is about that. Now do you want to talk or not?'

The bureaucratic model used for this interview came out of the continuity stable. Its values were: what we (selectors and organisation) know, what we can control, low risk, stability, a predictable future, and contentment. They were trying to recruit a manager who would fit in.

If instead the values had been: what we don't know, high risk, change, an unpredictable future, disturbance, and tension, then the process for selecting a suitable candidate would have been very different. Interviewers could have asked:

What would you want to do with the power to change things that this job would give you?'

They would then consciously be trying to recruit a leader, or at least someone with the interests and qualities associated with leadership.

What appears to have been missing in the selection process was an appropriate pre-selection conversation inside the organisation about what change it needed, what it needed leadership for, and therefore what it needed OD capability for. The price paid for missing this out was an inappropriate discussion at the interview and a risk of choosing the wrong candidate.

In a different transport company, an organisation which was in the process of being privatised, and thus being required to compete in a commercial marketplace for the first time, chose a new HR director based on the second set of values. He signalled HR's new change role, both within HR as well as to HR's customers, in a striking manner: he pinned badges on his senior managers labeled 'norm buster'.

MANAGERS' DUAL ROLES

If managers are to exercise leadership, their job has to change. Think of managers as having two roles:

1. Their first role is to do what they routinely consider their job to be (probably outlined in a job description). This requirement is to deliver results for the organisation through employees within the current paradigm (things as they currently are). This role calls for management. But it is not enough.

London Business School's (LBS) bold programme to shake and challenge today's model at its very core (discussed in this book's *Conclusion*) claims:

> 'Management is the last remaining bastion of organisational life not to have an inbuilt capacity for ongoing adaptation, reinvention or innovation. The world in which so much management practice resides is based on a conceptual model which separates the interests of the organisation and those of the person. It is as if the organisation is an abstract, personality free, objective entity, a mysterious cocktail of artefacts, processes and protocols. Emotional and relational-driven people are expected to use their skills and knowledge to further the goals of this disembodied structure. Management is a kind of go-between, linking these two universes, but constantly found wanting in its ability to connect them.' [22]

2. Managers' second role is to change the first – i.e. *improve* the way things are by asking challenging questions about their job. How is it adding value? Is it clear how the job is being pulled by customers' needs? How does it need to change? The aim behind this second role is to question and, if need be, change the paradigm. This role calls for leadership.

   > Ask: 'Why am I continuing to do what I am continuing to do the way I am continuing to do it?'

   How and *why* are strategic questions that draw on qualities of leadership. It is managers' second job role that gives them access to leadership characteristics in the list in Table 3 on page 46 – when it is appropriate and within their own sphere of influence.

Such a leadership role, in the manner defined here, goes some small way in giving the comfortable paradigm of management a good shake. But it may fall short of the revolutionary thinking that LBS's work calls for.

In the discipline of systems thinking, comparing roles 1 and 2 above, the *management system* that delivers today is separate from the *leadership system* that challenges, improves and thereby secures tomorrow. This concept is unpacked in Chapter 12, *Leadership and Systems*.

---

22   Middleton, S. and Matcham, A. (2008) 'Mindset management', *Labnotes 'TopCoder'*, No. 8. London: Management Lab, London Business School, May.

○ **Example: Invitation to tender**. This real instance from the world of local government illustrates the difference between managing and leading. In July 2008 an invitation to tender (ITT) was issued by a local authority's museums, library and archives services. The aim was to evaluate whether the authority was getting value for money in its use of leadership programmes for its managers (apt given the subject of this book). An upper limit for the piece of work had been budgeted at £5000.

A managerial mindset would say:

- We buy in consultancy services to provide us with answers to such questions.
- The system says we have to go out to competitive tender to obtain value for money for ratepayers.

By contrast, a leadership mindset would ask:

- Do we really want to spend the time and money preparing an ITT and then evaluating bids and interviewing a shortlist for a contract worth less than £5000?
- Is it fair to subject an unknown number of bidders to the time and expense of submitting competitive bids for a contract worth less than £5000, for which the total cost of their effort in competing for the work will probably exceed the value of the contract?
- Can we not in any case predict what consultants might say? What would our best instincts be?
- Are we really using the ITT process as a crutch? Could we use our best judgement, take a risk, and save everyone a lot of time and money?
- What would the private sector do in this situation, given that we are being urged to behave in a more businesslike way?

Having dual roles (or two hats, a *running-today* hat and an *improving-tomorrow* hat) can help to prompt the manager to think of what to do differently if donning the latter.

Over-managed and under-led. Over-led and under-managed

All managers need both to manage and to lead, but the mix varies according to a wide variety of factors and conditions. The same holds true for organisations. But some organisations are over-managed and under-led.

> 'Lead, not manage. There is an important difference. Many an institution is very well managed and poorly led. It may excel in the ability to handle each day all the routine inputs yet may never ask whether the routine should be done at all.' (Warren Bennis, 1989)

A poorly led organisation may be well-managed, and it may simply be over-managed. The latter is sometimes said of the UK's National Health Service. The reverse is possible: some organisations are over-led and under-managed; i.e. there may be no shortage of grand visionary statements about the future, but there may be insufficient managerial foot soldiers to follow-through and satisfy today's customers. A balance between managing and leading is therefore needed. In institutions relying on technical expertise, such as engineering and scientific establishments, and, indeed, the NHS, a further complicating factor is in play: that between managers and technicians. Ask this question:

In this organisation, have we got the right balance between leading and managing, and between managers and technical experts?

The explanation behind different perceptions may lie in what critics think managing and leading are and whether their focus is primarily internal or external. The history and traditions of the organisation will be a factor too.

Sharpening the distinction between managing and leading is helpful because it provides a way of understanding what is going on inside under-performing organisations and what we need and would like more of. It allows those who provide oversight (including politicians) to think clearly about appropriate measures of performance. A manager's two distinct roles and contributions can then be performance managed appropriately (discussed later in Chapter 14, *Leadership and Accountability*).

Turning managers into leaders

If the organisation's leadership strategies have been well chosen, made clear and integrated within the relevant HR systems (such as promotion criteria and appraisal documentation), is that enough? Will managers use the leadership strategies? Will they know *when* to use them?

There are three approaches that companies can adopt to help achieve their desire for increased leadership behaviour. These are presented here in increasing levels of radicalism:

- **Managers more like leaders**

    The name of the game with this strategy is to extend management activity in the direction of leading. Leadership competencies are therefore added to, and merged with, a list of management competencies (though these may confusingly also be called 'leadership competencies'). For example, the list of leadership competencies for managers published by Centrica, the company that owns British Gas, includes *Creates a compelling future* (i.e. leadership) along with *Delivers great performance* (i.e. management).[23] (See also Chapter 9, *Leadership and Competence*.)

---

23   Centrica (2005) www.centrica.com/files/reports/2005cr/files/leadership_competencies.pdf [accessed 11 March 2009].

- **Sometimes managers, sometimes leaders**

  Here, managers should make conscious choices to adopt specific leadership competencies when the need arises. Leadership competencies are therefore identified in a way that makes them distinct, helping managers to see the wider framework and understand which kind of behaviour falls under which category.

- **Leaders rather than managers**

  With this strategy the organisation has generally decided to favour leading over managing (possibly just for senior managers and maybe just at this time). This strategy highlights the contrast between managing and leading, and encourages the latter; for example, expecting this group of managers to concentrate on change, tomorrow and improving the system, while leaving front-line staff to be more self-managing for their everyday operational work.

  > 'In systems design, management's role is complementary. If the work can be controlled by the people who do it, why do we need managers? The answer is to act on the system, to take responsibility for all the things outside the control of the workers that have a bearing on how the work works.' (Seddon, 2008)

Most organisations adopt the first and easiest strategy by default. They have not worked out what the organisation really means by leading and what it needs. They are content to leave that distinction and practice to individual managers.

There are risks of leaving it open. Taking one crucial example, if managers are left to decide for themselves whether their unit needs more stability or more upheaval, the organisation may not get its needs met for one or the other, or the right balance between them. Managers' perceptions will differ on this, as will their disposition, comfort zone and skills.

In practice, the most likely outcome of this strategy will be excessive stability, with managers choosing not to behave as leaders of change unless pressed to, or unless it is made abundantly clear to them in a particular context that this is one of their prime roles and is required of them.

Of their own volition, managers are unlikely to choose consciously between a course of action based on stability versus change, but will simply muddle through, or follow a pattern that fits with their personality and preferred style. If a shake-up really *is* needed, then relying on a list of behaviours that blurs managing and leading may be neither sufficiently strategic nor sufficiently proactive.

MANAGING	LEADING
☐ Delivers today	☐ Secures tomorrow
☐ Works within the existing paradigm	☐ Changes the paradigm
☐ Uses the present business model	☐ Develops the next business model
☐ Manages the people for productivity, efficiency and effectiveness	☐ Manages the system for productivity, efficiency and effectiveness
☐ Operates within the system	☐ Steps outside the system to challenge and improve it
☐ Maintains consistency, ensures order and prevents excessive disturbance	☐ Questions current rules and norms and disturbs the organisation
☐ Executes existing directions as efficiently as possible	☐ Promotes new directions
☐ Has goals derived from necessities	☐ Has goals derived from desires
☐ Understands the present	☐ Explains current reality
☐ Achieves more with less and gets the work done efficiently	☐ Provides focused direction for the common good
☐ Does things right	☐ Does right things
☐ People, operations, information, finance	☐ Inspires and empowers people
☐ Processes, statistics, calculations, routines	☐ Envisions and communicates the future
☐ Planning, organising, monitoring and controlling	☐ Aligns people with the organisation
☐ Problem solving	☐ Provides meaning for people's work
☐ Science	☐ Art
	☐ Provides good governance
	☐ Balances long-term stakeholders' interests

Table 3: Managing versus leading

In the part of a manager's job that is concerned with relationships with people – i.e. leading and managing those who report to the manager – generic definitions of the leading and managing roles may suffice. But the organisation still needs a discussion about what it expects from its managers in their relationships. And the company has an additional agenda: it needs clarity about what leading and managing the *organisation* means, given the latter's evolving circumstances.

Once the distinctive meaning of *leading* versus *managing* is clear for the business, the organisation can design and run personnel systems for appointment, development, appraisal, promotion and reward more effectively. These systems can specifically target either leading or managing *where this distinction matters* (as the ITT case on page 43 showed). This helps to ensure that the organisation's need for managers to exercise leadership doesn't get overlooked in their pursuit of their management role. They need to know when to manage and when to lead, and they need to understand on what to concentrate their leadership role and energies.

FOCUSING LEADERSHIP ON THE ORGANISATION

If the ultimate purpose of leadership is to help an organisation continually to adapt, improve and change to safeguard its future, then its prime focus needs be on the organisation. Leadership's focus of people is to that end. That calls for an internal conversation about what the activity of *leading* means practically. What does it mean for the organisation now, given the demands upon it, the challenges it faces, with its current problems, aspirations, and change agenda? We take a look at two well-known and interlinked leadership challenges facing all complex organisations.

The challenge of life cycle

What does leadership mean for an organisation at a particular time in its life cycle, given the ever-present tension between the forces in favour of centralising, standardising and economising, and those favouring decentralising and local tailoring?

This tension is a major and a recurring issue that faces all large organisations. It particularly affects the public sector, including the organisation of police forces and local authorities – big, strategic, economies of scale versus local, nimble, in touch, manageable scale. The structures that result from oscillating between centralisation and decentralisation both have their own weaknesses. Solving one set of organisational problems brings with it the inherent weaknesses contained in its substitute. Eventually, the need for the countervailing set of forces again becomes apparent as the weaknesses overwhelm the substitute model and lead to a recall for the alternative.

Business organisations have their own life cycles, as we see in a moment. So do public-sector institutions, influenced by a government's own life cycle. In the UK's public sector, centralisation has predominated for many years, but predictably cracks begin to appear:

> '[Michael Fuller, Kent Chief Constable] took aim at the government's attempts to ensure the police are up to scratch. He said up to 13 bodies had the right to inspect his force: "There's always somebody inspecting us, or we're under the threat of inspection. It is a constant inspection process. Probably at least a third of my time is spent dealing with inspection, inspection processes, preparing for inspection, accounting to inspection bodies." He said some inspection bodies made contradictory recommendations: "It actually takes us away from our core role. There's been too many targets... We've been over-inspected by too many agencies who often don't cost their recommendations, who often don't talk to each other or share information ...".' [24]

Oscillations between pressures for central control and local freedom especially afflicts politicians. Take governments' growing reliance on tests, targets and

---

24   Dodd, V. (2008) 'Labour making our job harder – police chief'. London: *The Guardian*, 4 September.

inspections. Over time political leaders grow frustrated and lose their ability to trust others to deliver. So they install a regime of centralised targets, national statistics, inspections and testing. Inevitably, in due course, this 'Stalinist solution' suffers failure and is seen as heavy-handed, remote, costly and inflexible. There is a backlash and call for a policy reversal and more local discretion and accountability. Institutions are then again trusted to manage their own affairs and focus on their own priorities for improvement. A case in point is the UK government's decision in October 2008 to scrap National Curriculum Assessment ('Sats') tests at age 14 and hand responsibility back to schools to assess the children.

In the manufacturing sector, at one time Pilkington's federal structure meant that it had 27 different specifications for hard hats. There was a price to be paid for this. With such a proliferation of practices, centralisation becomes the logical way to regain control over standards and costs. But let go at the centre to allow local control, and a proliferation of standards will return.

The same happens with prices: Magnet Joinery's head office allows each branch manager to determine prices for their depot according to what they believe works best for them, their particular local situation, and their strategy for attracting custom to their store. As a result, customers find themselves shopping around between the company's branches in their region for the best price, and may need to venture further from home to make their purchase, with no immediate obvious benefit for the joinery company. In turn, that raises the dilemma of whether head office wants branch managers to compete with each other or cooperate.

Some organisation designers believe that the oscillation is wasteful and that there must be a happy medium between centralisation and decentralisation and recommend searching for it. But a counter school of thought argues that you have to be doing one or the other at any one time, otherwise you will experience the worst of both worlds and attend to neither. So eventually, the wheel turns again; concern about different standards or prices, coupled with impatience at the centre, results in a return to centralised control (Tate, 2003b).

    ○   **Example: IT purchasing system** The BBC is installing a centralised IT-based purchasing system. This has cut the cost of placing orders from £38 to £6. But licences on about 2,000 machines were never used and some 780 staff were removed from the system because it was costing more to license them to use it than any savings they were making. And managers spent more than £200m on buying equipment outside the system, through local deals, making almost 38,000 individual purchases from suppliers with which it had no central contract.[25] The BBC notes:

> 'While there is always more that could be done to further centralise suppliers, which can reduce central costs, the NAO's report notes "that there is a balance to be struck between centralising contracts and keeping the supply base open, competitive and innovative in order to attract smaller businesses".' [26]

---

25   Henke, D. (2008) 'BBC accused of wasting millions on props, costumes and catering'. London: *The Guardian*, 13 May.

26   Peat, J. (2008) 'The BBC is not wasting millions'. London: *The Guardian* (letters page), 15 May.

John Seddon (2008) points out that leadership of the system is exercised in a context of change and improvement. He particularly calls for managerial courage to resist certain fashions such as moves towards large-scale back offices, outsourcing and illusory economies of scale.

> 'At the heart of outsourcing is the Fordist faith in mass-production: specialisation, division of labour and economies of scale. But while the formula worked for Adam Smith's pin factory, the diseconomies of scale – in the shape of massive demoralisation and labour turnover – were already becoming apparent by the time of Ford's Model-T. HMRC, and the vast shared-service factories being imposed on local authorities and other public service providers, are today's equivalent of Ford's River Rouge plant. Behind the automated document handling and batteries of computers sits a rusting, outdated hulk of a management model.' [27]

This case from the UK government's Department for Transport shows what can go wrong:

> 'A Department for Transport efficiency drive brought in to save over £50m ended up costing the taxpayer over £80m. The cost had escalated from £55m to £121m, and the projected benefits had fallen from £112m to £40m. The department had attempted to save money by integrating the main DfT computer with its seven agencies, including the Driving Standards Agency, The Driver and Vehicle Licensing Agency, and the Coastguard. The project was to create a shared service centre in Swansea to provide human resources, payroll and finance support. Only two of the agencies were using the new system and the shared service centre was failing to meet most of its performance targets. The Public Accounts Committee accused the Department for Transport of "stupendous incompetence" and said that the service was worse than that previously provided.' [28]

The challenge of efficiency versus effectiveness

All these cases have at their heart issues of efficiency and effectiveness. These two goals of management are often mentioned in the same breath, but in reality they often find themselves in opposition. Things done in the name of efficiency gains can run counter to effectiveness. Centralising back-office functions, as in the decision on prison purchasing (portrayed below), can reveal flawed logic, short-sightedness and failure to anticipate consequences, as the following story tells.

> 'I was part of the team setting up Her Majesty's Prison Service shared service centre in Newport...
> '... there was a system in place in each prison that would allow the purchasing of equipment, clothing and food from suppliers. ... Most of the fresh produce suppliers were local and therefore knew what each prison wanted. Under the old system, the prison placed an order over the phone to the supplier who rocked up with the
> *cont. overleaf*

---

27   Caulkin, S. (2008) 'Painful truth behind the Revenue's slipped disk'. London: *The Observer*, 30 March.

28   Stratton, A. (2008) 'Whitehall efficiency drive cost £80m, say MPs'. *The Guardian*, 16 December.

produce. If there were any anomalies then the driver and the catering manager could adjust the invoice accordingly before submitting to the accounts payable clerk for paying. … In the new world, an order would be placed on the new computer system (usually from a catalogue), the goods would arrive and would be checked in and receipted by the catering staff and entered onto the system, the bill would then be sent to the shared service centre's accounts payable team for them to release for payment. The issue was (and probably still is) that the computer system is stupidly precise. What I mean is that if a prison orders 6kg of beans it shouldn't matter how they receive it. However, the catalogue system meant that if you ordered 3 x 2kg cans of beans then you should received 3 items to meet that order. However, if the supplier only had 3kg cans and only brought 2 then the system would reject the receipt and prevent payment. This was the same for every item. I was in Leeds and was watching a chap receipting an order. The prison had ordered 500 apples which usually came in 10 boxes of 50. However, on this occasion all the boxes had been bundled into 1 crate so there was only 1 item in the consignment. The chap receipting therefore entered the number being received as 1. The system then rejected the order as it required an additional 9 boxes to be delivered before it would pay.

'As a result of this fantastic system the team on the accounts payable section saw their work in progress escalate and the number of suppliers threatening to take their business elsewhere increase. … After nine months I left. Mostly because of the sheer blinkered view that centralisation cuts costs.' [29]

Such examples require leadership to bring about complex change, reorganisation and improvement. This applies both for those charged with taking controversial decisions and for the armies of managers who have to try to make a success of decisions taken 'higher up' or by politicians. A failure of leadership in cases like the above can include:

- failure to recognise when change is needed and when not
- failure to anticipate what might happen
- failure to understand the nature of systems
- failure to understand human dynamics

Knowing when or how to resist or to support controversial decisions, and how to behave loyally and responsibly with one's own team in times of uncomfortable change also calls on qualities of leadership.

---

29   Anonymous subscriber (2008) *Vanguard News*, August. Buckingham: Vanguard Consulting.

SUMMARY OF CHAPTER KEY POINTS

1. The act of leading/leadership is not the sole preserve of those designated 'leaders', nor is it tied to position. The role comprises a process, acts, activity, response, moment, or phase, and is open to anyone when called for. It is one part of every manager's job at appropriate times.

2. Leading/leadership is principally distinguished from managing/ management by its function; i.e. what leadership is for, what it achieves for the organisation, not what it looks like in managers' qualities, behaviours or personality.

3. The prime purpose of leadership and its main value to a business is to ensure that the organisation continually improves and changes to ensure that the business has a secure future. Management activity is more short-term focused and more concerned with meeting today's known challenges.

4. The more senior positions are more likely to contain a requirement for focusing a greater proportion of time on securing the future and on focusing on the organisation as a whole than on today's operations and managing individuals' performance.

5. An organisation needs to achieve an appropriately balanced state between stability and change, and between today and tomorrow.

6. It also needs its managers to achieve an appropriate balance between their managing and leading roles. The organisation should clarify, guide and encourage managers to choose appropriately and achieve that balance.

7. Talking the language of leading is important. It changes perceptions of managers' role, and it opens the door to organisations stewarding leadership separately from management.

8. When needing to appoint a senior executive, an organisation needs to do its homework beforehand, confronting the stark choice between choosing leadership/shake-up/risk qualities or management/stability/reliability qualities – especially for roles with an OD/change element.

9. Don't rely on lists of behaviours that blur managing and leading if you want the organisation to obtain, manifest and oversee the leadership it needs.

10. Don't confuse the drive for greater efficiency with the drive for greater effectiveness. The former may turn out to be a false god and come at the expense of the latter.

11. Lists of competencies that distinguish between managing and leading will not, on their own, ensure that managers will choose the leadership option or know when or to what to apply it.

CHAPTER 4:

NEW CONCEPTIONS
OF LEADERSHIP

- ☐ *Levels of leadership*
- ☐ *The need to manage leadership*
- ☐ *How leadership is changing*
- ☐ *Distributed leadership*
- ☐ *Leadership in, of, by and for the organisation*
- ☐ *Giving and receiving leadership*

Who are the carriers of leadership? We know that leadership may be exercised by a manager or other individual, as well as by a team such as an executive board or management group. Sometimes the term 'leadership' is applied to things like innovation and concepts – thought leadership, cost leadership and environmental leadership. This chapter takes this idea a step further. Another way of thinking about leadership is to treat it as a characteristic of the organisational system that surrounds managers and of which they are also a part.

In contrast to individual-centric and team-based models of leadership, the systemic route places the organisation at the heart of leadership practice and improvement. If personal leadership is thought of as level 1, and collective leadership teams as level 2, then systemic leadership is level 3.

Level 1	The individual leader and personal leadership	
Level 2	Collective leadership teams	
Level 3	Internal organisational system leadership/ systemic leadership	← The book's main target
Level 4	The business's outward projection of leadership	

Table 4: Levels of leadership

Level 3 addresses the organisation as a system, including what the organisation needs from future leadership and how the system delivers and uses leadership to become better led. At this third level, the actor, carrier, conveyer, source, owner and manifestor of leadership is the organisation. It is unusual to find leadership developers' interventions that think about, let alone target, the system in this way, though OD interventions achieve some of this. Level 3 is where this book's primary interest lies.

> 'People's heightened interdependence and need to exert authority and leadership at all levels calls for a focus on systemic leadership capacity. Focusing only on top executives as the sole source of organizational leadership hinders the confrontation of the more troubling, deeper problems contributing to the contemporary crisis in leadership.' (Krantz, 1990)

Arguably, there is a fourth level: the business entity that is the outward-facing manifestation of the organisation that supports it. A company can manifest leadership in terms of its reputation as a brand, price, market or sector leader. It may be recognised as a leader in corporate responsibility, governance or environmental matters. In the public sector, a council may provide strong leadership in local government ('leadership of place' is the jargon). I will touch on this fourth level only lightly.

MANAGING LEADERSHIP AS A RESOURCE

To study how the organisation as a system operates to foster and deliver leadership calls for novel ways of understanding what sort of thing leadership is. As we have seen, leadership is more than a job, a position, a level, a status. Leadership is more than what leaders do, more than their personality, behaviour, style, competence, and even more than the action they take and more than a process. The label 'leadership' may be used for all these things, but it is also a *resource*. As such, leadership can be thought of rather like other valuable intangible assets; for example, brand reputation and a loyal customer base. That way of thinking about leadership holds some important implications, which can be summarised in the question: What is this resource used for, and how is it best deployed and utilised?

Leadership can be thought of as one of the properties or defining characteristics of an organisation. Leadership lies at the heart of an organisation's governance and success. People recognise an organisation and they experience its brand as a result of the way the organisation is led. This is what makes leadership a key corporate *resource*, one that calls for serious stewardship.

So there is a need to manage leadership, however oxymoronic that may sound. Such a vital resource should not be left to find its own future, its direction, priorities, applications and meaning. Leadership and deciding the needs of their organisation cannot be left to individual managers and developers alone. Yet this is what routinely happens (i.e. develop leadership and then leave it alone: don't point it at what matters most, and don't manage its accountability).

As a key resource, an organisation's management of leadership entails being clear about:

- How the organisation defines and understands leadership.
- What the organisation currently needs leadership for.

- How that need is changing.
- What the needs of the organisation's stakeholders are to *receive* leadership.
- What the organisation's current priorities are for leadership attention.
- What is happening in the organisation's environment that holds implications for leadership.
- How leadership itself needs to change.
- How the leadership resource can be expanded and developed.
- How focus will be maintained and embedded, and not be today's good idea, only to be forgotten tomorrow.
- How the system will support the use of its leadership resource.
- How the organisation can prevent the waste of leadership.
- How managers' leadership will be performance managed.
- How leadership will be held to account, when most needed, and especially in cases of failure.

   ○ **Example: Accountability** A key aspect of leadership that is routinely under-managed is *accountability*. By that I mean having and operating clear and regular processes for explicitly holding managers to account for their leadership, including any lack of it. Rarely is it even clear where responsibility lies at senior executive level for ensuring that the organisation has a rigorous accountability system in place, one that is well designed, recognised, practised and respected.

Especially in the design of major change initiatives, it is rare to find accountability clearly specified and processes in place. Simply saying that the chief executive is accountable doesn't lead to anything different happening that contributes to a more successful outcome – which is the purpose of having sharpened accountability. (For guidance on how to manage this, see Chapter 14, *Leadership and Accountability*.)

Leadership needs to provide oversight and itself needs oversight. Leadership holds others to account and itself needs to be held to account. (This is why governance best practice calls for the separation of the roles of chief executive and company chairman.) Governance is an obvious example where people accept that leadership at the most senior levels needs to be managed, supervised and subject to proper scrutiny. The formalities of the governance process are relatively well-understood, specified and practised. But in most organisations accountability is given much less attention.

Sponsoring then abandoning leadership

The contribution that the system makes to the presence or absence of leadership needs managing too. The need to manage the process of leadership in the organisation is separate from the need to manage the people who lead (and manage).

In most organisations, the management of the leadership *process* remains loose – loosely specified, loosely targeted and loosely monitored. Leadership is developed at the behest of the organisation yet is then largely abandoned by the organisation. It should be maintaining an active interest in directly focusing leadership's effort, managing its usage, and exploiting its potential.

In many organisations, the process of leadership may be vaguely mediated via individual managers, but is left lacking any real corporate definition and steer and is somehow expected to look after itself. Indeed, one can think of the whole of this book as being about managing leadership and attempting to fill that vacuum. The consequence of the failure to manage leadership effectively is that much of this valuable resource goes to waste.

What does the organisation need leadership for?

- It is important that the organisation is clear about its needs for leadership, as media stories show time and again.

> In November 2007 two CDs went missing from the Child Benefit Agency in Wearside (part of Her Majesty's Revenue & Customs) containing 25 million data records containing names and bank account details. Investigations followed by the Independent Police Complaints Commission (IPPC) and the management consultant Kieran Poynter. On 25 June 2008 the Chancellor of the Exchequer, Alistair Darling, reported to the House of Commons the findings of those investigations. These included IPPC's conclusion that 'there was an absence of a coherent strategy for mass data handling ... and a muddle-through ethos ...', and from Poynter that 'A great deal of work will be needed to bring HMRC up to and to sustain the world-class standards for information security to which it aspires.' [30]

The IPPC's conclusion that 'there was an absence of a coherent strategy for mass data handling' and HMRC had 'a muddle-through ethos' highlights a need and priority for leadership attention. All companies face choices that need to be made at the macro level about priorities at a given time, and these choices affect the need for and focus of leadership. Some current examples of companies and their possible leadership priorities are listed in the following table:

BBC	Reduce profligacy; manage within its means
M&S and Tesco	Extend green credentials. Become more global
Airlines	Balance security and customer ease
Royal Mail	Improve productivity. Mend relations with unions. Manage loss of monopoly. Adjust to reduced mail volume from electronic messaging
Mowlem	Fend off predators
Banks	Improve public image. Improve risk management

---

30   (2008) *The World at One*, BBC Radio 4, 25 June.

BP	Improve safety. Reduce fat
Pharmaceuticals	Embrace social responsibility
NHS	Overcome MRSA and C Deficile
Farming	Transform role to manage countryside
Northern Rock	Improve governance

Table 5: Possible priorities for leadership attention

Note that some of these leadership priorities are external and business related, while others are concerned with the organisation that serves the business.

How is leadership changing for an organisation?

Changes in an organisation's environment, changing stakeholder expectations, and emerging priorities may dictate a change of style, culture, mood or pace, moving from the 'external what' towards the 'internal how'. Such considerations help to shape the organisation's new leadership agenda. For example:

Becoming more or less competitive/collaborative
Offering more or less security of employment
Putting the customer first
Shaking up or consolidating and calming down
Speeding up or slowing the pace
Becoming more innovative
Becoming less bureaucratic

Table 6: Examples of shifts with leadership implications

Fleshing out the leadership agenda is tough. Answers may not be durable, but that is not a reason to avoid them; the conversation is important. The main mental blockage for most organisations at the moment is that leadership – its practice and development – is seen as universal, timeless and context-free. It isn't. And because it isn't (i.e. there are choices) and because it is highly unpredictable, leadership needs to be managed.

What are the organisation's assumptions and expectations?

Many organisations behave as if they have little choice but to leave leadership to chance and that the best they can hope for is to develop leaders and then cross their fingers and hope managers will lead wisely. In most cases, the organisation's only or main contribution to improving leadership is to provide development opportunities. Those assumptions communicate a sense of powerlessness and an imagination void. They are diametrically opposed to the assumptions in this book and in the *Systemic Leadership Toolkit*. The toolkit directly addresses current leadership practice within organisations and the active role the organisation should play in getting its needs for leadership met. For example:

- When should managers manage and when should they lead?
- When should managers let others lead?
- In what circumstances would managers be permitted to lead?
- Is power distributed in a way that gives managers real power to lead?
- Does the organisation remove obstacles to managers taking a lead?
- What are the risks to managers' careers when they try to lead?
- What are managers focusing their attention on when they lead?

Who owns leadership?

If we identify leadership exclusively with individuals, the more likely it is that we will manage the subject as a branch of personal development. But if we identify leadership with the organisation, the more likely it is that the business's own needs for leadership will be met. And the more likely it is that the resulting leadership strategy will take account of society's, and other stakeholders', needs and expectations for business leadership in the new economy of the 21st century.

The conventional model for leadership improvement tackles the connection between the organisation and the individual indirectly: it naively assumes that the *sum* of individuals attempting to exercise leadership will somehow deliver leadership for the organisation as a whole and result in making it better led overall. It is not clear how this should be expected to happen. Some say via that mythical creature, the 'critical mass'. But even if members of this critical mass knew what to do, this doesn't provide the answer, as I explore in Chapter 1.

To achieve a beneficial outcome for the organisation overall, organisations must (among other things such as providing managers with the necessary resources) deliver a leadership agenda that includes:

- a shared, honest and valid purpose
- a path ahead and forward journey that is clear
- a safe and supportive leadership culture and climate
- a clear leadership structure that works fluidly
- both individual and collective aims and objectives
- clear priorities at this time
- a minimum of obstacles.

Leadership cannot simply be left to individual managers to work out for themselves. It cannot be assumed, for example, that managers will avoid the temptation of using leadership for personal benefit (misusing power, hoarding information, etc.). Organisations have an interest in knowing:

- What will managers do with their leadership?
- What *are* they doing with it?

- What are they *not* doing with it?
- What does the organisation need them to do with it?
- What will stop them?
- What will start them?

A reliance on trust, faith, a wing and a prayer is not enough. If organisations want to end up in a healthy place, leadership cannot be relinquished to agents such as management development (MD) departments or contracted suppliers of training. Delivering the leadership that the organisation requires, and improving the organisation's leadership, is a strategic activity before it is a training activity. The strategy – indeed the *lead* – needs to come from the organisation itself.

LEADERSHIP AND CHANGE

There is *always* a change agenda – known, emergent or suppressed. But where, or who, does it come from? Pressure for change may come from the top, middle or bottom. Resistance may come from the top, middle or bottom. But instructions to change come from the top. Hierarchical organisations still think that responsibility for knowing what change is needed and commanding that change (usually required of others) rests at senior levels, and that this view of responsibility determines who has a leadership role. But more organic views of the change process and people's role in it are taking hold, as this example from the company Google shows.

> 'Decision-making, he [Google's CEO Eric Schmidt] says, is the 'wisdom of crowds' model. Every issue, no matter how small, is debated – and seniority does not count. To get the best decisions, one of his most important tasks is to identify dissidents (good decisions require disagreement), but then to establish a deadline to prevent discussions from continuing indefinitely.
> '... As the fastest-growing company in UK history, says Schmidt, Google has faced every management problem ever invented, but simultaneously rather than in sequence. In an unpredictable future there will be plenty more. 'I try to anticipate the problem and say, "OK, you guys, you think you're so smart, what are we going to do about this?" And that provokes the internal debate.' [31]

Google's situation is unusual, but the trend it represents responds to more egalitarian and less deferential times than we have been used to in the past. It makes change seem a more natural way of conducting business for everyone, not dependent on an announcement from the boss, from 'management' or head office. It is also more likely that change suits people and is freed from the vested interest of the prevailing hierarchy: turkeys don't naturally vote for Christmas. But that still leaves some questions:

- Who maps the external environment? (This task is relatively easy.)

---

31   Caulkin, S. (2008) 'How to make $4bn without really managing'. London: *The Observer*, 27 July.

- Who thinks about the internal implications for the organisation? (This is more challenging and often not undertaken because the default assumption is often to address individual managers' required skills.)
- Whose job contains responsibility for ensuring the company gets the kind of organisation that is needed? How far can this responsibility be shared with managers? (The more senior a manager's position, the more an incumbent holds some accountability for the organisation's design and how well it functions.)
- Who knows best how the organisation is working, how it can be improved, and who has most to gain? (The answer – mostly it's front-line staff.)

'New notions of leadership stress that leadership is not simply the domain of the few, but is prevalent throughout the organisation in the untapped talent of all its employees. The role of the organisation and its formally appointed leaders is to create a culture in which such latent potential is nourished, recognised and released.' (Alimo-Metcalfe and Alban-Metcalfe, 2008)

This makes the case for a *shared, dispersed* or *distributed leadership* model, where the aim is to create an organisation which is 'leaderful', though this can easily drift into or amount to, distributed *management*, argues McCrimmon (2008).

■ Distributed leadership

Interventions using the *Systemic Leadership Toolkit* (drawing on an organisation's leadership resources to improve the way the organisation works) are founded on a particular model of *distributed leadership*. Substantial research has been undertaken by the National College for School Leadership (Bennett, *et al*, 2003). David Jackson (2004), chief executive of the college, points out that:

'Leadership is ubiquitous in the organisation, but the vast majority of its capital lies dormant among its employees ... The role of the leader, then, is to liberate, harness and focus it for the benefit of the organisation.'

A review by Richard Bolden (2007) of Exeter University's Centre for Leadership Studies decribes a model that contains the following elements:

- An emergent property of a group or network of interacting individuals (as opposed to a phenomenon arising from individuals)
- It entails concertive action (contrasted with numerical or additive action; i.e. the aggregated effect of a number of individuals contributing their expertise in different ways)
- Openness to the boundaries of leadership
- Varieties of expertise are distributed across the many, not the few.

Note the last point on 'varieties'. The distributed leadership model generates diversity, not multitudes of clones. I pick up this point later in my discussion of leadership competency frameworks.

At the other end of the leadership spectrum from distributed leadership lies *command-and-control,* where power is concentrated in the hands of a few. Nowadays, for most types of organisation for most of the time, commanding others to do things, including to change, by using top-down hierarchical power is rather outmoded and less successful. While the command-and-control model appeals to bullies, it owes more to a perception of how organisations are supposed to work than mere bossiness. Command-and-control remains the mode of choice, however, for many politicians and many of their appointees who are frustrated and impatient about the pace of improvement and change, are insensitive about the consequential long-term relationship issues, and have no understanding of the nature of the organisation as a system and its inherent capability (including to frustrate them). They think a strong man (and it is usually a man) is needed 'to sort them out'.

> 'Many people in the public-sector services describe Sir David Varney as 'god'. Formerly holder of top jobs in HMRC and British Gas, Varney is an adviser to the Prime Minister on public-sector reform. His view is that public services should be delivered through huge factories. Public-sector managers await his deliberations and decisions with a mixture of awe, disbelief, and concern. After years of being labelled 'producer interests', obstructive and resistant to change, they wait in silence, reluctant to express their concerns, to see what Varney's next ideas will be.' (Seddon, 2008)

A NEW ROLE FOR MANAGERS AND A NEW WAY OF DEVELOPING THEM

The above vignette shows how the strong-single-leadership-from-the-top approach sucks power out of managers. If managers are forced to swim in such a dirty environment, they cannot behave as leaders, cannot afford to take risks, cannot be brave enough to show initiative, and indeed are not asked to. Command-and-control leadership is exclusive. It confines and condemns leadership development to its familiar, local territory: the relationship that managers have with their own staff. It forgoes the relationship they have with the organisation – as it is now or how it needs to change.

The world is changing; it is becoming more complex and less deferential. The idea that leadership can be, and needs to be, distributed more widely has taken hold. This represents a loosening of the hierarchy and a change in managers' roles, inviting them to become involved with leadership matters that lie beyond their everyday managerial jobs and beyond relationships with their staff.

It follows that leadership development needs to change. It needs to become more organisational. Indeed, this can only happen if the organisation sees itself being run in a different way – the antithesis of the model favoured by David Varney in the above vignette.

If such a change in the leadership culture of an organisation is accepted as an inevitable trend, desirable for the organisation, and not undone by autocratic behaviour, then leadership development programmes need a change of direction as well as a change of gear. That begins by redefining what is expected of managers in their jobs.

MULTI-DIMENSIONAL LEADERSHIP

The democratic government analogy

Prepositions are important to language and to understanding. Systemic or organisational leadership is more than leading *in* the organisation. We can find other useful prepositions gleaned from the American president Abraham Lincoln. In his famous Gettysburg address in 1863, Lincoln was speaking about democratic government and the people. In our own case we are interested in leadership – a related but somewhat different focus.[32]

Using a licence to paraphrase Lincoln, we get:

> leadership
> > *of* the organisation
> > > *by* the organisation
> > > > *for* the organisation.

This analogy is not so far fetched or as high blown as it sounds. To succeed, systemic leadership needs to recognise and address all three facets. Here is how it works:

■ Leadership *of* the organisation

Every enterprise has both an external and internal aspect. The former is its outward-facing 'business' (focused on customers, products, prices, sales, etc.). At the service of this business is the (internal) 'organisation', and it's the internal organisational aspect that is the main interest of this book (See Chapter 1 for a fuller explanation of the difference between the 'business' and the 'organisation'.)

Leadership of the organisation is needed to ensure that the necessary structure, culture, communication, supervision, skills, systems, policies, codes, rules, relationships, supplies, etc. are in place and are being followed, monitored, updated and maintained. Leadership of the process of change happens here.

---

32   Abraham Lincoln (1863) *Gettysburg Address.* 19 November. Pennsylvania.

■ Leadership *by* the organisation

This focus is external. It refers to ways in which leadership is manifested to stakeholders and to the community. To take policing as an example, it includes the non-uniformed police constable (not seen formally as a 'leader' for development purposes) who nonetheless finds himself nominated to take the lead role of 'officer in the case', say on a particular serious crime assignment, and who has to display leadership both inside the organisation and externally in the community when representing the force or giving evidence in court.

Such leadership also includes sector leadership, market leadership, being a 'beacon' in local government, partnering schools, making inexpensive drugs available to impoverished peoples, pioneering new approaches in assisting society, developing new business models, using philanthropy wisely and generously. It means providing leadership to benefit all stakeholders, not just the shareholders, directors and employees.

■ Leadership *for* the organisation

An organisation has a legal personality. The directors owe their *duty* to the company, not to the shareholders (a popular misunderstanding). They also have multiple *responsibilities* to several stakeholder groups, some of which have long been enshrined in law, especially certain responsibilities for their employees:

> 'In the UK the 2006 Companies Act requires all directors for the first time to have regard for the interest of their staff, their suppliers and customers, and the community, and the environment.' [33]

Additionally, directors have to *account* to shareholders for how they discharge those duties and multiple responsibilities, and in doing so have to keep shareholders satisfied financially. But leaders work *for* their company. The table below shows how these different prepositional focuses are reflected in leadership's reputation.

LEADERSHIP REPUTATION

☐ An individual can have a reputation for *being a leader*. This usually refers to leadership *in* the organisation.

☐ A company can have a reputation for *being well led*. This is leadership *of* the organisation.

☐ A company can have a reputation *as a leader* – as brand, market or sector leader. It may have a reputation for *giving a lead* (e.g. in practising diversity). This is leadership *by* the organisation.

Table 7: Leadership reputation

---

33   CMI (2008) *Corporate Responsibility: Sustainable Business Practice*. London: Chartered Management Institute.

Giving and receiving leadership

Organisations and leadership depend on each other. Organisations are both givers and receivers of leadership. For organisations to provide leadership outwardly, they need to receive leadership from managers (to improve, grasp opportunities and overcome problems). To receive this leadership from managers, they need to give appropriately to managers ('give' in the sense of display, clarify, permit and resource). The organisation's relationship with its managers' leadership is thus symbiotic.

When it comes to improvement, there is a virtuous circle at work. An organisation can help improve managers' leadership, and managers in turn can improve the organisation in ways that make the managers' leadership improvement possible. Organisations can then provide leadership to the business, which in turn can give leadership to its sector and to all its stakeholders (as shown in Figure 1).

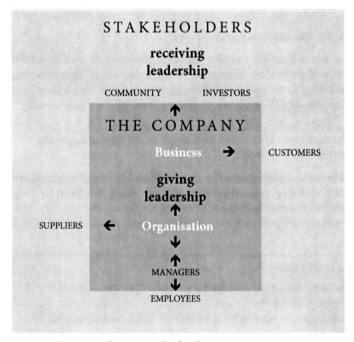

Figure 1: Giving and receiving leadership

The application of leadership is often left unspecified by the organisation. In other words, it is generally assumed that, once developed, managers (acting as leaders) will be free to choose where and how to focus their leadership endeavour. Little thought may be given to the various groups who might be on the receiving end of leadership, how they might benefit, let alone how they might be involved in, and contribute to, the overall leadership process and its success for the wider organisation.

Some fluidity is expected, even desirable. Not all needs can be predicted and specified. Managers have to be free to respond to events as they judge appropriate. But the contention here is that organisations can generally do more to make it clear to managers what the organisation's expectations of leadership are.

Leadership is not exercised in a vacuum. There are other parties to the process, including internal and external customers, and not forgetting followers. People, and even *things* in the system, are involved in giving or receiving leadership.

SUMMARY OF CHAPTER KEY POINTS

1. The purpose of the new systemic approach is to foster and bring about better leadership in, of, by and for organisations by understanding, developing, improving, expanding, releasing and applying organisational leadership capability.

2. At a systemic level, the carrier, conveyer, source, owner and manifestor of leadership is the organisation.

3. Leadership is an organisational resource. It needs to be managed.

4. The need to manage the process of leadership is separate from the need to manage the people who lead.

5. Compared with managing, leading has more to do with seeing the need to improve the organisation as a working system in order to secure the business's future.

6. There is always a change agenda. Make that agenda clear to managers so that they can see where their leadership role fits.

7. Recognise that responsibility for the leadership and change agendas benefits from being distributed widely among managers. In this model, responsibility and action on behalf of the organisation is widely distributed and shared through the hierarchy by interaction, rather than concentrated on a small cadre of individuals acting independently. It is the opposite of a strongly hierarchical command-and-control way of running an organisation.

8. There is a need to consider what are the needs of the organisation's stakeholders to receive leadership – what is leadership to be used for and for whom?

9. For business leadership to result, the relationship between the organisation and managers is symbiotic and operates as a virtuous circle. The organisation gives appropriately to leadership and receives appropriate leadership. Managers can help the organisation see how it can improve the way it helps managers give leadership to the organisation.

10. The application of leadership cannot simply be left to individual managers to work out for themselves.

11. Delivering the leadership that the organisation needs, and improving the organisation's leadership, is a strategic activity before it is a training activity.

CHAPTER 5:

SWITCHING THE LEADERSHIP MINDSET TO THE SYSTEM

- ☐ *The popular leadership mindset*
- ☐ *Supply and demand leadership strategies*
- ☐ *An alternative leadership mindset*
- ☐ *The developer's kitbag*

People's behaviour stems largely from their perceptions, preconceptions, worldview and beliefs, their actual experience of organisations, their likes and dislikes, what they know they are good at and what they like to avoid, as well as a multitude of assumptions about cause and likely effect, inputs and outputs, actors and audience.

Change and learning begins and ends with mindset. So this chapter confronts some of the most frequent mindset issues, in order to get you to make the mental shift towards a systemic way of thinking about leadership.

> *'Unless you change the way you think, your system will not change and, therefore, its performance won't change.'* (Japanese consultant in Seddon, 2003)

Whether as leaders, those being led, trainers, developers, consultants, critics, pundits, commentators or authors, few people seem to realise that there is a problem with the dominant mindset around leadership. It is doubtful that they spend much time thinking about it, or being worried by it. Instead, they think the problem is simply with particular individuals who are poor leaders. But it isn't: the problem lies in the collective mind.

The reality of near-universal practice by the leadership 'industry' suggests there is a deeply ingrained mental model, a misinformed and incomplete one, a mindset that serves to exclude consideration of important alternative ways of thinking. This chapter attempts to reframe that mindset.

The form and forming of mindset

Like most assumptions, the mindset around leadership and its development isn't consciously constructed. Suffering little challenge from ready alternatives, the mindset simply forms, takes hold, gets passed on, and is reinforced by the media, the market and business commentators.

The familiar way of thinking about leadership isn't seen as an option to be weighed and adopted. For its believers and those on the receiving end of its consequences, the current mindset is real and powerful. It determines most leadership-related activity in organisations: goal setting, rewards, accountability for success and failure, tenure, and especially leadership development.

In its focus on individuals, the popular mindset meets deep psychological needs and takes political pressure off organisations' leaders. It also provides a useful shared language and backdrop for discussing leadership in organisations. But there is a problem. The mindset is specious – plausible and convenient. It is narrow, limiting and misplaced. It constrains our thinking and the evolution of leadership. It cripples the expansion of leadership. It holds back improvement in organisations.

There is an alternative leadership mindset available, one that is more strategic and more directly focused on the organisation's needs. A nuanced dovetailing between the mindsets can be achieved – as this book aims to show.

But first, just what exactly is the popular mindset?

THE POPULAR MINDSET AROUND SUCCESSFUL LEADERSHIP BASED ON THE INDIVIDUAL LEADER

You will recognise most of these key elements and assumptions, most of which are erroneous:

1. The vehicle for leadership is the individual (whether highly concentrated on a few or dispersed among many) – as in 'If you want leadership, look for (and develop) leaders'. (False)
2. Leadership *for the organisation* will be improved by developing individual managers' understanding, focus, skills, behaviour and style. (False)
3. The route to improving leadership in the organisation is best achieved via individual managers' leadership. Organisations directly gain benefit on the back of the gains of the individual managers in their jobs. (False)
4. There is no need for a separate, conscious and distinctive leadership agenda for the organisation as an entity since the organisation's need is discharged through and delegated to individual managers and their developers. (False)

5. Organisations require, want and welcome extra leadership. They will make good use of any enhanced stock of leadership ability. (False)
6. The organisation's strength comes from stronger individual leadership, especially at the top of the organisation. (False)
7. Inside large organisations the most important, visual and talked-about activity concerning leadership is its *development* (usually carried out under the broad banner of management development – training, coaching, seminars, feedback, secondments, psychometrics, etc.). Ask about leadership, and you will probably be referred to the company's HR management development department. (True but undesirable)

The picture represented here is painted starkly to make its point. Of course, many organisations' practice is more subtle and advanced than this. But this mindset doubtless exists across many organisations and what it depicts is an unreal picture of how leadership really works. And, more important even than its relationship to reality, the mindset fails to deliver consistently high-quality leadership appropriate to serve the changing needs and challenges of a particular business and of its stakeholders – and of business in general. The chief point is that you cannot meet organisation-based needs with individual-based responses, whatever this approach may achieve for individual managers in their jobs and careers.

In *The Social Psychology of Organizations*, Daniel Katz and Robert L. Khan (1978) amplify the issue:

> 'Attempts to change organisations by changing individuals have a long history of theoretical inadequacy and practical failure. Both stem from a disregard of the systemic properties of organisations and from the confusion of individual changes with modification in organisational variables.'

The organisation's presumed role

In the popular mindset, the organisation's main role is to provide the necessary funds, time and other resources for leadership development to take place. By and large it then lets leadership developers, and indeed the resulting developed managers, get on with it.

The mindset treats the organisation as a grateful, largely passive recipient – like an open vessel into which developed leadership talent can be happily poured. Displays of leadership initiative will be welcomed, or so it is assumed and claimed. There are of course annual routines such as performance reviews to help keep things on track.

INTEGRATING SUPPLY
AND DEMAND STRATEGIES

Addressing leadership shortcomings and shortages requires a careful consideration of, and linking between, supply and demand strategies. But in most organisations there is a disconnect. A systemic leadership approach rectifies this.

The familiar mindset favours the supply side and indeed leaves most of the creative thinking, driving energy and qualitative decisions here. Most managers' development activity takes place because someone tries to sell it to them, before they even knew they were in the market and wanted to buy it. By comparison, a cornerstone of systemic leadership is that the organisation's role in leadership should expand and that demand-side issues should receive much fuller consideration than is typically the case.

The model of exchange between development provider and organisational client has traditionally been characterised by the parties' separation. Producers have been allowed to retain most control over the supply chain. The systemic leadership approach is different: it aims to connect the two sides of the problem-solution equation, welding the organisation's (demand) with development's (supply) in a more even-handed partnership.

The systemic stance draws on the discipline of systems thinking. As Seddon (2008) explains, the cardinal principle is: always understand what the customer is demanding before coming up with solutions and services. In the leadership context, the organisation is the customer. The organisation is where the needs are – needs to which individual managers, by giving their leadership, and the providers of leadership development should respond.

Instead of the supply side pushing its views, services, products and self-interests, the demand side pulls what it needs. 'Design against demand' is the byword. So you need a way of understanding that 'demand', and you need the door to be open.

Organisations' *de facto* supply-side strategy

The popular mindset that drives most training and development embodies a *de facto* supply-side strategy; it concentrates on increasing the supply of leadership talent – whether that means leaders to fill positions or an increase in leadership skills. The mindset assumes that all will be well with the organisation if there is a sufficient supply of talented individuals. It assumes that this is what the organisation needs in order to be well led and to improve. Developers (the provider) and their corporate clients (on the user side) alike fall into this mental trap.

Most typical management development is supply-push in nature. Such strategies assume (wrongly) that pushing more talented individual leaders into the organisation *per se* will lead to the changes that the organisation requires for itself.

The popular strategy treats the demand side as little more than the volume of demand for training and development (often expressed as requests for places on programmes). To be fair to trainers and developers, that is how the demand side itself often sees its role.

An alternative, demand-side perspective

There is a different way of viewing demand. The 'demand side' can be thought of as what is happening on the user's side of the equation. This begins with:

- What is the organisation's requirement for leadership?
- What is the organisation's contribution to providing a solution?
- What is the organisation doing to define and pull in what it needs?

The demand-side needs are expressed as a clear requirement for the leadership that the organisation needs in order to address its own agenda. In systems thinking terms, the company is the customer and should put itself in a position where it can *pull* from its supplier(s) the leadership it needs to carry through its specific change mandate, including how well the organisation works as a system to deliver organisation-wide leadership appropriate to its business future. The 'supplier' includes provision of all sources of leadership talent, competence, development, performance management systems, succession planners, HR, OD, MD, coaches, development consultants and facilitators.

To get informed and objective answers raises a structural issue concerning the balance of power. Many organisations need to attain greater 'consumer sovereignty' in exchanges with developers. They need to avoid being beholden to producer power and professional self-interest, which pushes its own preferred, often generic, 'solutions'.

On the other hand, developers need to be treated as partners who can offer advice freely and have full access to the organisational issues. They mustn't always be biting their tongue for fear of saying more than the client is ready to hear about the organisation.

○ **Example: National leadership shortages** Attempts to solve skills shortages are addressed mostly one-sidedly by talent-push strategies. When it comes to shortages in the schools sector, for example (one in five schools is without a permanent head), the analysis is supply-side driven.

The instinct and habit is to jump straight to the supply side to find solutions. But, if asked, the demand side would have a lot to say about what is going on there which would suggest the possibility of demand-side solutions, as in the case of Bede College, Middlesbrough:

'Last Friday its principal, Miriam Stanton, had on her desk two 135-page documents from the LSC [Learning & Skills Council] relating her college's data to national data; her college's 135-page self-assessment; the 30-page extract she is required to make of that for the Ofsted website; her 50-page quality improvement plan; her annual internal development plan; her three-year internal development plan; and her quality improvement plan.

"'I have a vice-principal whose main duty is to prepare for inspections, and another teacher who spends four days out of five collecting data for quality assurance, and therefore only teaches the equivalent of one day a week," she says. "That is two people away from where they should be, supporting students and teachers. Yet quality comes from teachers in classrooms. ... When I came into the job I was involved with students every day. Now I spend most of my time dealing with documents and spreadsheets."' [34]

'Teachers who might have set their sights on headship 10 years ago may now be having second thoughts because of the increase in responsibility, accountability and vulnerability.' [35] (John Dunford, General Secretary of the Association of School and College Leaders.)

In the specific case of a shortage of headteachers, we should examine the school as an open system. This takes account of its interaction with government departments, showing that the problem on the demand-side is that the headteacher job is increasingly unattractive. There is a high turnover. And too few deputy heads want to become headteachers.

An employer's supply-side perspective advocates using higher pay and bonuses to attract more candidates. But the effects of this strategy will be limited and short-lived. Paying more to try to retain existing headteachers is unlikely to be any more successful. Pumping in more candidates to replace the losses isn't ultimately very successful because it doesn't tackle the root cause.

'We have to change from a punitive culture to a collaborative one ... so that the headteacher job is not seen as so vulnerable.' [36] (Mick Brookes, General Secretary of the National Association of Headteachers.)

---

34   Beckett, F. (2006) 'Another go at duplication'. London: *Education Guardian*, 2 February.

35   Dunford, J. (2008) 'NPHQ (National Professional Qualification for Headship) must have practical emphasis'. London: *The Guardian*, 4 November.

36   Brookes, M. (2008) 'We need a massive cultural change to liberate our heads'. London: *The Guardian*, 4 November.

This invites us to return to the demand side for solutions. Such a perspective points to a need to make the headship job more attractive. It might be of some help for the headteacher to create a new role of chief operating officer. This job would take on the management/administrative/bureaucratic functions currently performed by the head, giving more space for his/her leadership role, and perhaps even freeing up some time for teaching. To address this need there is, belatedly, a pilot scheme for school business directors. Another effective, demand-side response to the problem would be to question the reasonableness of the government demands on schools and their negative impact on headteachers' jobs. Organisational problems that call for demand-side pull action cannot be solved by relying on supply-side push methods.

To solve general problems of this kind:

- Look at the issue from both sides of the equation.
- Don't try to solve a demand-side problem without first analysing and understanding the problem from a demand-side perspective.
- Don't try supply-side solutions until you've first considered demand-side solutions.

What is in the developer's kitbag?

Lacking an OD appreciation and capability, most conventional management developers have only a supply-side mental model and only supply-push tools in their kitbag. Besides, their remit, structure and circumstances may force this position upon them. This happens where the suppliers of development are corporate 'universities' and management schools; it is their natural default and is built into their business model. Trainers and educators come ready made with solutions (which clients unthinkingly expect and accept) that sit entirely within the supply side. But it is unfair to lay the problem at the supplier's door. Clients get what they deserve.

■ Client/provider relationship

Organisations have a mental kitbag too. While, as client, they are located on the demand-side, most organisations themselves instinctively think 'provision' instead of 'need', having only supply-side solutions in mind. They neglect the wider part they could be playing on the demand side. In other words, there is a problem with the mindset concerning the roles of each party, and therefore with the resulting dynamic.

The effect of this is to occlude a potential demand-side perspective and intervention. It confines organisations' action to using funds to commission training and development type 'solutions' from suppliers (whether internal or external), rather than commission learning, understanding, research, investigation or analysis that would lead to a better understanding of the problems/situations/issues on the demand side. As such, it reduces the likelihood of an intervention that targets the organisation as a system.

■ Reputation

Clients are in a position to commission diagnostic or related services, but most prefer to hang onto a role that positions themselves as being in charge of strategy; that is, specifying the problem and defining the need, which they then hand on to others. That way they feel safer in their internal managerial relationships and those with external developers and consultants. Most clients want the contractor to provide the solutions that the client has predetermined, not to ask questions. They don't want to open the door to providers to intrude into their thinking space or strategic responsibility. It's easier and safer for them to keep the respective roles in their pigeonholes.

■ Control

So clients wish to retain control over the organisational half of the equation and access to it. In *Changing Conversations in Organizations*, Patricia Shaw (2002) advises that clients are suspicious of commissioning somewhat ill-defined consultancy in the spaces. I first mentioned these spaces on Warner Burke's flipchart, where I said that the organisation's competence resides, and can be lost, in the spaces and gaps between executives, more than they reside and are lost somewhere <u>within</u> each executive. The client manager is unlikely to see it as in his or her political interest to let development consultants roam free in this less bounded organisational area. Far safer for them to run a well-understood programme for individual managers.

There is a second space: that is the one that exists directly between the client manager and the (potential) supplier. Strategically minded suppliers may doubt the accuracy or wisdom in the client's brief. They may hope to be able to check it out in the organisation by talking to other managers. They may seek a more upstream and strategic role for themselves. And they may be hoping to talk to more senior and influential managers, including the chief executive. Client managers will usually be reluctant to agree to this, not least because it would mean ceding some of their personal control (both to other managers and to the developer). They might hear that their pet solution doesn't hold water, find themselves out of their depth, etc. So they keep a tight rein on the client-supplier relationship, on who does what, and what can be discussed.

(The politics of this are considered further in Chapter 8, *Leadership and Learning*.)

These elements of mindset tend to make the division of labour habitual and problematical. Thus developers are held firmly in the box marked providers of solutions – whether these are their own solutions or ones that come as a requirement from the client without real engagement. That intellectually restricted mindset can change only if key leaders understand that it is in their business's interest to do so and that it holds the key to unlocking their organisation's door to systemic leadership.

The ideal conversation

The ideal client/supplier relationship is for the parties to break with tradition and engage in a trusting intellectual partnership in which they allow themselves to be challenged. To do this they must overcome habit and resistance to the popular division of roles; i.e. whose job it is to be aware of and define the organisation's need and set the strategy, and whose job it is to design and deliver solutions. Such a healthy conversation would contain these elements:

- Establish the 'why' of development before the 'what'.
- Ask what the organisation needs to get out of this and let the design be pulled by that, rather than have a proposal pushed upon the client organisation by providers (internal or external).
- Be honest with clients who are reluctant to understand the point that developing managers is not the same as developing the organisation.
- Make sure that management development and organisation development resources are joined up in discussions.
- Make a record of the conversations to use subsequently to carry out evaluation of a programme against what the organisation says it requires in order to be different afterwards.

A MINDSET BASED ON ORGANISATIONAL REALITY

The abject case of two whistleblowers at Wakefield Prison (see below) provides a graphic 'warts-and-all' illustration of the complex messiness and toxicity of some systems' dynamics, and shows why an organisation's need for leadership improvement cannot be addressed by the conventional development model.

'There were extraordinary scenes at an employment tribunal last week when a judge demanded the head of the prison service, Phil Wheatley, apologise to a woman officer [Emma Howie] who was victimised by colleagues after blowing the whistle on assault and bullying at two high-security jails.

'... The tribunal is considering the level of compensation owed to Howie for bullying, discrimination and harassment, which have seen her absent on paid leave from Wakefield Prison for some four years. ... Howie gave evidence in a claim of similar treatment by another officer at Wakefield, Carol Lingard, who was awarded £480,000 in July 2005, a record for a whistleblower in the public service.

'Wheatley said after the Lingard judgment that the prison service needed "to learn the lessons and sharpen up our response to those sorts of complaints". Lingard was found to have been intimidated and put at personal risk by colleagues at Wakefield because she had reported wrong-doing at a high level.

'Howie's persecution over the same issue at the same prison has raised renewed questions of whether the service can protect officers who break ranks to report abuse.

cont. overleaf

> 'Referring back to the Lingard case, Judge Grazin said the prison service had
> "uttered fine words but failed to carry those through into meaningful actions".
> The tribunal found that Howie had been completely let down by the jail's internal
> investigation.' [37]

NB: This case is discussed more fully in Chapter 10: *Leadership and Culture*, where
the power dynamics in Wakefield Prison are examined (see pages 178-179).

In instances such as the torrid tale above, the problem isn't one of conventional
development. The popular mindset of individual leadership coupled with
personal development is of no help here. What needs targeting is the system.

'The system' means the prison service culture, the specific *leadership* culture within
that, the distribution of power, the legitimate and the unofficial communication
process, the relationships, the definition of acceptable standards, the performance
management process, etc.

There is also the governance system, not prison governors that is, but the system
by which the top managers are held to account, both within the professional
service and within the political system that surrounds it. What is that process,
and why isn't it working?

Crucially, there is a range of perceptions (the basis of behaviour) at work here.
These include:

- perceptions of the leadership role held by various parties and levels
  (e.g. 'Is it my job?' and 'What do my paymasters expect of me?');
- perceptions by key players in the system of what are the likely
  consequences of various possible courses of action (e.g. 'Are they
  likely to work?' and 'What will happen to me if they do/don't?').

One of Deming's key principles was 'first get knowledge'. In other words, begin
by finding out what is going on in the system and in people's mental models,
and gain a full understanding of how the organisation is working as a system
and what explains and lies behind this. This includes the way the leadership
component within the wider system itself operates as a system (or sub-system).

The organisation's needs and dynamics

In contrast to the popular mindset, the new systemic mindset acknowledges the
part played by the organisation, wittingly or unwittingly, positively (enabling)
or negatively (frustrating). It recognises that the organisation is a *system* and
behaves as an entity in its own right. The organisation is seen as a major player to
be factored into the recipe. It is itself a target for development action.

---

37   Allison, E. and Wainwright, M. (2008) 'Judge calls for prison service apology'. London: *The
     Guardian*, 9 April.

The parties would be well advised to adopt a more realistic mindset based on a healthy understanding of the organisation's dynamics that affect leadership, as set out below:

- Ultimately, managers' ability to exercise leadership (or not) depends almost entirely on what is happening inside the organisation and the part the organisation plays (usually unconsciously and by default). Managers can exercise leadership only if the organisation plays an active and positive role.
- Exercising leadership cannot be taken for granted. Nor is it easy, rational or predictable. Leadership is often not welcomed by organisations, despite what is assumed, what is needed, and what organisations say to the contrary.
- Organisations thwart the exercise of leadership as much as they value, license and make use of it. They are adept at putting obstacles in the path of managers who try to lead.
- Organisations unconsciously waste leadership talent. The open vessel having leadership talent poured into it is really a leaky pipe. One of the organisation's strategies should be to stop the waste, rather than continuing to have more talent pushed upon them regardless. (For a full discussion on leadership waste, see Chapter 7, *Leadership and Organisation Development*.)
- The status quo exerts a powerful hold.
- The natural forces of entropy continually erode good intentions. (For a full discussion on entropy, see Chapter 11, *Leadership and Decline*).
- Organisations are messy, confused and confusing places that usually leave it unclear what leadership is needed for and where and how it can be practised and best applied.
- Managers' leadership is relational: it cannot be considered and conducted independently of other people – their aims, needs, perceptions and beliefs.

SUMMARY OF CHAPTER KEY POINTS

1. The popular leadership mindset is powerful, specious, limiting, and needs to change.

2. Ask a question about leadership in an organisation and you will probably be referred to the HR/management development department. Don't automatically accept this.

3. Organisations excessively relinquish responsibility for leadership – its improvement, development and application – to its agents, especially developers and Human Resources professionals. A partnership is needed,

with more dialogue, joint analysis, shared responsibility and joined-up demand/supply interventions.

4. Organisational problems that call for demand-side pull action cannot be solved by relying on supply-push methods. Demand-side issues should receive much fuller consideration than is typically the case. Understand what is meant by the organisation's demand and what it comprises in a given case, then design against it.

5. The organisation's demand-side needs are expressed as a clear requirement for the leadership that the organisation needs in order to address its own agenda. In systems thinking terms, the organisation is the customer and should put itself in a position where it can *pull* from its supplier(s) the leadership it needs to carry through its specific change mandate. The supplier includes all sources of leadership talent, competence, development, performance management systems, succession planners, etc. (HR, OD, MD, coaches, development consultants and facilitators).

6. Developers' kitbags are full of supply-push tools and need more demand-pull ones rooted in an understanding of the (organisational) customer's needs. This can only happen and be useful if the demand side relinquishes its own supply-side predilection, and if it is prepared to let down its guard.

7. The organisation is a major player and needs to be factored into development, and is itself a target for development.

8. Despite assumptions and what is said, leadership is often not welcomed by organisations. Organisations thwart the exercise of leadership as much as they value, license and make use of it.

9. Managers can exercise leadership only if the organisation plays an active and positive role.

PART TWO

APPLYING THE NEW APPROACH –
THE INTERVENTION CHALLENGE

This second part builds on the theoretical underpinning offered by the opening five chapters in Part One. It consists of nine chapters that provide practical advice and numerous examples of how the new model of *systemic leadership* applies to a range of organisational contexts affecting specialists and generalists.

Chapters 6-9 focus on more specialist aspects of improving leadership that will be especially relevant to HR/Learning & Development professionals. Chapters 10-14 offer a new perspective from which to view managers' day-to-day experiences of organisational life; while they are more general in scope, they also contain advice that is relevant for HR specialists. The whole of Part 2 is designed to equip anyone who has a leadership interest and responsibility with essential knowledge and strategies for bringing about improvement on a systemic level.

Following Part Two, the book's messages are pulled together in Conclusion.

Chapter 6:

Leadership and Management Development

- ☐ *Management development's contribution*
- ☐ *Connecting management development to the organisation*
- ☐ *Becoming more strategic*
- ☐ *How to make the most of context*
- ☐ *A change strategy for management development itself*
- ☐ *Holding management development to account*

Many large organisations have sophisticated management development (MD) schemes, often accompanied by attractive website publicity. A typical policy statement looks something like this:

> *We believe that continuous personal development by managers is an important factor in our ongoing success. Therefore, the executive board fully supports the provision of opportunities for managers to identify and plan to meet their own development needs.*

Such policies spring from good intentions and fulfil most people's expectations of what a large organisation provides. But they often raise more questions than they answer. Whose needs are being met? Is this the company's sole development strategy? How does the organisation get its own needs met? Just what is going on in this company? What are its values and beliefs? What is its development philosophy?

In this chapter I explore these questions in order to examine the basis and the basics of management development as applied to leadership. I go on to suggest how management development can become a more strategic activity that is better connected with the organisation's goals, needs and realities.

What do the missing words tell us?

Taken on their own, the policy's words say nothing about the company's management and leadership – its business and organisation – and where it is headed. Such a sense of detachment can be inferred from '*… opportunities for managers to identify and plan to meet their own development needs*'. The implication is that the company's development strategy is designed around individual managers' needs. The 'opportunities' referred to may have little impact beyond individual managers' careers, marketability and own jobs. Even benefits in a manager's current job can be in doubt if the organisation and colleagues haven't been factored into the development process and favourable conditions aren't in place.

The lack of an explicit link to the organisation is widespread in management development. Some would say that it is unavoidable. But is it? How much does it matter? What are the risks? What are the alternatives?

Before considering these issues and exploring alternatives and improvements, below is my definition of management development.

THE CONTRIBUTION OF
MANAGEMENT DEVELOPMENT TO LEADERSHIP

THE NATURE OF MANAGEMENT DEVELOPMENT

☐ Develops the ability of currently employed managers in the organisation, using a variety of methods, forums, courses, programmes and media. Employs various techniques (e.g. 360 degree feedback and competency assessment) to measure the quality of individuals' leadership and their training and development needs.

☐ Concentrates on the *means* by which leadership in an organisation may be enhanced; namely, via individual managers' leadership. Leaves the *ends* (organisational benefit) to managers to work out after the learning event.

☐ Expects managers to decide for themselves, subsequent to their development, the purposes and activities to which to apply their enhanced leadership capability.

☐ Is predicated on a supply-side strategy, one which assumes that the organisation will be better led if it is supplied with more talented leaders.

☐ Develops managers' leadership skills, usually on their own, but sometimes with their team colleagues, when it may be aimed at enhancing leadership of or by the team. The true leadership aspect may become subordinate to team communication and team relationships.

☐ May develop managers' leadership skills either in a generic setting or in a specific local context.

☐ Targets the individual manager for diagnosis, assessment and training and development needs.

☐ Puts the main onus on the individual manager and places few demands on the organisation to think before engaging in development activity or to change afterwards.

☐ Views the organisation mainly as a passive beneficiary of the output and outcomes, not an active contributor to the input (other than providing funds, processes and definitions).

Table 8: The nature of management development

This raises an issue about how effective MD is, from whose point of view, and what the effectiveness issues are for the parties.

- For managers the issue is tactical. It principally concerns learning transfer (see Chapter 8, *Leadership and Learning*). The question is: How can managers make their learning count?
- For the organisation the issue is more strategic. The question is: How can the organisation best sponsor management development that is underpinned by the company's interest, is grounded in workplace realities, and is most likely to make a difference?

One company's management development department received feedback from its contracted providers of outdoor development programmes that the future leaders performed very well under training when the rules were clear, but were floundering when the situation was ambiguous and there was no clear structure to 'tell them what to do'. The implication was that there might be something about the organisation's culture, systems, recruitment, promotion or reward criteria that was obstructing the kind of creative and risk-taking leadership deemed necessary for the future. This convinced the company to take a serious look at itself, clarify where it was headed and what leadership would mean in its future, and make changes to its culture, systems and processes, rather than rely alone on traditional development programmes to deliver suitable leaders.

This company knew that its environment was fast changing and that its future would be very different. It would be less easy for managers to predict what actions would be appropriate on their part and what would work. With increased partnership working, boundaries would become less clear and change the leadership challenge and who would need to be involved in that. And the idea that managers would be in firm control of events, confined within their company's boundary, would largely be a thing of the past. All this resulted in a new consideration of what it would mean to develop what is known as *adaptive capacity*.

Whose needs?

The fictional MD policy mentioned at the beginning of this chapter refers to '... *development by its managers is a key factor in the ongoing success of the organisation*'. This implies that a connection between the managers' development and the fate of the organisation is expected. However, there is nothing in the statement to suggest that the linking happens other than by the efforts of the managers themselves. This is most organisations' default assumption.

■ Needs rooted in the individual

The conventional focus on individual managers is mirrored in the way that training needs analysis (TNA) is typically conducted. If the analysis comes out of individuals' performance reviews ('*What training do you think you need?*'), the link with the organisation's own needs may be tangential. It is the wrong question to ask, certainly as the first question.

The policy speaks of '… *continuous personal development*'. A strongly individual approach may express the company's commitment to *continuing professional development* (CPD) and a belief that it is the company's responsibility to provide the opportunities.

There is a legacy of large organisations viewing their responsibilities in a paternalistic way, especially in the public sector and in corporations that have been privatised. It was all part of a piece with the central planning of managers' long-service careers. Some organisations are now letting go and placing a greater onus on individuals to take charge of their own development and careers. The quoted policy's reference to managers identifying and planning to meet their own development needs may suggest that this trend is being recognised; less centrally mandated, marshalled and monitored TNA processes reflect the changing pattern.

■ So where does this analysis take us?

I am not claiming that individuals do not have training and development needs or cannot benefit from personal learning, or that such needs are insignificant when compared with those of the organisation. There are, however, three important issues:

- Is the organisation getting its priorities right and putting its energy and resources into activities that yield the highest return?
- Is responsibility for managers' development being located in the best place to achieve an appropriate sense of ownership and economy?
- Could policies, processes and arrangements that are acceptable for management development be unacceptable for leadership development?

There is a danger of organisations getting the worst of all worlds. On the one hand, they may be taking too much responsibility for individuals' development. On the other hand, they may be squandering that investment in time and energy by taking too little responsibility for the *organisation's* development, which calls for greater leadership.

An option available to organisations is to make individual managers' training and development and their personal training needs analysis the responsibility of the individual manager. Similarly, managers can be made responsible for 'pulling' their own appraisals and 360 degree feedback. The organisation (i.e. the HR department) doesn't necessarily have to police such administration or insist on uniformity, as some do.

A good question for policy-makers to ask is:

What are we doing out of habit as a legacy of the past that is not strategic for the business and may no longer deserve such a high priority and investment of energy and resources by the company?

The converse is also pertinent:

What are we not doing at the moment that would be strategic for the business that may deserve a higher priority and investment of energy and resources by the company?

There are two other reasons to question the dominant focus on individual managers' development:

- This book's opening story about Warner Burke's diagram (see 'A Personal Story') asserted that 'What happens at the edge of a job matters more to organisational effectiveness and performance than what happens at the heart of the job' (with the obvious conclusion: concentrate the organisation's improvement effort on the periphery, interfaces, interactions and interstices, more than attempting to improve competence of the parts in isolation – namely individual executives).
- If this were not enough, consider the system's power to shape, distort and thwart individuals' best intentions to apply their learning and become better managers.

If these points are accepted – however reluctantly – then one also needs to be cautious about organisations giving undue focus, attention, energy and funds to conventional approaches to individuals' competencies, coaching and 360 degree feedback. And where used, such practices need a solid organisational foundation to complement, channel and support them.

Needs rooted in the organisation

Managers' development needs can spring from the organisation's thought-out requirements, especially any planned organisation-wide change. Consider these two examples.

> 'Richard Baker, the incoming chief executive of Boots the Chemist in 2004, gave his diagnosis of the stores' ailments. The store chain, he said, "was introspective, slow to respond, not focused on customers, poor at taking money in an orderly fashion, and lacking basic shopkeeping skills". ' [38]

Baker's analysis provides a context and some specifics for how leadership of Boots the Chemist needed to improve. In the second example (below) the Council's aspirations feed directly into its leadership programme.

---

38   Finch, J. (2004) 'Boots sacks one in three at head office'. London: *The Guardian*, 12 January.

> In tune with the local government sector generally, a review by one of the county councils mentioned earlier identified the need to:
> ☐ become more innovative
> ☐ take more risks
> ☐ take decisions more rapidly
> ☐ manage in a more businesslike way.

In instances like the two cited, managers' training and development needs and subsequent provision can be given a sound strategic platform. In other cases where the diagnosis isn't so obvious and isn't provided, a general way into a relevant diagnostic discussion is to ask:

What does the organisation need more of and less of at this time?

Some aspects of an organisation's diagnosis feed MD provision of management and leadership development, but others call for the application of organisation development (OD) methods, as discussed in the next chapter.

Development for maintenance or change

When the fictional MD policy speaks of the '*ongoing success*' of the company, it implies that the purpose of development is one of maintenance rather than of change. It sends a 'steady-as-she-goes' message, which may simply be a piece of copywriter's puff, or may have been thought through carefully as making a choice – i.e. favouring stability. The stance may reflect the absence of any desire or strategy for changing the way the organisation operates. Alternatively, these words might be a reflection that:

- The organisation recognises no role for MD in the process of change.
- The MD scheme is complemented by other programmes or activities that *do* address the need for change.
- HR plays a purely tactical role in the success of the organisation.
- Leadership and responsibility for change is not distributed down to the level of managers that is affected by the MD scheme.
- The organisation is unable to see a direct role for itself and believes it has no choice but to relinquish responsibility for the organisation's future to individual managers and their development.

Semi-detached development and developers

The picture painted is the familiar one of semi-detachment for management development, about which there are mixed opinions.

> 'Whilst there is a danger that development activity is insufficiently related to the business, the opposite may also be true. There is a risk of development being too engaged with current issues and supportive of how the business is now, thereby maintaining the status quo and the current regime's interests. It may also rely on what is currently known about the likely future.' (Tate, 2004a)

The secret lies in building a relationship between development and the business that is close but not too close. Developers must remain mindful that they exist to serve the needs of the business. Business leaders must remain mindful that developers need the freedom to develop managers and strategies for leadership with abilities, energies and ideas that may be uncomfortable for the organisation. Developed managers may (and ideally should) challenge the status quo, but not alone (they should watch their backs if they try, because the system will resist change and make it difficult, wearing, risky and political). Managers and developers should have an interest in securing a future for the organisation that the present leaders may not be able to see.

Developers can find themselves walking a tightrope. They risk being accused of colluding with learners in subverting what they may together perceive as dysfunctional in the organisation or with their bosses. On the other hand, if they accept things as they are, their measures may be insufficient to help the organisation improve. Their supervisors must be sensitive to this predicament.

In reality, most organisations, most developers and most managers probably give such strategic and philosophical issues little conscious thought. The management development department simply does what it does. Its contribution is tactical and attuned to individual managers' needs. It keeps its nose clean and provides a service. But it doesn't have to be like this.

Developers can be business partners

Ideally, developers should know the organisation's direction, long-term plans, goals, business strategies, problems and opportunities. Otherwise, development will take place at arm's length from the organisation's realities and will only be able to concentrate on individual managers' characteristics, qualities and capabilities.

Except where rotated as part of a career programme – like the Royal Army Education Corps – developers are usually dedicated specialists. As such, they become typecast and pigeon-holed, kept in their box. Clients may not expect or want them to ask searching questions about the business and organisation. Let them loose in the organisation and you don't know what might happen! They might have conversations or see things they shouldn't. They may be idealistic and subversive.

When Head of General Training in the early days of British Airways in the mid-1970s, I tried to break out of the box. I asked if I could visit managers who were sponsoring people for management training. I wanted to engage in a conversation about the organisational background for their training. I was firmly told to go away and stick to my own patch. All that the sponsoring managers wanted from me was a menu of training courses that they could nominate people to attend; I didn't need to know why, they said.

A common feature in any organisation's shadow side (protecting turf) was rearing its head. I received no backing from those above when I tried to redefine the scope of the management training department.

Politics apart, developers themselves may have neither the interest nor the capability in extending their learning territory. Their own self-image, expertise and interests may stop them requesting such information. Even if they had the information, many would not know what to do with it.

The upshot is that both parties may be comfortable with the strong ring-fencing that frequently encloses development activity. Yet this isolation is unhealthy and is not a sustainable arrangement if development activity is expected to make a more direct contribution to the business.

For external providers, isolation is a structural problem. But even in-company developers can find themselves treated in the same way. Many even see themselves in this semi-detached position and are content with the arrangement.

Management development's reputation

Some commonly held views about management development include:

- Management development must be doing some good *for the organisation*, though we can't put our finger on it.
- It is there because it has always been there.
- It is rather peripheral.
- It is what is expected of a large organisation.
- It shows the organisation as a caring employer.
- It is politically correct.

What this says is that whatever is happening to the business – its ups and downs, whatever crises the organisation faces, whatever its plans for the future, however dysfunctional the organisation – the management development department will continue to make personal development opportunities available.

Mostly then, such arrangements stand alone, often based on annual routines for identifying managers' training and development needs. Occasionally they may be mirrored by a parallel strategy for identifying and planning to meet the *organisation's* own needs using OD methods, but the channels may not be connected.

The chasm between effort and benefit, and between individual and organisation, may result from an inability – of developers and clients alike – to see the potential benefits to the business of having a closer connection. Developers may themselves lack strategic awareness of the business or even have much active interest in the business. They may lack the ability to think strategically. Many organisations mistakenly appoint top trainers rather than strategists to lead the development function.

MAKING MANAGEMENT
DEVELOPMENT MORE STRATEGIC

Some organisations and some developers will have higher aspirations for the management development function. They will want it to become more strategic, more closely connected with the organisation's agenda, more influential. In short, they will aim to move upstream.

> 'There are bodies floating down the river. You think it's your job to fish them out, resuscitate them where possible and return them. But it's not. Your job is to go upstream, find out who is throwing them in and stop them.'[39] (Dr Nick Georgiades)

Here are some first-level questions for the strategically minded developers to ask – of the learners, of themselves and of the organisation:

FIRST-LEVEL QUESTIONS FOR MANAGEMENT DEVELOPERS

☐ How will the organisation support the application of what is learnt?

☐ Once the manager has learned 'how', to 'what' should the 'how' be applied?

☐ If learning and development are the means, what are the ends?

☐ If real projects are part of the learning process, how can the organisation sponsor them?

☐ How will individual managers' efforts be combined to make a collective impact?

☐ If development is about 'doing things right', how will managers know what is 'doing the right things'?

☐ How and when will managers know when to manage and when to lead?

☐ What distinction does the organisation make between management and leadership activity in managers' jobs?

Table 9: First-level questions for management developers

Many management development departments are left to get on with their programmes in a detached way, with little serious steering or interest shown by the organisation in what effect they are having, if any, beyond individual managers' jobs. The best organisations have strategically considered programmes, resulting from serious analysis of how their organisations' management and leadership need to change. Hence, they distinguish between managing and leading. One such example, from the University of Essex, appears below.

---

39   Based on Georgiades, N. (1984) Address given to British Airways HR Department by incoming HR Director.

'Management development is not solely concerned with the mechanisms for learning how to perform as managers (e.g. training, coaching, mentoring, action learning). It is also concerned with appropriate structures: e.g. the ways in which teams are used; the systems for performance management and reward; and methods of identifying and selecting people for management. These all play a part in enabling learning to be transferred and become effective in the organisation.' [40]

MAKING THE MOST OF CONTEXT

The context for improving and applying managers' leadership cannot be given too much attention. There are several ways that are used to think about context. They mostly involve the letter 'c'. Context can embrace:

- circumstances
- concerns
- challenges
- colleagues
- culture
- climate

In *A Manager's Guide to Leadership*, Pedler *et al* (2004) claim:

'Leadership is always situated: always done *here*, with these particular people; it is always local and contextual. Context is vital: what works here and now may not work in another place and at another time. There is no right way to lead: if you do get it right here and now there is no guarantee that this will work in the same way in another situation, or even in the same situation some time later.

'Generic leadership characteristics are context-free, but leadership challenges are always contextual.'

For these authors, the memorable code lies in three domains: what are the leadership *challenges, characteristics* and *context*?

- *Challenges* are the critical tasks, problems and issues requiring action.
- *Characteristics* are the qualities, competencies and skills that enable us to contribute to the practice of leadership in challenge situations.
- *Context* is the on-site conditions found in the challenge situation.

The challenges give the characteristics their point; the context gives reality to the setting. But context can mean much more than this, as will become clear.

---

40   University of Essex (2008) *ibid.*

Using context in coaching

The importance of considering context is recognised when coaching senior executives. A Corporate Research Forum workshop suggested these elements:

- What the organisation wants and needs (its purpose, direction, goals, success measures, etc.), and whether these are clearly communicated, understood and respected.
- The particular urgent and important current and future challenges facing the organisation and the executive.
- The organisation's culture – its values, beliefs, traditions and norms – what it's like round here (e.g. its degree of centralisation and control).
- How the organisation is expected to function (its hierarchical structure, policies, processes, rules, protocols, accountability framework, reward and promotion system, feedback provision, spending levels).
- Colleagues, and their feedback, whose support can enable, or if unknowing or withheld, can frustrate the executive's plans.
- The nature and potency of the organisation's darker side: its political nature, social hierarchy, bullying, power bases and struggles, turf wars, morality, favourite sons, level of toxicity, messiness and craziness, the undiscussed and undiscussibles.' [41]

Why context alone is not enough

The injection of context is a big improvement on generic, one-size-fits-all approaches. But, while *awareness and inclusion* of the organisational context is necessary, it is an insufficient condition for the successful development, improvement, conduct and expansion of leadership. It is insufficient on three counts:

■ Combining learning and doing

There appears to be a common assumption that learning leadership can still be successful if separated from doing it. Even learning leadership is rarely what it claims: it is often learning about leadership (for example, discussing lists of leadership competencies). The legendary turnaround king Jack Welch, erstwhile CEO of General Electric, offers two-day events where people learn from him 'the key characteristics of effective leaders and how to put them into action'. Such learning takes place in the head, whereas real learning (if anything is to change) is visceral and entails interaction and doing it for real.

---

41   CRF. (2006) *Managing Coaching in Organisations* (workshop notes). London: Corporate Research Forum.

■ Learning is a means. To what end?

Learning is often treated as an end in itself. If you want to check this out, just look at what is evaluated. Learning should be treated as a means towards a clear end, and an active interest in what happens organisationally following formal learning should be demonstrated. (For a fuller discussion on means versus ends, see Chapter 8, *Leadership and Learning*.)

■ Organisations need to do work on themselves

The target of most authors' advice on context and challenges remains individual leadership, or more probably development of individual leadership. Advice stops short of recognising that organisations need to do work on themselves. That means examining the system, which calls for an OD approach.

MANAGING
MANAGEMENT DEVELOPMENT

Moving deeper into the organisation

If management developers make progress with the first-level questions on page 89 and have the appetite and courage to press further, then here is a range of more challenging questions:

SECOND-LEVEL QUESTIONS FOR MANAGEMENT DEVELOPERS

☐ What is happening in the organisation at the moment that management development activity should know about and try to take into account?

☐ Where in the organisation is management and leadership performance currently deficient?

☐ Where is the respective balance of responsibility for the managers' performance improvement between the organisation and the individual?

☐ If managers try to manage or lead in a different way, what will happen, and what will obstruct them?

☐ What risks will they be taking with their careers?

☐ How are managers' jobs structured to separate their day-to-day delivery role from their role of questioning for tomorrow?

Table 10: Second-level questions for management developers

A change strategy for management development itself

It is quite common to find little dialogue between top line managers and trainers, educators and developers, and it is worthwhile trying to improve the level of engagement. Getting into a dialogue via the questions above makes management development more relevant to the future of the business. It shifts the developer's focus and energy:

AWAY FROM		TOWARDS
a provider mindset	→	a business partnership mindset
an interest and expertise in inputs	→	an interest and expertise in outputs and outcomes
self and client perception as internal 'outsider'	→	self- and client perception as mainstream contributor

Figure 2: Shifting the developer's focus and energy

In themselves, these shifts amount to nothing short of the basics of a strategy for management development *itself* to become more organisational. Such a challenge should be formally laid at the door of every head of management development.

Shifting MD to make it more organisational brings mixed comfort. The change falls short of organisation development (OD), leaving the action remaining within the ambit of management development (MD) – just. In other words, it still targets the manager, but is now more strategic in being more closely tied to the organisation. Such an approach is sometimes termed *organisational management development.*

Even Georgiades' fabled 'go upstream young man' to find out who is behind the drowning bodies floating in the river is still looking for dysfunctional managers rather than a dysfunctional system. Yet that system might bear responsibility for the managers' behaviour and ability to perform.

'As Newcastle (United football team) began the process of replacing (Kevin) Keegan, who resigned on Thursday, the board's modus operandi faced a twin attack, with (Alan) Shearer ... stating: "I'd like to be a manager at some point but I want to control who comes in and out of the club."

'Describing the internal structure at St James' Park as "strange" the former Newcastle captain, added: "If you've got three, four or five players waiting for you and you don't know who they are, then you've got the right to ask yourself, 'can I manage this club?' A manager lives and dies by his decisions. If he can't do that is there any point in him being there? It's dangerous when you go into a club and the director of football is not appointed by you."'

Shearer was clearly referring to Keegan's emasculation at the hands of Dennis Wise, Newcastle's all-powerful director of football, and Mike Ashley, the club's owner. ... (Richard) Bevan (chief executive of the League Managers Association) insisted that Ashley's largely London-based management structure was doomed to failure: "If you look at a football club when people are running it from different parts of the country, when you've got a manager who doesn't know who is being signed, who is leaving and who is coming in, it's a recipe for disaster. Newcastle looked a bit like an orchestra with four conductors. It was going to break down sooner or later." ' [42]

The football club case reveals the complex organisational structures, reporting arrangements, responsibilities, accountabilities, communications and dynamics that need considering quite separately from an individual manager's capability.

---

42   Taylor, L. (2008) 'Knives out for 'disaster' club Newcastle'. London: *The Guardian*, 6 September.

Hence, compared with OD, MD's ability to make an impact on the organisation at large is limited. However strategically informed and conceived, management development in itself doesn't change an organisation or any of its variables such as its reporting structure. To achieve more, managers' efforts need reinforcing by making changes to the organisation as a system and therefore to what *surrounds* them.

Holding management development to account

Once management developers accept the need to engage in greater and more meaningful dialogue with the organisation if their activities are to become strategically significant in the company's fortunes, then this raises a fundamental governance issue: For whom, and to whom, is management development responsible? And how practically can management development be held to account? Here are some questions for chief executives to ask of management developers:

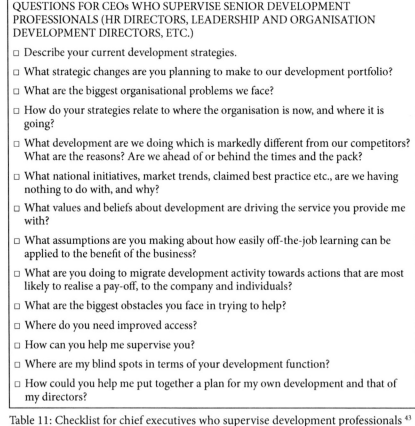

QUESTIONS FOR CEOs WHO SUPERVISE SENIOR DEVELOPMENT PROFESSIONALS (HR DIRECTORS, LEADERSHIP AND ORGANISATION DEVELOPMENT DIRECTORS, ETC.)

☐ Describe your current development strategies.

☐ What strategic changes are you planning to make to our development portfolio?

☐ What are the biggest organisational problems we face?

☐ How do your strategies relate to where the organisation is now, and where it is going?

☐ What development are we doing which is markedly different from our competitors? What are the reasons? Are we ahead of or behind the times and the pack?

☐ What national initiatives, market trends, claimed best practice etc., are we having nothing to do with, and why?

☐ What values and beliefs about development are driving the service you provide me with?

☐ What assumptions are you making about how easily off-the-job learning can be applied to the benefit of the business?

☐ What are you doing to migrate development activity towards actions that are most likely to realise a pay-off, to the company and individuals?

☐ What are the biggest obstacles you face in trying to help?

☐ Where do you need improved access?

☐ How can you help me supervise you?

☐ Where are my blind spots in terms of your development function?

☐ How could you help me put together a plan for my own development and that of my directors?

Table 11: Checklist for chief executives who supervise development professionals [43]

---

43   Modified extract based on Tate, 1995a.

Management development strategy

Henry Mintzberg argues pragmatically that there is always a strategy, even if it exists by default and is simply a consistent refection of a position, one which may never have been published formally as such. This is what he calls *emergent strategy*. Mintzberg (1987) talks about the Five P's of strategy. Whether emergent or well-planned and communicated, strategy may be reflected in a:

- plan
- position
- pattern
- perspective
- or ploy

Mintzberg's model provides a checklist or lens through which to view and review a company's actions, including those affecting its management and leadership development.

■ Training's weakness

Leaders sometimes invoke training either naively or as a strategic ploy (Mintzberg's fifth P) to point the finger elsewhere or to try to reassure the market and investors, as in this example from the pensions mis-selling scandal:

> As an explanation of the finance sector's scandalous mis-selling of pensions and endowment mortgages in the 1990s, poor training was a convenient target for blame. Equally conveniently, redesigned training was held out to the public as offering hopeand reassurance to customers for the future. Training and retraining individuals conveniently points the finger elsewhere. Training is a quick, easy and visible reaction by managers who need to be seen to be doing something. Training is far easier than questioning the values, culture or systems of the institution or sector for which, in any case, the leaders may lack mental models and have only a vague understanding. But you cannot solve a dysfunctioning organisation or sector that has low ethical standards and a flawed business model with individual-based solutions.

Even when not used as a ploy, trying to improve people's performance and leadership through training, without regard to what the system is doing is especially fraught with the risk of failure.

> 'Training is frequently undertaken without sufficient regard to the systemic properties of organisations. As such, it confuses individual changes with modification of system variables, such as the business's mission, structure and reward system. … W Edwards Deming, the American thinker and teacher behind the Japanese quality revolution, argues that most improvement in productivity comes from improving the system (the way the work works) not the people (the way the people work).' (Tate, 2005)

Questions to consider include: How does work come in, how is it parcelled out, how much discretion do people have, who checks whose work, who is responsible for coordination across functional teams, where does accountability lie? It's worth bearing these systems design and flow questions in mind when pointing the finger at training – whether for solutions or blame.' (Tate, 2005)

Sir Michael Lyons, Chairman of the BBC Trust, has done something similar in the wake of the Jonathan Ross/Russell Brand scandal involving foul-mouthed humour on Radio 2. Following his enquiry, Lyons refers to a 'review of the calibre and training of editorial executives'. [44] Instead he should look at what surrounds those executives, such as what market the BBC wants to move into, in what direction it is trying to shift its ethos, what brief it gives to senior executives, who should employ programme producers (Brand employed his own producer) and whether there is a conflict of interest, and what achievements the executives get rewarded for. (See Chapter 12, *Leadership and Systems*, for a systemic analysis of this case.)

John Browett, the new chief executive at DSG International (the renamed Dixons Group and owner of Currys and PC World) makes the same mistake in launching a sales training programme for 20,000 store staff.[45] It is not just a case of the company's values, which are in danger of being overlooked in this approach (i.e. an element in its organisation model), but in this case the flawed analysis may be found in the business model and the impact of internet sales. Training alone risks missing the point.

Ed Balls, UK Secretary of State for Children, Schools and Families, makes the same mistake in calling for better training of social workers in the wake of Baby P's murder in the London Borough of Haringey (see pages 157-159 for case study).

What these three cases amply demonstrate is the need for interventions that can reach more deeply into the organisation than can be achieved by management training and development. For this reason, organisation development methods are the subject of the next chapter.

---

44   Midgley, N. (2008) 'Calls to break BBC's monopoly on licence fee after damning Sachsgate report'. Telegraph.co.uk, 21 November.

45   Finch, J. (2008) 'Financial Viewpoint: No quick fix for DSG's electrical faults'. *The Guardian*, 27 June.

SUMMARY OF CHAPTER KEY POINTS

1. Company statements of management development policy bear careful consideration and skilful and informed crafting. This may lead to a healthy re-questioning of the underlying strategy, which might simply reflect a historical pattern and exist mainly by default.

2. Individual managers' learning and development is important, but organisations can take too much responsibility for planning and managing it, while correspondingly showing too little interest in the organisation's development.

3. There is usually plenty of scope, and benefit to be achieved, by linking management development activity more closely to the goals, needs and realities of the business and its supporting organisation.

4. Equally, developers require a degree of respectful freedom to develop managers to be able to see things that their sponsoring managers cannot see, and to challenge the organisation and the status quo.

5. Organisations and management developers may learn much and find benefit from rethinking and renegotiating their psychological contract. Developers' activity may be able to move further upstream.

6. Taking account of the various elements of 'context' is fundamental to successful management development, including coaching.

7. The management development function needs its own strategy for improvement and change.

8. Management development needs a formal process by which it is held to account.

9. Management development lacks organisation development's (OD's) ability to intervene in system variables, and how the system may be failing and obstructing leadership.

10. A request from 'on high' for leadership development for others is an opportunity to move upstream and talk about doing something more strategic.

CHAPTER 7:

LEADERSHIP AND ORGANISATION DEVELOPMENT

□ *Re-engineering the context*
□ *Grounding development in the system*
□ *The contribution of organisation development*
□ *Minding the gap*
□ *Minding the waste*
□ *Minding the perceptions*
□ *Minding the fishtank*

There is no leadership without an organisation to lead. The organisation determines the leadership it gets. The organisation gets the leadership it deserves (not necessarily what it needs). Every organisation wastes leadership – it escapes down gaps of various kinds. There is rarely an acute shortage of leadership talent available to the organisation, if only it will see it, release it, support it, hang onto it, apply it, and choose to make the most productive use of it.

This chapter looks at a number of deep-seated issues that are common to all but the smallest of organisations. Addressing them calls for organisation development. 'OD' works by pulling on several levers. It includes but reaches beyond managers and managerial teams, to focus on the organisation as a system and how the various components interact. Management development – the subject of the previous chapter – is unable to address these wider organisational needs and dynamics because its remit is more narrowly focused on the development of managers' capability. But OD can go deeper than MD to develop and use the kind of leadership that is needed to deal with systemic problems.

An OD approach recognises the reality that the economy is dominated by organisations, not individuals, as Simon Caulkin has noted.[46] This fact explains much about the reality of leadership and about organisations' dominion over it (much of it negative) and of which they are mostly in denial. Organisations typically shoot themselves in the foot when it comes to leadership because they behave as though we live in an individual economy. This leads to their pointing leadership interventions at their managers. If they want to improve leadership they should first turn the spotlight on themselves. As we said earlier, if you want leadership, look inside the organisation.

---

46   Caulkin, S. (2008) 'Workplace skills are hard to find at head office'. London: *The Observer*, 10 August.

Systemic diagnosis

The systemic leadership diagnostic process penetrates the organisation deeply. The approach treats the organisation as a system and investigates what is going on there, and what needs to be going on there. It seeks to discover what is supporting leadership and what is blocking it. It anticipates what the organisation's future needs are – for the organisation itself and for the kind of leadership it will require if it is to change. Such a diagnosis is essential if leadership is to improve and be successfully applied. Typical questions include:

- Where in the organisation is leadership deficient?
- How does that deficit show?
- How well are leaders combining their efforts?
- How does individual leadership effort contribute to the organisation being better led?
- What and where are the gaps and what is falling down them?

The systemic approach to improving leadership draws on organisation psychology and uses organisation development methods rather than management development ones. The two approaches can be integrated, with OD helping to build a strategic platform for MD.

Managers alone cannot achieve organisational change. They have little leverage beyond their own small 'patch'. At the same time they need things to be changing in the system in which they are working. Taking account of the organisational context in their personal development is not enough: the context itself needs re-engineering.

Re-engineering the context

As previous chapters have shown, management development doesn't directly set out to challenge, improve and change the organisation. It doesn't see (and may not be permitted to see) that the organisation system itself can and should be a target for a leadership intervention. Warner Burke (1972) offers this advice:

> '… individually oriented strategies of change, such as training, are not effective in bringing about organizational change. This is due to at least three basic problems. The first relates to the age-old issue in training – transfer of learning. The simple fact that most training occurs in a location other than the individual's work space produces the problem of re-creating the training milieu and learning back on the job. Critical mass is a second problem. How many people must one train to obtain the desired impact on the organization? … A third problem relates to the social psychological principle … that individual behaviour in a group context is considerably shaped and regulated by social norms. Individual training often requires individual deviance from accepted norms. … Trainers … do not understand that groups are easier to change than individuals. … Training should facilitate change, not attempt to provide it.'

OD is called into service both as a complement and a foundation to management/leadership development. It is the organisation that is the powerful springboard for leveraging improved leadership processes, contributions and practice. Recognising this means taking action that targets non-people factors in the system, as well as people ones.

THE CONTRIBUTION OF
ORGANISATION DEVELOPMENT (OD)

What is OD?

OD is concerned with how organisations work. As McCrimmon (2008) points out, its focus has always been on the 'soft' side of human interaction (culture, team relationships, communication etc.), rather than on the 'hard' side (strategy, IT, logistics, key performance indicators, etc.).

But from its broad beginnings in the mid-20th century, OD has morphed into many specialisms, such as culture change, change management, talent management, and leadership development. Its concentration on the internal organisation has highlighted a weakness: OD's neglect of organisations' external environment. A summary today would look like this:

A DESCRIPTION OF ORGANISATION DEVELOPMENT

☐ OD activities intervene in the system. Their purpose is to improve the way the organisation functions to better serve the business and lift overall performance.

☐ The whole organisation or a substantial unit is worked on, capturing the interdependencies and how it all comes together holistically.

☐ The focus of capability is collective and systemic rather than individual.

☐ In working on the organisation, interventions engage with people, but as agents or means to improving the organisation as a system.

☐ Interventions may target structural issues, culture, climate, relationships (team, inter- and intra-departmental, hierarchical, partnership, etc.), work flow, waste, bureaucracy, turnarounds, merging and demerging, building organisational capability, performance management, putting the customer first, etc.

☐ Diagnosing what is happening relies on obtaining people's perceptions ('soft data'). Such diagnosis aims to find out what the real needs and issues are; these may not be what they are initially claimed to be or are believed to be.

☐ Data gathering is an active part of the OD intervention, not just a prelude to it. Data gathering is itself an important part of the learning and improvement intervention. The conversations that occur during the beginning of this process begin to change perceptions and influence attitudes towards improvement and change. Nothing is ever quite the same afterwards as it would have been without the conversation. Every conversation changes the future.

☐ OD activities are usually seeking sustainable improvement – long term rather than a quick fix.

Table 12: A description of organisation development

'OD is not about today's programmes; it's about the programmes for tomorrow. It is looking ahead to what we want to achieve in future years and making sure that we have the skills and capacity in place to do it.' [47]
(Chris Hyams, Assistant Director of Human Resources and Organisation Development, Bolton Metropolitan Borough Council)

Systemic leadership approaches draw on the above principles and apply them to make the organisation as a whole better led, in the manner shown in the box below.

HOW ORGANISATION DEVELOPMENT IMPROVES LEADERSHIP

☐ Keeps focused on the *end result*; that is, improved and appropriate leadership *practice* in the organisation that benefits the enterprise.

☐ Diagnoses an organisation's unique leadership culture ('what leadership is like round here'), where it is functional and dysfunctional in relation to the enterprise's aims, and attempts to improve its characteristics.

☐ Ensures that appropriate systems are in place, and excessive restraints absent, to support the application of sound leadership.

☐ Recognises that the organisation itself is often an obstacle to leadership being practised, and identifies and removes any such barriers.

☐ Ensures that all HR activities that bear on leadership are joined up, and that leadership talent is appropriately defined, acquired, recognised, developed, utilised, appraised, promoted, rewarded, retained and terminated.

☐ Examines the nature of the gap between what organisations say and do around leadership (rhetoric versus reality), and seeks to bring them closer together.

☐ Is clear about the difference between leadership and management and what this means for the organisation, for the process of change and for securing the organisation's future.

☐ Views leadership as a component in a holistic systems model for understanding organisational dynamics, performance delivery and the process of change.

☐ Uses systems principles to apply leadership to improve the way the organisation works as a system.

☐ Has a clear understanding of what the organisation needs more of and less of if it is to succeed, and the implications for leadership.

☐ Understands the business's need for improved leadership; what leadership is currently most needed for, to what it will be applied, and what it needs to achieve.

☐ Clarifies what it considers to be appropriate and inappropriate leadership, and how leadership in future will need to be different.

☐ Specifies what groups, levels and roles will be expected to deploy leadership.

---

47   Hyams, C. (2008) quoted in *Making Successful Change Happen* (report). London: Improvement & Development Agency.

☐ Identifies the organisational challenges and agenda that will be used to provide a real-live context for individual leadership development.
☐ Balances and integrates demand- and supply-side strategies.
☐ Uses diagnosis, assessment and development to directly target the organisation.
☐ Ensures that the organisation actively shapes the leadership strategy by contributing its own direct needs and change agenda, purpose, direction, challenges, dynamics, culture, climate, system, structure, processes, definitions and funds.
☐ Puts the onus firmly on the organisation and challenges it to think deeply about its own requirements, where the organisation needs to be taken, and how leadership will be used to change its future and the way it works.

Table 13: How organisation development improves leadership

MINDING THE GAP

Gaps are both inevitable and fundamental to systemic leadership, and may be positive or negative. Some gaps become cracks, gulfs and chasms, affecting how the organisation works together and threatening the organisation's wellbeing. Silos are often cited as an example.

Some gaps qualify as 'spaces' – healthy, vital and containing opportunities. Spaces are interfaces, points of connection. Spaces are where individuals and functions come together in cooperation. Whereas individuals may be creative, innovation takes place in spaces. Whereas individuals may be competent, sparks are generated in spaces. Partnerships thrive where the space is alive with energy, goodwill, trust, respect, common purpose and conversation. Spaces hold opportunities for synergy and for building social capital, for deciding plans and agreeing improvement action. Spaces need to be given special attention.

So some gaps act as a spur to reform, but many become a source of cynicism, mistrust and resistance. Things escape down gaps, including leadership and the potential for leadership. Communication, trust and dialogue can all fall victim to gaps. Waste finds its home in gaps. Most of an organisation's ailments are found either in dysfunctional, neglected and poorly managed gaps, or in a failure to take advantage of spaces.

'A newly appointed chief executive to a Swiss engineering conglomerate announced his email address and said he would be happy to receive emails from anyone in the company. A consultant working with the company cited this as a welcome development and indication of a new style of management. A manager responded that he would not dare email the CEO: if his immediate superior found out that he had bypassed the chain of command to communicate directly with the chief executive, that would be a career-limiting move. The chief executive remained unaware of why he received so few emails.' (Tate, 1995b)

As in this example, the gaps depicted in Burke's model at the start of the book were relational: they were between people, between functions and departments, and between levels in the hierarchy. But there are many other types of gap calling for analysis and action.

A range of gaps

The table below presents a long list of gaps, with possible labels/issues/ explanations shown in brackets. Some of these are serious weaknesses and need remedial action. Some of the other gaps are not evidence of dysfunction; e.g. the inevitable gap that exists between various stakeholders' interests and those of the organisation. All types of gap call for the exercise of leadership in one form or another.

TYPES OF GAP

1. Leaders' rhetoric and the organisation's current reality (*out of touch*)
2. Leaders' rhetoric and their privately held values and beliefs (*cynical*)
3. Leaders' aspirations and the organisation's current reality (*unrealistic*)
4. Leaders' aspirations and the organisation's current backing (*unalignment*)
5. Leaders' aspirations and individuals' competence to deliver (*incapability*)
6. Leaders' aspirations and the organisation's capacity to respond (*lack of capacity*)
7. The organisation's claimed skills and resources and those actually available (*under-resourced*)
8. Leaders' required skills and know-how and their current skills and know-how (*individual learning*)
9. Senior management's perceptions versus those at lower organisational levels (*hierarchy*)
10. People's private convictions and the demands of their role (*authenticity*)
11. Relationships between key individuals (*teamworking*)
12. Relationships between departmental functions (*silos*)
13. The organisation's social goals versus entrepreneurial goals (*corporate social responsibility – CSR*)
14. Stakeholders' needs and those of the organisation (*stakeholder dialogue*)
15. Different stakeholders' conflicting needs and expectations (*stakeholder management*)
16. Legal obligations and the organisation's current behaviour (*compliance*)
17. Voluntary regulation best practice and the organisation's current behaviour (*governance*)
18. Official targets and the organisation's current performance (*performance shortfall*)
19. What the organisation needs to know and what it actually does know (*organisation learning need*)

---

20. What the organisation doesn't know it needs to know and what it does know (*blind spot*)
21. The organisation's legitimate system and its shadow system (*politics, etc.*)
22. Managers' performance and being properly held to account (*accountability*)

Table 14: Types of gap

You can use this list as a checklist to see where the biggest gaps are in your organisation, and prioritise them for action.

Gaps in competence

Judging from most training and development activity, appraisal practice, and needs analysis, you might expect the most crucial gaps in an organisation are to be found in an individual's competence, but this is not so. HR's easy question 'What training do you need?' receives undue attention when compared with other potentially more challenging and valuable gap-closing questions concerning the system. The ambitions of the Financial Services Skills Council (FSSC) are illuminating:

> 'The FSSC is licensed by the UK government to work in partnership with employers to provide strategic and responsible leadership for training, education and development for the industry in the UK, the world's leading international financial services centre. … provides strategic leadership for training, education and workforce development in the industry. Employer-led, the Skills Council is licensed by government to:
> – coordinate improvements in the sector's skills base;
> – raise productivity; and
> – improve business performance.' [48]

In aiming to raise productivity and improve business performance in specific sectors and in the national economy, a government and its agencies have their hands on few levers beyond generic skills (even accepting that the word 'skills' is nowadays used as a catch-all term for a wide spectrum of learning and a range of capabilities). But while the Government's assumptions about the crucial importance of skills have a superficial attraction, they are overstated in business terms, as are the claims of the FSSC. There are two related problems, explained below.

The first is that the distance between individuals' generic abilities and a specific company's productivity and business performance is simply too wide. These needs are a matter for those particular businesses; a sector agency that concentrates on developing individuals' generic skills can play only a small 'scattergun' part in achieving such specific goals.

---

[48]   FSSC (2008) www.fssc.org.uk/429_14.html?i=1 [accessed 11 March 2009].

Commenting on the Government's 2006 report by Lord Leitch, *Prosperity for all in the Global Economy: World Class Skills*, Simon Caulkin observed:

> 'One of the fallacies earnestly and unquestioningly maintained [by the UK Government] is that we live in a primarily individual economy. We don't. … The consequence of living in an organisational economy is that management – the orchestration of collective activity – matters greatly: as least as much as individual ability and skills. … [Leitch] is the latest in a line of hand-wringing reports going back at least 150 years linking the UK's poor productivity record with our shortcomings in education and training and attempting to solve the first problem through the second.' [49]

This highlights the other problem. In the FSSC's backyard, just look at the performance and reputation of banks. This was already low even before the 2008 banking crisis. In the UK alone it has been necessary to bail out Northern Rock, Bradford & Bingley, Halifax Bank of Scotland and Royal Bank of Scotland, and investment banks have failed across the globe. Skills cannot remedy a flawed business model, flawed ethos and values, and a flawed fishtank milieu that surrounds managers. Skills councils don't let a company (let alone a sector) off the hook from examining and improving itself.

The most important gaps in an organisation are not identified by analysing skills gaps. The important gaps don't owe their identity to under-developed people. They result from flaws in the wider organisation and beyond. So when developers are considering who they should be trying to help, instead of assuming that performance problems and learning needs reside in individuals, they should first search for other kinds of gap.

Talking about improvement rather than development can make it easier to think about organisational gaps. Max De Pree, erstwhile chairman and CEO of Herman Miller Inc, a United States furniture company, has surely got it right when he asks his directors a range of thought-provoking questions, a few of which are repeated below:

MAX DE PREE'S QUESTIONS
☐ What are a few of the things you expect most and need most from me?
☐ In what significant areas of the company do you feel you can make a contribution but feel you cannot get a hearing?
☐ What examples of budding synergy do you see in your area? How can we capitalise on them?
☐ What signals of impending entropy do you see in the company? What are you doing about it? [50]

Table 15: Max De Pree's questions

---

49   Caulkin, S. (2008) 'Workplace skills are hard to find at head office'. London: *The Observer*, 10 August.

50   Modified from Tate, 1995a, with acknowledgement to De Pree, M., 1989.

MINDING THE WASTE

Every organisation claims to value leadership, saying that it needs and wants managers to exercise leadership. Many organisations make expensive provision for leadership development programmes and other MD and OD improvement interventions. Yet every organisation scandalously wastes leadership.

> 'An executive being headhunted for a top job at Marks and Spencer turns it down saying, 'Marks and Spencer's bureaucracy strangles leadership; you can't get anything done'. He could see trouble ahead. Yet his own leadership wasn't in doubt – in his own mind or that of Marks.' (Tate, 2007)

A lot of money is spent on developing talent and then wasting it. Rather than stopping the misuse and haemorrhaging, organisations instead choose to put all their energies into leadership acquisition strategies. On this basis you would expect an organisation in due course to attain massive leadership capacity, but it doesn't turn out that way of course. The reason is not that leadership talent leaves (some does, of course), but mainly that waste continues. First stop waste.

> *'If the capacity of the system is the work and its waste, the way to improve capacity is to get rid of the waste ... the waste is caused by the regime.'* (Taiichi Ohno in Seddon, 2008)

Waste of leadership takes several forms. There can be massive waste in where and how leadership is applied, in the development of leadership, and in the potential for leadership. Below I review the sources of waste identified by Taiichi Ohno to gain valuable insights into how leadership is wasted in practice. Ohno is usually referred to as the father of the Toyota Production System, which is the basis for what is considered in the West as *lean management*.

Categories of waste

Ohno identifies seven categories of waste. His model is shown below in simplified form, with some of the manufacturing emphasis and language removed. Ohno's model offers some help in understanding some of the ways in which leadership is wasted; but the model does not make a perfect fit: not all his categories have leadership waste easily matched against them, and there are additional forms of leadership waste that don't map against his model. But the depiction may help you see your own organisation's waste of leadership more clearly:

Category	Interpretation	Applied to leadership
1. *Defects*	Failure to meet specification. Switch from quality control to quality assurance. Devolving efforts to getting the improvement process right rather than inspecting the results.	□ Shortfall in leadership capability. Poor choice of leaders. □ Premature promotion. □ Person-job mismatch. □ The Peter Principle (promotion based on success in previous job, resulting in elevation to level of incompetence). □ *Buggins' Turn*: 'I've been around a long time waiting for my turn in this job.' □ Developing generic capability that relates poorly to particular challenges. □ Hanging on, tiredness, past sell-by date. □ New appointees building up to speed.
2. *Over-production*	Having only the quantity required.	□ Developing too many leaders. □ A mismatch between supply and demand (e.g. more admirals than ships). □ Costly severance.
3. *Waiting*	Under-utilisation. Using time effectively. Preventive action.	□ Promoting people to the next higher grade based on competence while waiting for a vacancy to arise (Civil Service practice). □ Waiting until an incumbent departs before beginning replacement process. □ Finding a suitable post on return from full-time development programme. □ Waiting for committee decisions. □ Waiting for bureaucracy to work. □ Delays, deferrals, queues and bottlenecks. □ Incurring fixed costs rather than on demand.
4. *Transporting*	The cost of separation of the parts.	□ Excessive travelling cost.
5. *Movement*	The amount of time and effort making the connections.	□ Excessive travelling time.

6. *Inappropriate processing*	Doing only what is appropriate.	☐ Involving too many leaders in too many baton passes, approval steps, decisions and meetings.
		☐ Too much or too little delegation.
		☐ Allowing the urgent – however trivial – to drive out the important.
		☐ Micro-management.
		☐ Taking piecemeal decisions in the absence of a plan.
		☐ Requiring managers to try to work out what are the organisation's needs.
		☐ Allowing the various functions to develop into silos.
		☐ Measuring success of the individual parts, rather than the system as a whole.
		☐ The perfect is the enemy of the good.
7. *Inventory*	Inappropriate stock. Stock hides problems. Holding just the right amount.	☐ Misusing and misjudging the resources available, including one's own and one's boss's time.
		☐ Allowing talent to languish in backwaters. Placing the most talented leaders in the least crucial jobs.
		☐ Misusing the hierarchy as an available resource.
		☐ Not suited to the customer's needs.
		☐ Not available when needed. Otherwise engaged.
		☐ Damage, wastage, scrap and turnover.
		☐ Allowing providers to decide what you need.

Table 16: Seven categories of waste

'On the eve of a European Union summit meeting, Prime Minister Gordon Brown was emailing top civil servants late in the evening and early the following morning asking them what they thought should be the deposit on a supermarket plastic bag.' (BBC Radio 4 interviewee)

Avoiding the waste of leadership

Table 17 suggests some actions you can take to avoid wasting leadership:

HOW TO AVOID WASTING LEADERSHIP

- ☐ Place talented leaders in the jobs that face the most important challenges. Don't allow them to languish in backwaters.

- ☐ Make sure that managers know what the organisation most wants from leadership. Don't leave them in the dark to try to work this out for themselves.

- ☐ Design programmes that are driven by the carefully thought-out and express needs of the organisation. Don't allow developers to choose whether or not to align individual learning with the organisation's agenda.

- ☐ When choosing in-house administrators of programmes, check that they possess the necessary strategic OD understanding, especially when working with external developers/consultants.

- ☐ Foster close liaison and coordination between managerial colleagues. Don't allow learning and energy to be squandered through a lack of communication or protected role boundaries.

- ☐ Facilitate the transfer of learning to daily work situations. Don't allow good intentions to fall victim to the difficulty that individuals can face in grounding their learning back at work.

- ☐ Make sure that managers' attempts at providing leadership are free from obstructions, especially by bureaucracy.

- ☐ Ensure that top management provides any leadership development activity with a framework of strategic guidance, supervision and challenge.

- ☐ Define the improvement of leadership broadly to include a range of possibilities, of which developing individual capability is merely one.

- ☐ Ensure that managers apply their leadership talents to doing the right things (not just doing things right), especially those that are ethical.

- ☐ Learn from terminations (both voluntary and involuntary) of leaders.

- ☐ Ensure that all HR specialisms act in a joined-up way at the service of improved leadership. Don't just leave it to the Management Development department or Learning & Development.

- ☐ Monitor leadership to be sure that it is being used honourably, ethically and not for personal gain.

- ☐ Help the organisation to be clear about what its needs are for leadership, so that it can pull to itself what it requires rather than have suppliers' interests dominate the provision agenda.

Table 17: How to avoid wasting leadership

'Where customers can "pull" what they need from the organisation without friction or

*barriers, wasted effort can be rigorously
stripped out and, critically, the capacity of the
system increases.'* [51] (Simon Caulkin)

MINDING THE PERCEPTIONS

Perception is the new reality

Since Isaac Newton's time the dominant psychology that is assumed to explain people's choosing to take action has been based on *stimulus and response* theory. The assumption has long been that external forces are always needed. This belief underpins the familiar tools in HR's armoury: external controls, hierarchy, targets, monitoring, rewards, recognition, incentives and punishment.

The perpetrators of extrinsically based policies will probably claim that reliance on external forces is not needed in their own personal situation, but for other people they are still necessary. Extrinsic motivation remains the default perception, exemplified in the bizarre and ill-thought-through NHS Primary Care Trust policy below:

> 'A scheme which pays bonuses to GPs for not referring patients to hospital was criticised as "absolutely ridiculous" by a patient group. The policy introduced by Oxfordshire Primary Care Trust will see average-sized doctors' practices earning up to £20,000 for reducing referrals. The cut could cost the Trust £1.2m, which is seen as justified because the increasing number of patients being sent to hospital costs an estimated £6m. [The chair of a patient group] said: "It seems to imply that GPs aren't making good judgements and need financial incentives." ' [52]

The popular perception of physicians' Hippocratic Oath may be under challenge by the NHS: *'To practice and prescribe to the best of my ability for the good of my patients* [substitute PCT], *and to try to avoid harming them'*. And: *'Never to do deliberate harm to anyone* [substitute PCT] *for anyone else's interest'* [substitute patients' interest]!

The PCT is confusing two different types of 'survival' system in society, or two ways of making a living. In *Systems of Survival: A Dialogue on the Moral Foundations of Commerce and Politics*, Jane Jacobs (1992) identifies these as a 'commercial syndrome' and a 'guardian syndrome'. The latter is based on values of loyalty, honour, tradition, exclusivity and prowess. Trading is anathema to it. This guardian syndrome governs the behaviour of public services. Jacobs'

---

51 Caulkin, S. (2008) 'Thank you, readers. I couldn't have done it alone'. London: *The Observer*, 6 January.

52 Press Association (2008) 'Trust pays GPs bonuses to cut hospital referrals'. London: *The Guardian*, 20 October

syndromes behave as systems: their internal elements interact with one another. Tamper with one element and you risk producing a 'monstrous hybrid':

> 'The disastrous results of the GP contract can be traced directly to the government's determination to turn an essentially guardian organisation into a commercial one. GPs have responded to incentives in textbook fashion, by finding ways to meet targets. The government has changed their motivation from intrinsic (the work itself) to extrinsic (outside rewards). But, as a patient, which GP would you rather consult, one motivated by money or by doing the best medical job?' [53]

■ The extrinsic/intrinsic debate

Call centres are an extreme manifestation of the extrinsic model at work. Hierarchical controls, externally set targets, regulators and audits are all constructed on this basis. This model leads to passivity, negativity, resistance to change and injunctions, cynicism and cheating.

> 'A multi-billion pound BT contract to run Ministry of Defence phone lines was branded a "real-life Whitehall farce" after it emerged that the telecoms giant's staff made sure they met call-answering targets by ringing each other. BT was forced to pay the Ministry of Defence £1.3m in compensation after the fiddle was uncovered.' [54]

There is, however, a growing challenge to the assumption that people cannot be trusted and relied upon to do the right things, behave appropriately and work hard enough without external controls and incentives, punishments and rewards.

For example, teachers who don't decide things for children or impose their decisions on them, and who don't reward and punish but instead facilitate those children in taking responsibility for their own shared decisions, report a greater degree of responsible and mature behaviour. So it is throughout life.

> Following the murder of Victoria Climbié, directors of children's social services in local councils were instructed to cooperate with other authorities such as the police. The Government addressed this need by creating another tier of bodies called Children's Trusts to oversee and enforce cooperation. A 'Duty to Cooperate' law was passed. Various reports now show that this external model isn't working. The Audit Commission's study reports that there is 'little evidence of better outcomes for children and young people' and too much time is being spent on 'structures and process' at the expense of improving the lives of children. The report also comments that: 'on the ground, professionals are working together, often through

---

53   Caulkin, S. (2008) '198 reasons why we're in this terrible mess', London: *The Observer*, 9 March.

54   Churcher, J. (2008) 'Phone target fiddle a real-life Whitehall farce'. *The Independent*, 30 October.

> informal arrangements outside the trust framework'. The Audit Commission's chief executive says that improvements to children's services have happened in spite of the trusts, rather than because of them.[55]

Chapter 12, *Leadership and Systems*, offers a different way of getting groups who are locked into silos to choose to cooperate for themselves, without the need for a legal 'duty to cooperate', additional and costly structures or targets, inspections and incentives.

■ Perceptual Control Theory

A significant development in motivational theory is *Perceptual Control Theory*, developed by William T. Powers (1973). This theory challenges the Newtonian-based extrinsic philosophy. Powers posits that we can decide to act for ourselves provided that our own perceptions are legitimated and aligned. Interpreted by others, and at its most simple, people ask themselves:

Is there a gap between what I perceive and what I want to perceive?

And to decide whether to close that gap,

Do I perceive that I am in control, or that others are in control?

People will act themselves to bring about change if they freely perceive a desired state, perceive a present state that is different, and perceive that they themselves have the means (authority, skill, etc.) to close that perceived gap.

The RAF was interested in exploring some perception issues in their structures and how a more bottom-up approach might be used to solve any problems highlighted. The RAF used the systemic leadership[56] methodology to examine how the role of leadership was perceived at various levels in the hierarchy from senior non-commissioned officers (NCOs), through junior officers, to the station commander and the executive group. Unexpected problems of perception and practical communication issues between the levels were highlighted and subsequently addressed.

There were two major outcomes from this RAF investigation:

The first revealed that managers at the lower two levels were frustrated at being required to pass matters upward for decision and felt that they were not trusted to manage. Managers at the most senior level were frustrated at having too many matters referred to them for decision by subordinates who seemed unwilling to take decisions for themselves!

The second outcome revealed that managers believed they were under an injunction from the level above them not to communicate outside of their

---

55   Audit Commission (2008) *Are we there yet?* (report). London: The Audit Commission, 29 October.

56   At the time this was referred to as 'organisational leadership'.

technical stream (silo), but always to pass matters upwards until a level was reached where a senior manager had enough confidence/authority to speak to his or her opposite number in a different discipline – e.g. Operations talking to Engineering or Security. (See page 262 for an example of using the accountability system to address this problem.)

In most organisations, running sores like this can remain unhealed indefinitely, reduced to the level of dark mutterings. The system design/operational issue may already be known but cannot formally be acknowledged and acted upon until there is data to prove it and the right people are in the room together to hear it, discuss it and resolve it.

> 'We shall not cease from exploration and the end of all our exploring will be to arrive where we started and know the place for the first time.' [57]

Who owns the gap?

If someone perceives there is a gap but then expects someone else to close it, there is a risk of breaking the cycle through which people accept responsibility for taking remedial action and sense that they have the necessary practical and psychological control.

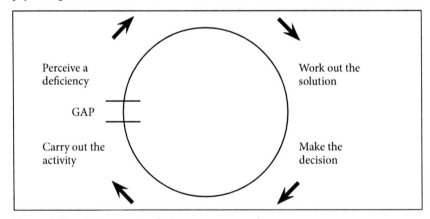

Figure 3: Perceiving a gap in the improvement cycle

An analogy to the improvement cycle is found in a thermostat. The mechanism that detects a temperature deficiency is directly connected with a pump, which gives a boost (heating or cooling). Contrast that with full-time quality inspectors in organisations whose job it is to inspect and reject *other people's* work. Professor Julian Birkinshaw gained an insight into how this feels in a domestic situation.[58]

---

57   T. S. Eliot, 'Little Gidding', *The Four Quartets*.

58   Birkinshaw, J. (2008) 'What does it feel like to be managed?', *Labnotes 'Renegade Thinking'*, Issue 9. London: London Business School, September.

'Try putting yourself in the shoes of an employee once in a while, and see how it feels. For example, last week, my wife asked me to help clean up the house, because there was an estate agent coming round the next day to give us a valuation. I was confused because I didn't see the importance of making the house spick and span for the valuer. And I didn't know what to do – because my standards for what passes as "clean" are much looser than those of my wife. So I started behaving like a recalcitrant employee – working whenever under observation, playing with my Blackberry when out of sight, and generally doing the bare minimum while she got the rest of the work done. For two hours, I was a confused and cynical employee. The next day, I was back in position as a manager of others – and with a much greater sense of empathy for their fears and their needs.' [58]

A break in the improvement cycle occurs frequently in training needs situations. Someone identifies a gap (say, a lack of customer focus) and then calls for staff to be trained. The latter have not been involved in perceiving that a gap exists. They do not feel they have sufficient control over what is happening, do not feel that they are part of the problem, let alone the solution, and may thus resist improvement and training.

MINDING THE FISHTANK

Recalling my fishtank metaphor in Chapter 2, most managers see only the fish (the staff). They train the fish. When the fish still don't sparkle they blame the fish:

'If you have an aquarium where the fish lack lustre, the typical development paradigm says brighten them up with some training, but don't bother to clean out the fishtank. In fact it's worse than that: don't bother to examine the tank for toxicity. We expect the fish to shine regardless. We probably don't even notice the tank; we've been trained only to see the fish. ... We look straight through the organisation and don't see the effect it's having. By contrast, the new paradigm puts the organisation itself under the spotlight and wants the cleaners to start their work there.' (Tate, 2007)

Criticising the fish is convenient for senior managers as it takes the spotlight away from themselves and points the finger at others – away from the system's impact on leadership, and away from their own responsibility for the system. While political, it is probably a natural rather than conscious act.

Christine Gilbert, the chief inspector of the education sector's regulator Ofsted, claims to have identified a new problem with the UK's teachers: some of them are boring. They need to be routed out and removed.[59] How easy it is to pronounce as an inspector. Teachers reply that it's the system:

'Most student teachers start out enthusiastic. The reason far more lessons are routine ... is that now there is in place a rigid tracking and testing regime that remorselessly marginalises creativity and fun ... children constantly being drilled for tests causes the disenchantment Gilbert highlights. A more creative curriculum based on reading, inquiry and investigation should be introduced. The main responsibility for that shift lies with policy-makers rather than teachers'.

'This one comes from a government that has done its best to remove every scrap of initiative and imagination from the teaching profession. Not that long ago teachers were free to write their own syllabuses to make them relevant to their pupils' abilities and interests, and were free to use any teaching style they wished. Now not only does the government, through the national curriculum, dictate the content of what must be taught but also the way in which it is taught (the sacrosanct three-part lesson)'.[60]

In case we needed reminding, the quality of teaching depends on both supply- and demand-side issues. To better understand the teachers' perspective, Ofsted would do well to take a look at the factors that spring from the demand side that affect teachers. In other words, it is unfair (and unproductive) to complain that the fish lack lustre until you have checked the fishtank for the quality of what the fish are expected to swim in (i.e. the system).

A further dynamic arises from the role expected of the assessor, judge and inspector. It is popular to rate and score. The UK government has launched a scheme whereby members of the public can rate their local NHS general practitioner. But Professor James Munro of Patient Opinion questions whether learning and improvement can happen when professionals feel that things are being done to them, rather than with them.[61]

Aware and astute managers understand these dynamics. They recognise the need for a frequent detox to return their organisation and themselves to full health. The process entails identifying and removing toxins and adding essential minerals, aiming to make the culture and systems easier to navigate, lighter to penetrate, less abrasive to pass through, and more benign in intent.

To undertake their purification role, managers need a conceptual framework for understanding toxicity and their role as leaders in this 'shadow system' (see Chapter 13, *Leadership and the Shadow*).

---

59   Curtis, P. (2009) 'Ofsted's new mission – to get rid of boring teachers'. London: *The Guardian*, 5 January.

60   Letters (2009) 'Primary rules for interesting lessons', London: *The Guardian*. 6 January.

61   Letters (2009) 'Plan to rate GPs should get a score of zero'. London: *The Guardian*, 1 January.

Swimming with the fish

A problem is that managers themselves are in the tank, and they have to be able to see the tank objectively and see how people's environment needs improving. To achieve this outsider's perspective, managers have to reposition themselves physically (taking time out from their daily work). The *Systemic Leadership Toolkit* offers a method for doing this. Managers can then be reminded of their responsibility as purifiers and be able to see their task more clearly. This is a key leadership role and important skill.

This isn't an easy task. Managers are fish as well and swim with other fish, sometimes in shoals and sometimes alone. They too have to do their best to survive organisational life and achieve their goals while swimming in these murky waters – the *system*. Managers' education does little to help them see and understand their environment as a system. Like real fish in water, they cannot appreciate what they are swimming in until they are taken out of it and given a lens through which to view it.

Trainers are usually handed fish (by managers) who have been plucked out of the water; the trainers scrub them clean, then return them to be dropped back in the same dirty water. As their environment is unchanged, the fish – the employees and managers – quickly return to their normal lacklustre selves. The fish cannot change themselves if the system is not changing. Hence the logic of focusing on the fishtank rather than the fish.

The fish are not free

Swimming in a fishtank (aka working inside an organisation) necessarily imposes constraints, as the fish are obliged to conform to the house rules and the culture's norms and protocols. The degree of compliance, compromise and deference required of people can be substantial and may carry a heavy personal toll. The stress and frustration arises from not sufficiently allowing people to behave in a way that is congruent with their true selves.

> I once experienced an occasion where a company's HR Director held one of his occasional 'informal' lunchtime gatherings with members of the HR department. These were opportunities for him to speak to the 'troops'. One HR manager saw it as an opportunity to ask the director an unplanned question. This broke a taboo, because it risked catching the HR director off guard. The deputy HR director whispered to me that the HR manager "has just made a career-limiting statement". This shocked me at the time. Here was the deputy director effectively colluding with me, rather than seeing that he held some responsibility (with the HR director) for allowing a state of affairs to continue in which such toxicity was seen as normal and humorous.

Aside from hierarchical pressures, there are two further straitjackets to bear in mind:

- The system will have its way.
- The group will have its way.

■ Complying with the system

Many people know of colleagues and bosses of whom it is said 'but he/she is a very different person outside work'. The most bullying, secretive and controlling manager may otherwise be an empathic, light, funny and sociable person when freed of the role, hierarchy, power and culture imposed by the workplace system. The halo and horns are easily exchanged. Organisations and the power they confer – both explicit and implicit – do strange things to people.

As an example, take HM Government's Home Office and the position of Home Secretary. It is sometimes remarked that all home secretaries demonstrate fascistic leanings in such a role. Few resist that tendency, the most notable and reforming exception probably being Roy Jenkins, later Lord Jenkins of Hillhead, Home Secretary from December 1965 to November 1967. More typical was the experience of David Blunkett, Home Secretary from 2001 to 2004.

> 'Blunkett defined his four years in the Home Office with a draconian mantra of toughness, and a rise in the prison population of almost 10,000. ... But in Banged Up [a reality TV show] he talks to the young offenders almost tenderly about their hopes and dreams for the future. ... "I actually felt, towards this particular group of young people, that they were very vulnerable." ... It's not uncommon for former ministers to reveal a more subtle or sensitive side. ... The nature of our political system, he argues, prohibits presenting a fully nuanced account of his beliefs. ... People who know Blunkett often say that his instincts are more progressive than the populist lock-'em-up position he used to present to the media. "The question we have to ask is, are there ways in which we can change the political climate and culture to enable us to do progressive things more readily. We've got to try to create a political tide which is feasible for progressive politicians to ride." ' [62]

Systems are not mutually exclusive: they are multiple and overlapping. Each exerts its own pressures and holds its hostage captive. For Blunkett, more than the internal Home Office civil service system, it was the *political system* that held most sway. The political system comprises the party system, the House of Commons adversarial debating system, and the electoral voting system. Also ever present in the room – the elephant if you will in this argument – was the tabloid press and its influence on the large swathes of the public, the press and public support or hostility to the government, and the public's expectations of harsh treatment for offenders. All these work against nuance, learning, understanding, humility, honesty and valuable doubt.

Taking a different political example, a systemic analysis of ex-President of South Africa Thabo Mbeki's unwillingness to denounce Robert Mugabe would reveal

---

62   Aitkenhead, D. (2008) 'Taking Liberties'. London: *The Guardian*, 7 July.

that the origins of his reticence lie in their shared cause as former freedom fighters in Southern Africa. For Mbeki to denounce a fellow freedom fighter would be to call into question his own background and values. When facilitators of constellations search for explanations of behaviour in a group, they physically bring into the room somebody who can serve as a token representative and reminder of past influences in order that such significant factors can be discussed and taken into account.[63] In this instance, Mbeki's past was in the room, an ever-present reminder of all the influences present in the system.

> When arriving as chairman of state-owned British Airways in 1981 with a brief to modernise the airline, one of (then plain Mr) John King's first dictats to managers was to replace the plates on their office doors with ones giving their name rather than their job title. In writing memos to each other, they were to write from their name, not from the job title they held (or worse, the job's initials). King's aim was to loosen the culture to free people to be more themselves. Yet they had to fall in line! Compliance with King replaced compliance with the system's bureaucratic norms.

■ Falling in line with the group

In the case of systems, the individual feels the pressure to conform with the expectations of others. But with decision-making groups, the pressure to conform arises more from feelings of belonging *within* individual members. Where they have a choice, people slide into a group where they feel at ease, and slide out when they are out of step, especially if they wish to avoid conflict.

'Groupthink' has acquired distinctively pejorative connotations since its original conception by sociologist William H. Whyte (1952) over 50 years ago, who accentuated the positives, saying:

> 'What we are talking about is a rationalised conformity – an open, articulate philosophy which holds that group values are not only expedient but right and good as well.'

Groupthink was initially seen as an expression of collective wisdom, and healthy and good for members' sense of wellbeing. But major incidents and systemic failures have inclined the term and the concept towards the negative aspects of group compliance. Commonly cited cases are the 1961 Bay of Pigs invasion and the 1986 Challenger space shuttle launch decision and subsequent disaster (Vaughan, 1996). An up-to-date example is the 2008 collapse of the UK bank Northern Rock and the wider international banking crisis that followed their high-risk, herd chasing of the sub-prime mortgage market, especially in the United States and copied in the United Kingdom:

> 'When a man is alone he feels relatively alright. But when in a group he can give way to impulses that do not really belong to him at all.' (Jung, 1964)

---

63   Abbotson, S. (2004) *A Brief Overview of Organisational Constellations:* Nowhere Foundation, www.nowheregroup.com [accessed 11 March 2009].

Irving Janis (1972) has done most to popularise the current, more negative, usage of 'groupthink':

> 'A mode of thinking that people engage in when they are deeply involved in a cohesive in-group, when the members' strivings for unanimity override their motivation to realistically appraise alternative courses of action.'

This has led to today's view of groupthink as 'The act or practice of reasoning or decision-making by a group, especially when characterised by uncritical acceptance or conformity to prevailing points of view'. [64]

Janis devised seven ways of preventing groupthink:

SEVEN WAYS OF PREVENTING GROUPTHINK

1. Leaders should assign each member the role of 'critical evaluator'. This allows each member to freely air objections and doubts.

2. Higher-ups should not express an opinion when assigning a task to a group.

3. The organisation should set up several independent groups, working on the same problem.

4. All effective alternatives should be examined.

5. Each member should discuss the group's ideas with trusted people outside of the group.

6. The group should invite outside experts into meetings. Group members should be allowed to discuss with and question the outside experts.

7. At least one group member should be assigned the role of Devil's advocate. This should be a different person for each meeting.

Table 18: Seven ways of preventing groupthink

'By following these guidelines, Janis claimed that groupthink can be avoided. After the Bay of Pigs fiasco, John F. Kennedy sought to avoid groupthink during the Cuban Missile Crisis. During meetings, he invited outside experts to share their viewpoints, and allowed group members to question them carefully. He also encouraged group members to discuss possible solutions with trusted members within their separate departments, and he even divided the group up into various sub-groups, in order to partially break the group cohesion. JFK was deliberately absent from the meetings, so as to avoid pressing his own opinion. Ultimately, the Cuban Missile Crisis was resolved peacefully, thanks in part to these measures.' [65]

Of course, there is much more to decision making, and to group dynamics in general, than the effect of groupthink. Other considerations include:

---

64 Answers.com (2008) *Groupthink*.

65 Wikipedia (2008) *Groupthink*. wikipedia.org/Groupthink, 9 July.

- What is the power distribution? Is the leader's office one of *primus inter pares*, the original first-among-equals role of prime minister, with the power to hold people together but not to order them? Or is it a more presidential role, at its most extreme when acting as commander-in-chief, as in the US constitutional *unitary executive theory* of presidential power? Is the role shifting from the former towards the latter?

- What are other participants' perceptions and expectations of the boss's role? How strong a lead do they want from the top, and how much deference does the system expect?

- Then there are personality differences, especially the divide between those with strong beliefs on the particular subject and whose chief interest is in their view of the singular 'rightness' of a decision, and on the other hand those who are comfortable with a range of possible decisions provided that there is a consensus.

Where there is a strongly directive style of leadership rather than a more consensual one, the leader may or may not be privately scornful of colleagues' opinions. Regardless, support for the leader's opinion brings political capital. Conformity can come about through patronage, persuasion, coercion and manipulation. Both the process and the outcome suffer. Compare JFK's handling of the Cuban missile crisis with the UK Government's decision to embark on the Second Gulf War.

> If he had behaved as a 'first-among-equals' prime minister, how might Tony Blair have seen his role in relation to his cabinet colleagues when deciding to go to war with Iraq? He might have said to his fellow ministers:
>
> 'My job is to help you to arrive at the conclusion that enables you to look yourself in the mirror, to enable you to face your families and friends, to act consistently with your personal values and beliefs and remain authentic, to speak to me on this matter from your heart, without being concerned how it will affect your remaining in a cabinet post. My role is to ensure that you have all the relevant information you need to arrive at the right decision as you judge it and to express that view freely. I also need to give you time to reflect on this and not feel bounced into taking an immediate decision.'
>
> Such imagined language would be a model of the leader's role to support and serve others.

Compare this fictional speech and idealised prime ministerial role with today's assumed 'leader' role (for many top leaders, not just prime ministers): to decide and then persuade others. Such a role leads to information being edited, timed and manipulated to obtain others' agreement. Used in this way, it prevents people from marshalling their thoughts, arguments, doubts, and how to plan safe ways of expressing them. The familiar tactic is to neutralise potential opposition, making the leader's chosen role of persuasion that much easier.

As Lord Butler (Cabinet Secretary) commented on this in his report of the enquiry into the use of intelligence to support the decision to go to war with Iraq:

'Without papers circulated in advance, it remains possible but it is obviously much more difficult for the cabinet outside the small inner circle directly involved to bring their political judgement and experience to bear.' [66]

This discussion (albeit it in an unusual and highly politicised context) contrasts the command-and-control leadership model with that offered by distributed leadership. When the leadership model requires the leader to win, and the leader's credibility in that chosen role depends on winning, the cabinet example perfectly shows how power (i.e. the power 'system') corrupts the process. All stakeholders, and this includes those who simply watch the games – the fish playing in their toxic fishtank – end up paying a heavy price. As we said in starting this section, the fish are not free.

SUMMARY OF CHAPTER KEY POINTS

1. The systemic approach to improving leadership draws on organisational psychology and uses organisation development methods rather than management development ones. The two approaches can be integrated, with OD helping to build a strategic platform for MD.

2. Managers alone cannot achieve organisational change. At the same time they need things to be changing in the system in which they are working. Taking account of the organisational context in their personal development is not enough: the context itself needs re-engineering.

3. Things escape down gaps, including leadership and the potential for leadership. Communication, trust and dialogue can all fall victim to gaps. Waste finds its home in gaps. Most of an organisation's ailments are found either in dysfunctional, neglected and poorly managed gaps, or in a failure to take advantage of spaces.

4. We live in an organisational economy, not an individual economy.

5. The most important gaps in an organisation are not identified by analysing skills gaps. The important gaps don't owe their identity to under-developed people. They result from flaws in the wider system.

6. A lot of money is spent on developing talent and then wasting it. Rather than stopping misuse and haemorrhaging, organisations put all their energies into leadership acquisition strategies.

---

66 Review of Intelligence on Weapons of Mass Destruction: Report of a Committee of Privy Councillors, chaired by Lord Butler of Brockwell. HC898, July 2004, pp 146-148.

7. The traditional model that assumes that people will only do the right thing, behave appropriately and work hard in the presence of external controls, hierarchical structures, power differentials, targets, inspections, incentives, punishment, etc. is under challenge from a model based on intrinsic motivation theories which encourages self-responsibility.

8. People will act themselves to bring about change if they freely perceive a desired state, perceive a present state that is different, and perceive that they themselves have the means (authority, skill, etc.) to close that perceived gap.

9. Managers have a tendency to follow a pattern of complying with the system and with the group. Wise leadership recognises and attempts to counter this.

CHAPTER 8:

LEADERSHIP AND LEARNING

- ☐ *Contracting out development*
- ☐ *Education versus training*
- ☐ *Convergent versus divergent learning*
- ☐ *Means versus ends*
- ☐ *Transfer of learning*
- ☐ *Multiple ways of improving leadership*

This chapter looks at a range of learning and development-related options, choices and decisions aimed at improving leadership or applying leadership to improve organisations. Some of these are strategic, such as considering when it is best to permanently subcontract development and OD expertise, and when it makes more sense to retain expertise in-house. Some decisions are more tactical, such as how to evaluate leadership development. I consider all these matters under the heading 'Making Choices about Learning and Development'. I will then move on to consider a range of means of 'Improving Effectiveness', before looking at 'Multiple Ways of Improving Leadership Besides Learning and Development'.

MAKING CHOICES ABOUT
LEARNING AND DEVELOPMENT

Generic versus bespoke programmes

From a provider/developer's perspective, the traditional, generic leadership development course (in-house or external) is convenient, repetitive, fun to deliver, and importantly isn't very sensitive and doesn't tread on people's toes. For clients, it is familiar, simple to recognise and understand, easy to budget for, is low risk, relatively low cost, requires little or no outside access into the organisation, requires minimum preparation time, and is safe to spend money on.

These strengths contain the seeds of its weaknesses. Some of the pluses signal a lack of integration with the reality of the organisation as a business and the reality of organisational life as a system. The result is an inability to respond to the organisation's unique needs and circumstances.

Typical development characteristics are:

- Takes place off the job (classroom or outdoors).
- Develops transferable skills and understanding.
- Assumes universal leadership truths.
- Assumes that tomorrow will be broadly similar to today.
- Develops learners as individuals, in isolation from their real environment, including their colleagues.
- Assumes that any changes that result will be confined to the learner and the learner's job.
- Employs well-researched, easily presented case-study learning material unrelated to the particular organisation.
- Relies on a subsequent transfer of learning (usually unspecified and uncertain) if learning is to be applied and have an impact.
- Ring-fences development activity and practitioners.
- Does not take practical account of currently live issues facing the learner's organisation.

Developers' expertise and confidence resides in their material, in teaching and learning methods, and in managing learner relationships. They may know little of the learner's organisation, its problems or agenda. The few who are interested may reasonably claim that they have difficulty gaining access and that, in any case, the clients don't want their organisation to be invaded. Many companies trust developers to work with their managers, but not to solve the organisation's problems.

Contracting out development

The generic scenario described in the list above is, in its own way, an informal contracting out of development, whether to an in-house, stand-alone facility, or to a management centre or other provider in the marketplace. Such top executives have chosen to remain at arm's length and not get too closely involved, either with thinking about and specifying the organisation's needs, with what the developers are doing to and with managers, or with what happens afterwards.

Many organisations go further and formally contract out development to an external provider. They may do so without thinking through and realising the risk they are taking in potentially widening the gap between an organisational problem and development solution. Or they believe that it is possible, clearly and cleanly and without risk, to separate management development from the organisation's own development; they see value in developing managers' generic skills and hope that they will be applied. Either way, they are operating within the popular mindset described earlier. For an example of why this mindset can be problematical, take a high-street bank's corporate university:

> A bank was experiencing a poor link between its corporate university and the rest of the business. It turned out that:
> - The organisation was unclear about the role of its managers.
> - The 'university' was told that the business wanted it to deliver a more 'intrapreneurial culture', but the university was not clear about what it needed from the organisation.
> - Visiting speakers provided a business context, but neglected an *organisation* context (e.g. 'what does the organisation need more and less of, how will the system behave, etc.?').

In instances such as this, thinking is usually supply-side dominated. The rationale is based on increasing skill in the organisation, which is deemed an unquestioned good. Understanding the demand-side (the organisation's needs, context, and what it does with 'graduates') is less well developed:

> 'The current perspective of the police service is that leadership development has not been led by the service itself. That it has become over time disconnected from operational needs and has become in part a generic management offering which neither takes full account of the professional customer, nor embodies the distinct professional and accountability requirements that fit with the needs and context of policing for now and the future. ... This has allowed leadership development in effect to be subcontracted out from the service and at times detached from the operational priorities and organisational culture of forces. Bramshill has declined as a centre of excellence and has moved from being a staff college to in effect a conference centre.
>
> 'Bramshill needs to be re-established as the leading campus of a national college of policing, which aims to be a catalyst for professional development in the Service and to grow as a research base for policing with strong links to academia.' [67]

Education versus training

The word 'training' is commonly used nowadays to provide portmanteau cover for a variety of learning experiences, even a university education; but that loose usage may mask important differences in principle and stop people reflecting on them.

In one of his most thought-provoking books, the television celebrity and writer Stephen Fry (1992) makes a telling point about the merits of education over training. Albeit in his case the sentiment was applied to children, but it transfers well to a business context.

> 'Education means freedom, it means truth. Training is what you do to a pear tree when you pleach it and prune it to grow against a wall. Training is what you give to an airline pilot or a computer operator or a barrister or a radio producer. Education is what you give to children to enable them to be free from the prejudices and moral bankruptcies of their elders. And freedom is no part of the programme of today's legislators. Freedom to buy shares, medical treatment or council houses certainly, freedom to <u>buy</u> anything you please. But freedom to

---

67   NPIA (2008), *ibid.*

think, to challenge, to change. Heavens no. The day a child of mine comes home from school and reveals that he or she has been taught something I agree with is the day I take that child away from school.'

There is a difference and a tension between training- and education-based approaches used to bring about learning. The two approaches hold implications for management and leadership development.

> 'The effect of pure training is convergence of ability around an external view of best practice. It helps deliver performance against currently known and agreed business goals. By contrast, the effect of pure education in development is divergence. This capitalises on the rich variety of views, ability and values found in humankind. Divergence is especially important for innovation since it generates both the freedom and the ability to challenge the status quo.' (Tate, 2004a)

A careful balance between convergent and divergent learning approaches is needed to manage both today and tomorrow. The precise balance, and who needs which, depends on the business agenda, the form of organisation, and the operating environment.

> *'Diversity is consistent with flexibility, innovation and autonomy, whereas uniformity tends to be associated with efficiency, stability and centralised control.'*
> (Jake Chapman, 2002)

Choosing convergence (a training-based approach)

The convergent approach may suit the organisation when:

- the future is already known and highly predictable
- best practice is undisputed and advocated by a professional body
- standards are laid down as the basis of gaining recognition or a qualification
- you want to constrain people to think the 'right' way (your own, or the organisation's).

While this list of conditions may reasonably be thought of as holding true for some jobs, it applies less to top jobs, especially leadership roles. Very different leadership styles, perceived roles, backgrounds, skills and values may be equally successful, and this is especially true at the top of an organisation. Peter Drucker sometimes likened leadership to conducting an orchestra:

> 'The successful recipe for what makes a great conductor has always been difficult to discern. What they have in common is their remarkable degree of individuality and the fact that this often correlates with their achieving remarkable results. Fritz Reiner hardly moved, controlling the players with glaring eyes. Herbert Von Karajan kept his eyes closed. Leonard Bernstein controlled with his mouth and highly animated body gestures.

'This parallel with the idiosyncrasy of top managers is not so far-fetched as it might seem; after all, there are now training courses teaching, for example, baton technique for budding conductors. How come? Leopold Stokowski used no baton! The answer may be simple. In both the musical world and business there is a trend towards greater conformity, perhaps resulting in part from less tolerance of a dictatorial style by those who are managed/conducted, and as a result of more training now being expected and available. In the case of the now-dead conductors mentioned, they had to discover for themselves what worked, and they arrived at personal conclusions.' [68]

Choosing divergence (an education-based approach)

For leadership roles, a more education-based approach to development is more likely to be successful. This is especially so where the future is uncertain and where divergence is both realistic and important. In such situations you want to expand people's thought horizons. The example below from the world of politics (the decision to go to war in Iraq) sharply brings home the need for choosing divergent thought.

Lord Butler referred to the psychological phenomenon known as 'groupthink' in the report of his enquiry into the use of UK Government intelligence to support the decision to go to war with Iraq. The US Senate intelligence committee made similar references.

The term was devised by Irving Janis, who analysed group decision making in the Bay of Pigs fiasco in the 1970s. He defined it as a form of decision making characterised by an uncritical acceptance of a prevailing point of view. 'It is a form of collective delusion, where bizarre policies are rationalised collectively, and contradictory evidence is discredited. Members of the group suffer an infusion of both vulnerability and morality, and construct negative stereotypes of outsiders.' [69]

While it is not universally accepted that the decision to go to war was wrong, it is generally agreed that a fair and open debate was obstructed by groupthink mentality (a phenomenon examined more fully on pages 119-120). A full discussion with divergent voices would have improved the political outcome for the government and the country alike, whether the actual decision to go to war was ultimately affected or not.

■ Ashby's Law of Requisite Variety

Ashby's Law states that any living organism needs to have sufficient variety in its armoury to cope with the potential threats in its environment. This rule of nature lies at the heart of the strategic diversity agenda and the need to let go at the top and empower individuals to lead. The law states:

---

68   Tate, W. (1995b) *ibid.*

69   Barkham, P. (2004) 'Group think theory of error'. London: *The Guardian*, 15 July.

'For an organisation to survive in a complex environment (business, technological, political and social) calls for its internal resources to be equally diverse. Organisations can learn from nature: without such a multi-response capability an organism cannot compete and will die.' (Tate, 2003c)

This principle is becoming increasingly important for organisations, given the prominence of the diversity agenda, albeit driven more by political reasons than strategic ones. Growing complexity means that opportunities and threats are becoming more diverse and rapid. Future challenges are becoming more difficult to predict. Old skills and responses may be insufficient to meet them. What does this mean for the aforementioned bank's corporate university?

If a company gets too firm a grip on its corporate university, the students' experience may become one of training rather than education. That is dangerous. It may serve to confirm the organisation in what it is already doing, which always needs challenging and changing. To develop that healthy challenge means giving developers the freedom to open doors in learners' world-views, lives and learning experiences that the business doesn't even recognise. Indeed, the business's top managers might be anxious if they did; while they might talk change, they may privately find comfort in the status quo.

But if the gulf between development and the business, and between developers and business managers is too wide, the learners may return to jobs and then experience frustration because their manager and the wider company cannot handle them. High turnover often follows.

'When managers attempted to implement their learning, their suggestions for improvement were rejected or ignored by their somewhat defensive and/or reactionary bosses.' (Alimo-Metcalfe and Alban-Metcalfe, 2008)

The contract between the parties needs trust, respect and dialogue, so that people feel safe and have informed expectations. If this doesn't exist, there are personal risks, frustrations and inefficiencies.

Distinguishing means from ends

Training and educational activities alike are intended to develop individual managers' leadership skills, roles, qualities and know-how. However worthwhile, the resulting development remains a means to an end. It is an *input* towards improving the quantity and quality of leadership in the individual manager's organisation (*applied* at the individual's whim in the individual manager's job – if the system and colleagues permit it, of course). Beyond these improvement outputs what ultimately matters are *outcomes* that are beneficial to the business, but that linkage is usually simply assumed. What client businesses should be less interested in is leadership development as an input; they are certainly not seeking an intellectual discussion of various historical figures' leadership styles (however interesting and entertaining). The example below shows how, with the best of intentions, it is easy to confuse means and ends:

> 'The OD resource pack in *Transforming Your Authority*, published by the Government's Communities and Local Government department, repeats the familiar argument for injecting context into development programmes. While you can't argue against that advice, it isn't enough to qualify as OD. The examples given in the pack are cases of the development tail wagging the dog. The advice positions the organisation as the means by which development (the end) is made more effective. But development should be the means, and organisational transformation the end.'
> (Tate, 2007)

So, relevant and well-designed development is a *means* of achieving organisational *ends*. Development is not the *end* to be improved by organisational means. Instead of 'How can the organisation improve leadership development?' ask 'How can leadership development improve the organisation?'.

Evaluation

There is a good test of what are means and what are ends. Ask yourself: 'What would the client *ideally* like to be able to measure as a sign of success and of a worthwhile investment?'. The chances are that it is not the development input, or even whether managers learnt something, but whether there was an effect on the organisation; i.e. level 4 in terms of the Kirkpatrick 1975 model of evaluation (in essence: 1. Did you enjoy it?; 2. Did you learn from it?; 3. Are you using new behaviour at work?; 4. Have the changes had an effect on the organisation?). These levels are increasingly difficult to measure as one progresses up through them.

Trainers, developers and facilitators show most interest in the low-level questions. That is where their interest and expertise lies. It is where they believe they have some control. They are interested in the short term, and they evaluate the event. But this is not about leadership; it is about learning, and whether presenters did a good job.

By contrast, a leadership perspective on evaluation is longer term and is concerned with the high-level question 4. And beyond this there is a neglected further level that is not normally considered: 'Has the business benefited?'. This cannot simply be assumed (the organisation may change but not bring business benefits).

■ Evaluation before as well as after the event

Evaluation is routinely conducted as an after-the-event concern. But Paul Kearns (1995) argues that this is both too late and that the questions are back to front. He proposes an alternative model that repositions initial consideration of evaluation as a strategic pre-event planning activity, with the aim of securing bottom-line improvements for the sponsor. The first question becomes 'What effect do you want on the organisation?'. Working backward from the organisation's need, you pass through what do managers need to do differently, what do they need to learn, leading to suitable training and development activity then being identified, proposed, designed and undertaken. It is claimed that the perennial problem of transfer of learning is thereby largely overcome.

This approach forces organisations to think clearly up-front about their own needs rather than accept generic development for individual managers as though it is an end in itself. In other words, this is a top-down, inside-out, demand-pull approach originating with the organisation, versus the more familiar bottom-up, outside-in, supply-push approach beginning with individual managers. However, the latter is still favoured by most developers and organisations because it is easier and a lower risk.

Who is serving whom?

In the practical development process and associated improvement activities, whereas management developers treat the individual learner as their client, organisation developers treat the organisation as their client. Instead of the individual needing to change, the organisation needs to change.

Where the agenda should clearly belong to the organisation (i.e. in OD interventions), the question of who is supporting whom comes into sharper relief. Instead of developers asking for the organisation's support (as is commonplace with MD programmes), with OD interventions the organisation calls on (or should call on) HR developers to support the organisation's leadership strategy.

Management development

HR	asks →	the organisation's leaders	to support →	management development's strategies and initiatives

Organisation development

The organisation's leaders	ask for →	HR's initiatives	to support →	the organisation's leadership strategy

Figure 4: Who supports whom: MD versus OD

In practice, organisations are rarely as proactive as this because they don't know what they need. They may not even have realised that this is something that they need to be thinking about. So HR takes the lead and thus requires support. But where pressure needs to be put on line managers to be supportive or compliant, the request or edict should come from the chief executive, not HR.

IMPROVING EFFECTIVENESS

Effective or successful leaders

What do organisations need and want? Are leaders who are successful also effective? And what is the difference? Those with an interest in career planning and development rarely appear to question this important distinction. Bosses, even chief executives, make the same mistake and promote the wrong managers.

It is often assumed that job effectiveness equates with career success, and that career success is a measure of development itself having been effective. But as Fred Luthans (1988) points out, success is judged and determined by bosses, and is generally measured by how rapidly and high up the career ladder the manager has climbed. This is regardless of whether or not he or she is good at the job. Parents are similarly proud of their children's success but unconcerned with their effectiveness.

Career success is achieved by managing upwards. It is bosses who must be impressed, as they decide promotions. By contrast, the accolade of being judged effective is awarded by a different constituency: customers, peers and one's staff. Effectiveness is achieved by managing downwards and sideways.

Discriminating between success and effectiveness enables development planners to be more circumspect in identifying worthy high flyers, and helps them choose the most effective senior managers as role models for junior managers.

> Succeeding in business is not the same as having a successful business: in fact, without careful management, the abrasive qualities that the unscrupulous use to elbow others out of the way as they move up can, and often do, tear the fabric of the organisation to bits. Assholes may 'succeed', but they often wreck the business in doing so.[70]

Can do. But want to do? Enabled to do?

In terms of the inputs-outputs-outcomes continuum, conventional development primarily concentrates its expertise on the efficacy of the inputs. But if potential is to be realised, it requires two further ingredients: *will* and *opportunity*. In the view of the coach Timothy Gallwey, 'performance is potential minus interference'. He is referring to personal psychological obstacles, but the concept can be extended to the organisational level.

> 'There is a need to reflect on the consequences for individuals who undertake some form of leadership development activity and become strongly excited by the experience, the affirmations it brings and the new possibilities for behaving in ways that are more fulfilling for themselves and their colleagues. But those individuals might then become more aware of the dissonance between these

---

70   Caulkin, S. (2007) 'With an asshole in charge, we all get a bum deal'. London: *The Observer*, 20 May.

possibilities and the reality of the less-than-effective leadership practised in their organisation. Expectations may be dashed by the desolate culture in which they work. The effect on their morale, performance and well-being, can also bring negative responses to the organisation.' (Alimo-Metcalfe and Alban-Metcalfe, 2008)

Instead of concentrating solely on developing individual managers' *can do* skills, it is important to recognise the part also played by their will/effort (*wanting to do*) and work opportunities (*enabled to do*). The organisation plays a key role in shaping people's perceptions in these two respects, whether deliberately or by default. (See Figure 5.)

The organisation provides a purposeful context, important problems to solve, a supportive framework, permeable boundaries, an absence of obstacles and restrictions, the least bureaucracy and protocol, a minimum of needless checks, etc.

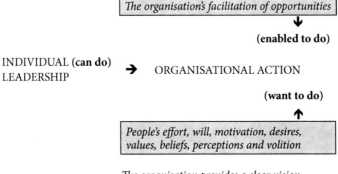

Figure 5: Converting individual leadership ability into action

Most development activity enhances can-do potential but does nothing about interference from above or below. The organisation can play a role in both boxes in the diagram. Not only does it provide the opportunities and a conducive environment in which managers can apply their leadership capability (the top box), it also helps to shape managers' perceptions and beliefs (the bottom box).

Shaping perceptions and beliefs

People behave appropriately to their perception of the situation, or the meaning they imbue it with as they mentally process it unconsciously, by comparing what they are experiencing with past memories, real and imagined. You can think of it as what's going on in their personal 'thought-bubble'. [71] Other people's perception of the same experience may be very different.

A good example of this is a ski instructor offering a row of beginners advice about how to make turns. The instructor might think that everyone is listening to the instructions, but some may be thinking about the après ski, others that what the instructor is wearing looks attractive, while others are scared of falling over, etc. The instructor knows none of this, and believes they are all ready, motivated, listening and learning. People on the giving end make the mistake of behaving as though meaning is 'out there' because they mentally project it 'out there', but it's inside people's heads.

People work together well when they have common or compatible meaning in their 'thought space'. Unfortunately, you cannot simply tell people what should be in their thought bubble. Nor have you any way of knowing what it is unless they tell you or otherwise convey it through their body language. Yet organisations can help shape these thoughts, and it is in their interest to do so.

Organisations and managers can help to influence people's perceptions favourably by changing their frame of reference from their standard one, explains Robson.[72] Moving outside one's daily workplace and standing to one side of the routine situation, as on an awayday, provides an opportunity for people to reframe their perceptions. Embedding the distributed leadership model depends on such a change of perception. A method of intervention that I recommend in the *Systemic Leadership Toolkit* involves inviting managers to enter into discussions with colleagues about corporate leadership issues that go beyond their regular managerial limits.

> *'The perception of leadership as a one-man show will give way to the idea of distributed leadership throughout the organization.'* [73]

Robson advises reversing the usual flow of learning, communication and accountability. He suggests that people are asked to convince their manager, instead of the other way round: those below leading rather than following.[74] (For an example, see page 217.)

Managers may think that it is part of their job to coordinate the activities of those who report to them, but this is generally not a successful strategy. Instead of managing the people, it is better for managers to see their job as managing the things that surround people. This includes those things that people take

---

71   Based on the work of Robson, I. (2006) *Perception Dynamics*. www.perceptiondynamics.com [accessed 11 March 2009].

72   Robson, I. (2006) *ibid.*

73   (2008) Respondent to Professor Gary Hamel's question: 'What does the future of management look like to you?', *Management Lab*. London: London Business School.

74   Robson, I. (2006) *ibid.*

from their surroundings concerning what the organisation expects from them. The aim is to change people's perceptions so that they regard coordination with their peers as their own responsibility, not something for them to dump on their manager.

Consciousness and volition

There is a so-called 'consciousness and volition' school of thought. This says that what goes on in a person's heart and head is of greater significance to their performance than what goes on in their hands. Research claims that developing people's self-confidence and esteem, energy, commitment to their organisation, beliefs about likely success, and courage to tackle difficult situations has a higher payoff than training in job skills.

Transfer of learning

A typical management development programme contains subjects such as 'managers will understand how they typically react to change' or 'learn how to lead people through change'. But what change? Whose change? Is the role of the managers to lead change or to receive news of it from above?

Returning to Perceptual Control Theory discussed in Chapter 7, do the managers perceive themselves to be in control or that others are in control? Most programmes don't face up to these matters: they simply teach the topic, unconnected with the company's context. So what are the learners expected to make of it?

The material used to assist most learning is generic and abstract. The issue at stake then is how to make such learning 'land' in the workplace, probably at some future date, when the circumstances will be different and memories will have faded. This gives rise to the problem known as *transfer of learning*.

Learning appears most likely to be effective in realising improvement back in the workplace if it:

- takes place with colleagues rather than strangers;
- develops collective capability;
- focuses on the organisation and business, not just the individual's skills;
- integrates with complementary action that is designed to improve other related system variables;
- makes use of real material rather than abstract/generic examples.

There are several options available to developers in choosing learning material that is most likely to connect with the organisation's reality (see Figure 6).

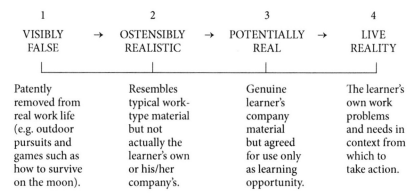

Figure 6: False-real learning material continuum (Tate, 2005a)

In the best cases the material used for learning will be live reality, that is really real, not merely realistic. So in the above example of 'leading people through change', the change being discussed will be actual change that is happening or is about to be announced. But such direct approaches to learning are rare. Programmes are put together by developers without significant input by organisation managers who know what is going on in the organisation and what lies ahead. Development, as said earlier in the book, remains semi-detached.

■ Using real-live material

Other than in coaching, it seems to be a given that learning has to be separated from doing; you learn something that is not your current work challenges and then try to apply that learning to those work challenges. This assumed separation needs to be challenged. Live organisational material *can* safely and practically be worked on during learning. In some cases the gulf can be bridged entirely; for example, developing a personal vision during the learning experience, rather than learning *how to* develop a personal vision. Here is an example that I experienced during my time working for British Airways:

> 'The airline designed a management development programme aimed directly at the real business. It got its senior management, again learning off the job in teams and under expert tuition, to examine the changing nature of the competition. The managers learnt the techniques and skills of competitor analysis by working on current material about Air France, Lufthansa, KLM, etc. They not only acquired new skills that they could use in the future, they took away with them completed up-to-date competitor analyses which they could immediately use back at work.' (Tate, 2004a)

While it is well recognised that learning needs to be transferred to the real work situation, the assumption continues to be made that it will happen largely unaided. Learners mostly confine themselves to notifying bosses and colleagues and asking for their support.

There are several common obstacles to improving the connection between learning and real work situations. A prior discussion should take place to try to identify and agree upon an important live issue that matters to the organisation. Surprisingly, even this can prove extremely difficult. In addition, line bosses often have low expectations of any impact arising out of management development and can remain disappointingly sanguine about development's semi-detached status:

> 'British Bakeries used to train its heads of departments in the skills of developing strategies for their own functional areas. To do this it asked them, as a group, to produce a radical business strategy for the company. They were then required to present their new business strategy to the board of directors. Having worked on this over several months, they became very attached to their strategy and considered it superior to the board's. They were then shocked when the board politely listened but then did nothing with their strategy, correctly saying that it was no more than a learning exercise (i.e. Position 3, Potentially Real) because that is the deal they struck with the developers.' (Tate, 1995a)

IMPROVING LEADERSHIP IN MULTIPLE WAYS BESIDES LEARNING AND DEVELOPMENT

Managing leadership along the employment spectrum

Throughout this book I have observed that development programmes are the default approach for the vast majority of organisations seeking to improve their leadership. I have given several examples that show how such programmes can add considerable value if they are cleverly designed. But I have not yet paid much attention to the alternatives. So, in case you are thinking 'how else might an organisation improve leadership?', there are other ways – development is only one improvement strategy. You can improve an organisation's leadership by many HR actions that bear on managers' employment, including:

EMPLOYMENT ACTION TO IMPROVE LEADERSHIP

1. *defining* leadership
2. *specifying* the organisation's leadership requirements
3. *identifying* managers with leadership qualities
4. *recruiting* leaders from outside
5. *selecting* managers to fill leadership vacancies
6. *spotting* the managers who will make good leaders
7. *rewarding* the managers with high leadership ability
8. *developing* leadership talent

9. *developing* leadership processes

10. *placing* and *utilising* leadership in the key jobs

11. *appraising* managers' leadership performance separate from their managing

12. *promoting* managers with leadership qualities

13. *retaining* managers with leadership talent

14. *rotating* managers proactively to reinvigorate and broaden their leadership

15. *planning* for the succession of leaders

16. *removing* obstacles in the path of managers and their leadership

17. *plugging* relationship gaps between executives, hierarchical levels and departments

18. *managing* and *limiting* the tenure of senior executives

19. *moving* managers who are poor leaders

20. *retiring* leaders who are past their sell-by date

21. *facilitating* the holding of executives to account for their leadership

22. *rejuvenating* the leadership culture

Table 19: Employment action to improve leadership

Some of these activities would not qualify as leadership development, but they do qualify as leadership improvement. The remit of HR Development departments usually spans training, education, appraisal and succession issues. Responsibility for recruitment, reward and termination may fall outside this definition. Focusing on *improvement* (and not just on development) embraces a wider range of efforts. These include:

- other relevant HR activities besides development
- other relevant HR specialists
- activities that call for OD rather than HR expertise.

■ An integrated model

Businesses may be described as being vertically or horizontally integrated. So too development. Thus far, the discussion in this book about linking development more closely with the business mostly assumes vertical integration; i.e. linking the individual manager, through the organisation, to business purpose and beneficial outcomes. But scope exists for horizontal linkages too.

> In 2005, Sir David Calvert-Smith, former Director of Public Prosecutions and chairman of the enquiry by the Commission for Racial Equality into racism in the police, admitted to the failure of diversity training to tackle the problem. Indeed, he said, it probably made things worse. The problem with the training, he suggested, was that it was not integrated with other policing action.

An integrated model seeks to establish horizontal links between development and a range of other HR interventions that together increase the chance of obtaining the desired outputs for the business. By contrast, organisations that lack joined-up thinking across HR activities risk:

- developing leaders at considerable expense, then letting them languish in unimportant functions where their talents cannot be used fully
- structuring the HR function in such a way that one department recruits talent while another selects people for redundancy on the cost criterion rather than ability
- failing to act as soon as poor leaders become part of the problem rather than part of the solution
- pouring leadership talent in at one end of the employment pipeline, and then carelessly letting it escape at the other

An integrated approach calls for a structure, culture and licence for those with strategic HR responsibility to have access to relevant decisions affecting recruitment and selection, training and development, career and succession planning, manpower planning, reward and recognition, severance and so on. It also requires a spirit of cooperation between these specialisms, rather than competition or a silo mentality.

■ Joined-up HR

Besides the ubiquitous default development programme, there are a wide range of related issues and opportunities to be thought about. These arise at several places on the employment spectrum with which HR plays a role. Questions to be asked include:

1. What leadership talent needs to enter the system?
2. How can the most talented leaders be allocated to the most important jobs?
3. Should newly developed leaders receive a change of job?
4. What criteria are used to assess the effective practice of leadership?
5. How is good leadership recognised and rewarded (and bad leadership 'punished')?
6. What criteria are used to assess suitability for promotion to senior positions?
7. What provision is made for successors?
8. How is leadership talent escaping unplanned from, as well as formally exiting, the organisation?

OBTAINING LEADERSHIP TALENT	→	DEVELOPING LEADERSHIP TALENT	→	UTILISING LEADERSHIP TALENT	→	LETTING LEADERSHIP TALENT GO

Consideration of:

Recruitment	Development	Assessment	Retention
Appointments	Qualifications	Promotion	Limiting tenure
Succession	Mentoring	Job rotation	Exiting
Talent audits	Coaching	Assignments	information
and spotting	Conferences	Leadership climate	Severance
Assessment	Projects	Leadership obstacles	
		Appraisal	
		Rewards	

Figure 7: Managing leadership along the employment spectrum

■ Issues of tenure

From the organisation's point of view, broadly how long is it ideal for a senior executive to remain in post, and who should have their hands on that lever to bring change about when it's the right time?

> In 2004, the spat between David Blunkett, then the British Government Home Secretary, and the Humberside Police Authority over the suspension and probable termination of their Chief Constable David Westwood following the Soham murders debacle raised the question of when is it the right time for a leader to step down.
>
> Leaving aside complaints about Westminster interference in local government matters, Westwood and his supporters made two claims. One, he had learnt the lessons from the Bichard Enquiry. Two, he owed it to the parents of Holly Wells and Jessica Chapman (the murdered children) to remain in post and put things right.
>
> The trouble with these claims is that they could apply to any failed leader. Even Saddam Hussein might have been able to claim that he has learned the lessons and that he wants to be given the chance to put things right. Even if this were actually true, the trouble lies with the past record not with the leader's future career aspirations. From Westwood's/Saddam's point of view, being given the benefit of the doubt makes sense. But the past record of mistakes might still make this an unacceptable future for the majority of stakeholders who are still focusing on what went wrong in the past. The chances are that someone else who didn't make those mistakes might appear to have a more credible claim to 'put things right' and 'learn the lessons'.

There is a common presumption in the case of 'permanent employment' contracts that the incumbent leader has a right to remain until either he/she decides to terminate the arrangement or has it unilaterally terminated for specified failure or misconduct. In other words, as things stand, the onus for making the case for his/her remaining in post does not usually lie with the incumbent; they have the equivalent of squatters' rights. The assumption is that someone who might do a better job cannot have it because it would be unfair to the incumbent.

But it can be argued that, for top leadership jobs, the balance of the right to remain and the right to be replaced should shift in favour of the latter. Incumbency advantages the jobholder beyond the interests of stakeholders. A change that might be considered is to reverse the default. Instead of a case needing to be made for a leader to go (as happens now in most instances), a case would need to be made for a leader to remain after more than, say, five years. If that case isn't made successfully, then the leader's time is up. This would change both parties' expectations and sense of their rights versus their obligations.

Besides the question of who should have the power to divest someone else of theirs is the question of how long leaders should broadly expect to remain in post.

> 'I believe to lead lasting change, the tenure of a CEO should be more than the current three-year average in today's organisations.' (Will Hutton, Work Foundation)

Opinions on this vary widely. Hutton may be right about three years. But the greater risk may be hanging on too long, remaining past one's sell-by date. There is a saying that 'a new broom sweeps clean'. There is no equivalent for an old broom; but old brooms get worn out and don't continue to sweep clean after several years. The difficulty is in noticing that the place has become dirty. Moreover, the dirt may be coming from oneself. See the discussion in the Chapter 11 about the effect of entropy on leaders following long tenure.

SUMMARY OF CHAPTER KEY POINTS

1. Be clear about who is the client: the organisation or the individual learner? And who is required to support whom – is the developer helping the organisation, or the other way round? Clarity over the customer and what are means and what are ends helps to focus goals and evaluation on the ultimate purpose.

2. If an organisation wants a real payback and value for money it first needs to understand its own needs, the nature of the connection and dynamic between the manager's learning experience and the organisation, the strength of the tie between developers and the client, and the provider's needed contribution and expertise.

3. The respective merits of control and freedom in the client organisation's relationship with the development provider calls for carefully considering, weighing and balancing.

4. They may all be called 'training', but learning experiences are different in principle depending on whether they are underpinned by training- or education-based principles. A choice has to be exercised about which

approach is best suited to meeting a given need considering the respective merits of convergent versus divergent behaviour and performance.

5. Managers can only realise benefits from development if there is help from the organisation in providing the necessary opportunities to apply learning, and if the organisation encourages managers' will (or at least doesn't discourage it and demotivate).

6. Senior executives can help shape junior managers' perceptions (for example, that it is the junior manager's responsibility to coordinate their work with colleagues), thereby freeing the senior executive to focus on the system and boundaries so that staff can get on with their job unimpeded.

7. Learning becomes most readily transferable to the work situation the more closely it resembles real work.

8. There are many ways of improving leadership other than by development, by intervening at multiple points along the employment spectrum.

9. There are always opportunities to better join up the various HR activities to serve the cause of improved leadership in the organisation.

10. Organisations should have more active influence over how long a senior manager should remain in post, and not cede control to the individual.

11. Don't confuse effectiveness with success. Identify and choose effective leaders as role models.

12. Contracting out development holds risks for the business if the hoped-for contribution is strategic and integral to organisational performance.

Chapter 9:

Leadership and Competence

- ☐ *Competency rationale*
- ☐ *Competency context*
- ☐ *Using leadership competencies*
- ☐ *Managing the organisation's competence*

This is a controversial subject. But why? We all 'know what we mean when we say that we hope managers will be 'competent' or possess 'competence'. Competence is an everyday word, which has existed with a commonsense meaning as long as people can remember. But in the early 1980s, in the US and the UK, the language of competence was taken up by various schools of thought and applied to different models concerned with the definition, assessment and development of competence. The result was organisations applying 'competency' models and frameworks, comprising 'competences', 'competencies' and 'elements of competence', each with precise meanings (see Tate, 1995b).

The subject became arcane, replete with ultra-nice distinctions drawn between the competing models and philosophies that exist to this day. Some frameworks and some consultancies concentrate on behaviours, others on knowledge and skills, qualities, attributes, characteristics, attitudes, standards, practices, etc. Some focus on *developing inputs* for performance (what you need in order to be able to perform), and some on *assessing outputs* (what you are doing when performing). Arguably, all have a place and are part of the rich and almost indefinable mix that together comprise people's performance. But some of these terms find no place in some of the competing frameworks.

Some frameworks are intended to be company specific, some profession/occupation specific, and others consist of universal and timeless behavioural dictionaries.

Since the early days of the movement, some purists and scheme designers have persisted, but others have become more pragmatic and have mixed and matched philosophies (input and output) and various types of content to suit a given organisation's needs and wishes.

Some of the most trenchant critics of leadership competency frameworks – of which there are many – identify severe flaws in all such individually focused models. Faced with this, my response in writing this chapter has been to be equally pragmatic, not wanting to discount any approach or even the commonsense experience of 'competence'. While I briefly explain the differences where that is necessary, I have largely glossed over them and confined myself to principles rather than the fine details of particular models.

The issues

- If competencies are used to specify managerial roles in an organisation, does the methodology transfer to managers' leadership?
- Should the target of a competency approach be leaders or leadership – the individuals or the process?
- Besides individuals' competence, what about collective or corporate competence, that of a team, a departmental function or the whole organisation?
- What about the organisation's *relational competence*, given that individuals' competence can get lost and wasted down the organisation's gaps?
- If *system competence* (the ability of all the organisation's component elements to work together effectively) is ultimately what matters most, why are organisations obsessed with individual managers' competence? After all, this is just a means towards a means.
- What does the organisation need to do to release and realise meaningful competence?

Let us remind ourselves of this book's core message: *'It's the managers' environment, what the system surrounds managers with, and the milieu that they have to work within and wade through, that contributes most to attaining and releasing (or blocking) leadership'*. Company HR policies and practices are part of that environment, which by definition includes any competency frameworks that the employer uses as the basis for individual leadership. To be successful in their careers, managers have no choice but to sign up to any such company framework; as Graham Salaman (2004) puts it, the first competence sought by the employer is commitment to its competency framework. Yet – paradoxically – to demonstrate and apply personal leadership competence, managers have to be surrounded by positive relational and situational elements; without those external factors being present and supportive, competence will remain captive, and the organisation won't release the leadership potential that is relevant, needed, and ultimately must be applied collectively and systemically.

This serves to remind us of the lesson from Warner Burke's flipchart in the book's Preface: 'What about those spaces between managers?'. Competence can get lost down unmanaged gaps and missed opportunities provided by spaces. For the organisation there is more to leadership competence than individuals.

COMPETENCY RATIONALE

The pros and cons of using leadership competencies mostly follow those of competencies in general, with some additional considerations. Many of the larger companies, consultancies and institutes publish lists of competencies (they may be called something else: management practices, occupational standards, leadership qualities, etc.).

Advocates of competency frameworks claim that competencies can be used to drive and horizontally integrate recruitment, appraisal, promotion, development and reward systems. They can also be used to vertically integrate managers' behaviour with the business's goals and organisational needs. They communicate what the organisation values in managers and what is considered to be best practice (that is, for individuals).

The assumption behind the approach is that people will be more effective if they possess the required pre-specified attributes, and that the route to this goal is via their organisation providing them with individual *development* opportunities and *assessment* of pre-existing or developed competence.

Competency frameworks can help individual managers' professional development; this may be what an organisation most wants and considers it needs at a given stage in its development. But it is important to recognise that individual elements ('competencies') are derived from people's past experience and experts' views of best practice, so they may incline towards professionalising the status quo – an important consideration for organisations in fast-changing environments; this may be true for both the content of competency frameworks and for the appropriateness of the methodology. Adherents of universal models claim that, by definition, their behavioural competencies are always relevant independent of context. In spite of this, the models are updated from time to time, which might suggest otherwise.

One of the attractions of formal competency frameworks is their face-validity. Their individual competencies possess natural appeal: they seem worthy and potentially useful for any organisation. Competencies are usually marketed as timeless and free of context, even when developed by and for a particular employer. For some, this is part of their attraction. For others this is a fatal flaw. Here follow some examples of such frameworks.

NATIONAL OCCUPATIONAL STANDARDS
FOR MANAGEMENT AND LEADERSHIP

In the UK, the Management Standards Centre (MSC) located within the Chartered Management Institute (CMI) publishes national occupational standards for management and leadership (most recent update November 2008). The MSC states: 'Upgrading the skills of managers is fundamental to the government's aim to raise UK productivity and competitiveness'. But as we saw in Chapter 7, *Leadership and Organisation Development*, the government's responsibility for the wellbeing of the national economy is quite different from that of individual businesses. Furthermore, compared with a company and its specific context, government and national institutions such as the CMI have very few levers to pull on – hence their attachment to individuals' generic skills and competence.

The model is a well-researched and long-established competency model relevant to leadership. The MSC has expressly chosen to merge management and leadership, and is not unique in so deciding. Some other frameworks claim to spotlight leadership, but this sometimes comes over as nothing more than an attempt to move the brand upmarket.

The MSC's set of 'standards' describes 'the level of performance expected in employment' in six areas:

Figure 8: The National Occupational Standards for Management and Leadership, published by the Management Standards Centre

The MSC has a tortuous history, as successor to the Management Charter Initiative (MCI). The framework began life in the early 1990s as one of many national occupational standards, using an output model for assessing managers' demonstrated performance elements – 'Can they do (the parts of) the job?'. It then had underpinning knowledge and understanding added (an input, used for assessing what a manager needed to know and understand in order to be able to 'do the job', thought to be more helpful for development purposes. The model's formal definition is said to contain three levels: '... the outcomes, behaviours and knowledge required to deliver identified management functions ...' [75]

---

75   MSC (2008) *National Occupational Standards for Management and Leadership*. London: Management Standards Centre (part of the Chartered Management Institute).

At first glance this seems a neat solution to the problem of combining these quite different but important elements, but it leaves some unresolved issues:

- While the CMI promotes a joint purpose and definition for management/leadership (see page 37 in Chapter 3: *From Managing to Leading*), the model states 'to provide leadership in your area of responsibility' you have to 'know the fundamental differences between management and leadership' (though it doesn't say what these are).

- The MSC claims that the model helps explain the function of leadership. In practice this amounts to laying down behaviours relevant to that function (e.g. 'articulating a vision'), but the overall function has to be deduced from the statement of the joint management/leadership role.

- The term 'knowledge' is inadequate as an explanation of 'input'. Admitting this, MSC expanded that category to 'knowledge and understanding'. Context-specific understanding, it says, includes knowing one's own *values, motivations* and *emotions*, though no 'standards' are specified for these. So one might conclude from this that a bully who enjoys bullying and knows it can easily jump this hurdle. (To specify what those 'correct' values etc. are would be near impossible, but it shows just how difficult it is to capture the richness and subtlety of performance in a workable model. Its very blandness makes it practical to prescribe but blunter in application.)

- There is no acknowledgement of the importance of managers' *perceptions* and *mindset* as triggers of behaviour. They would be difficult to assess, but the model could simply call for awareness of them (see above).

- The model is unclear on *skill* and *capability as* inputs to performance behaviour. Purists maintain that skill is not the same as competence, allocating skill a meaning that is more technical. The MSC rolls these terms together, using skill loosely as in the expression 'a skilled economy'.

- What initially seems like a useful three-level framework (building from knowledge, through behaviours to outcomes) is effectively two steps. *Outcomes and Behaviours* combine to become the National Standard, with *Knowledge and Understanding* combining to underpin the Standard.

- While *outcomes* are clearly an important element in performance, in this model these are at best *outputs*, and at worst the same as *behaviours*. E.g. 'Motivate and support people in your area to achieve their work and development objectives and provide recognition when they are successful' – is labelled an *outcome*. '(Consistently) encouraging and supporting others to make the best use of their abilities' – is labelled a *behaviour*.

- The model implies that competence can be assessed as an outcome from using assessed competence as an input. But conflating means and ends risks confusion. A manager may have the means (inputs) to achieve ends (outcomes) yet have those ends frustrated by others or by the system. Indeed, by definition, outcomes can be realised for the organisation only when they are not frustrated. Even if an outcome is limited to behaviour, the behaviour depends on a sympathetic relationship with another party. (Try negotiating alone, and who says you are good at motivating people?)

All this highlights the root problem of circumscribing individual managers' competence in the first place. Every competency model must, of necessity, fall short of identifying true outcomes for the organisation. It means admitting that competence is not the same as performance, and that the results the organisation requires of managers need handling elsewhere. The model only seems to work if you take the organisation and its needed outcomes out of the equation, and concentrate attention on individual managers' input competence.

(Note that, by comparison with the MSC, the widely used performance framework (not a competency model) from the European Foundation for Quality Management (EFQM) uses a structure of 'enablers' (inputs) and 'results' (outcomes). These are mediated or converted via processes or activities (throughputs). At a basic conceptual level, the EFQM approach is easier to grasp. But it too has staunch critics.)

As we shall see later in the chapter, such problems of definition are less significant in how they impact on developing and managing leadership performance when compared with organisational factors (culture, climate, procedures, bureaucracy, etc.) – in other words, with managers' daily environment.

The next section looks at some specific leadership competency frameworks and lists of competencies.

SPECIFIC LEADERSHIP COMPETENCY FRAMEWORKS

■ Centre for Tomorrow's Company

A simple list of timeless, generic leadership competencies researched for the Centre for Tomorrow's Company (Gamblin, C. *et al*, 2001) appears below.

ESSENTIAL LEADERSHIP COMPETENCIES
☐ Knowledge
☐ Courage
☐ Integrity
☐ Being purposefully awkward, and challenging the status quo

☐ Paradox management' – not 'either/or', but 'and'
☐ Vision
☐ Being an exemplar
☐ Helping others in the organisation change and feel comfortable with change
☐ Acting consistently in an ambiguous environment
☐ Listening to and understanding how others feel and make decisions
☐ Personal awareness and strong emotional intelligence.

Table 20: Essential leadership competencies

In preference to national occupational standards (which are mainly used to drive the award of national vocational qualifications (NVQs) at more junior levels), most companies choose to invest in their own research and develop and publish their own branded set. The irony is that what distinguishes the resultant lists from those of other companies bears almost no relation to the unique circumstances of that company, or at that particular time. This happens because researchers don't ask that question. Published managerial and leadership competencies turn out to be near universal. Whatever the chosen words may say, the sentiments are always very similar.

Some of the companies that have developed their own leadership competency frameworks include Shell, BAe Systems, Lufthansa and Centrica.

■ Centrica

Centrica's competency framework[76] concentrates on five leadership competencies, which, in simplified form, cover the following:

CENTRICA'S LEADERSHIP COMPETENCIES
☐ Creates a compelling future
☐ Inspires others to achieve
☐ Learns and shares knowledge
☐ Demonstrates a passion for customers
☐ Delivers great performance.

Table 21: Centrica's leadership competencies

Such frameworks break down into greater detail in a familiar pattern. Each of Centrica's items is expanded into 'key attributes' and is accompanied by definitions at five performance levels.

The public sector has gone down the bespoke road too; prominent users include the National Health Service.

---

76   Centrica (2005) www.centrica.com/files/reports/2005cr/files/leadership_competencies.pdf [accessed 11 March 2009].

■ National Health Service

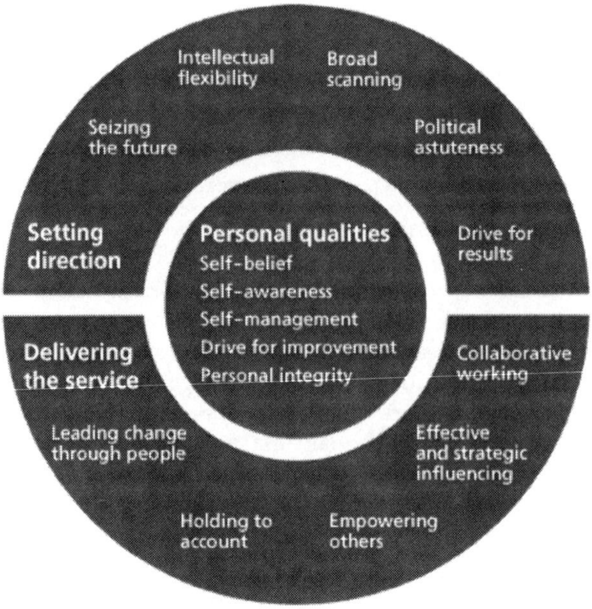

Figure 9: The NHS Leadership Qualities Framework

The NHS makes the following claims:

There are opportunities, it is said, to use 'The Framework' both on an individual basis and within the wider organisational context. It is grounded in research with 150 NHS Chief Executives and Directors of all disciplines. The framework 'sets the standard for outstanding leadership in the NHS, to which any leader should aspire'. It describes the qualities expected of NHS leaders, now and in the future. The framework has been tested within the NHS and validated in the context of *The NHS Plan* and its *Shifting the Balance of Power* programme (see page 154).

The framework is said to have a number of applications:

- personal development
- board development
- leadership profiling for recruitment and selection
- career mapping
- succession planning
- connecting leadership capability
- performance management

There are fifteen qualities, arranged in three clusters: **Personal Qualities, Setting Direction** and **Delivering the Service**. These are defined at levels that identify both effective and outstanding leaders (note the individual focus).

The framework describes a set of key characteristics, attitudes and behaviours that leaders in the NHS should aspire to in delivering *The NHS Plan*. It is said to provide a foundation for:

- Setting the standard for leadership in the NHS
- Assessing and developing high performance in leadership
- Individual and organisational assessment
- Integrating leadership across the service and related agencies
- Adapting leadership to suit changing contexts
- Benchmarking – by enabling the development of a database about leadership capacity and capability.

Analysis and comment

Lists such as those developed by Centrica and the NHS have a habit of mixing quite different ingredients (as does the MSC), such as managerial competence and behavioural competency. For the most part they fail to explain the *function* of leadership; instead they concentrate on qualities such as characteristics, attitudes and behaviours – *what* leaders do, rather than saying *why* leadership is needed (especially instead of management).

In the view of Richard Bolden and Jonathan Gosling (2006), such frameworks favour measurable features and outcomes and may therefore omit more subtle qualities, interactions and situational factors. And they may confuse behaviours that are causes with those that are responses.

Additionally, statements such as 'Delivers great performance' or 'Intellectual flexibility' say nothing about leading that doesn't equally apply to managing.

A key question is whether what the company wants day in and day out is what matters most and requires most attention and resource. It could be argued that a more important task – one with greater transformational potential for the organisation – is embedding and delivering competence from the perspective of what the company needs at a given time in order meet a specific agenda. For example, if the company is undergoing change, if it knows that it faces difficult issues ahead or a new set of opportunities, if it needs to modernise and shed out-of-date competencies, or if the organisation needs a change of style. Such radical change might be needed, say, for a government department gaining agency status and becoming self-financing.

However, note that the NHS Framework claims that its qualities are relevant for the future as well as now. How can that be? The NHS, we are frequently told, is undergoing massive change. Most NHS hospitals are currently seeking 'foundation' status, which will give them freedom and independence from the government's Department of Health. Yet, by having a fixed framework of leadership qualities, the implication is that it still needs to be led in the same way. This does not tally with the NHS's own account of the amount of change happening there.

Not least, the NHS is undertaking a radical *Shifting the Balance of Power* programme, which it describes as a 'culture change'. In that context of major change, at the start of this book we raised severe doubts about whether managers – however competent, and however relevant their competencies – could bring about culture change, with or without a critical mass (that is not how change happens, as explained elsewhere).

Nonetheless, in spite of all those reservations, with generic lists like those above, you can see why many large organisations are attracted to leadership competencies. Why would you not want your managers to have such competencies? Sadly, life isn't as easy as that. It is all too easy to come up with a list of what a company thinks it 'wants' from individual managers. However, what the organisation gets and how useful these frameworks are in practice is quite another matter.

Prime unit: manager, organisation or relationships

As the above examples show, competency methodology makes the unquestioned assumption that the prime unit of an organisation's efficiency, effectiveness, productivity and performance, and therefore the proper focus for development and assessed capability, is the individual. But that assumption is flawed. While individual competence is undoubtedly important, the methodology for specifying, assessing and developing it disregards the powerful contribution made by the organisation. Yet it is the organisation that affects the application of competence and its effect on performance – for both good and ill. The methodology also disregards team and system competence. And it may close doors to valuable consideration of how to extend leadership more widely through the hierarchy and in the spaces between managers.

> 'Within the UK we increasingly hear talk of 'distributed, collective and emergent leadership, yet the individualistic nature of most competency frameworks and the performance mechanisms they put into place severely limits the possibility of this occurring in practice or even being discussed ... Competency frameworks tend to reinforce individualistic practices that dissociate leaders from the relational environment in which they operate and could, arguably, inhibit the emergence of more inclusive and collective forms of leadership.' (Bolden and Gosling, 2006)

Given this book's spotlighting of gaps down which individuals' leadership competence easily gets wasted and the spaces where it is needed but underused, *relational competence* may provide a focus and an antidote. Relational competence does not refer to individual managers being personally competent at their relationships – with their team, with peers, customers, suppliers, senior executives, etc. – though this matters, of course. Nor does it refer to good teamwork and frequent team-building activities. An organisation's relational competence means that it takes the quality of all its relationships seriously; it identifies the relational pressure points and it manages them. For example, it looks out for and does not allow silos to build and thwart the collective business. It checks the prioritisation, nature and level of engagement with each of its stakeholder groups to which it owes responsibility. It keeps an eye on the relational operation of the hierarchy.

> 'Fred [Goodwin] was revered within the bank as some kind of founding father, and we all wasted a lot of time and energy discussing how to manage him and trying to second-guess how he would react to things.' [77] (Former RBS employee)

In metaphorical terms, the climate of apprehension that surrounds 'force of nature' bosses is the toxic content in the 'fishtank' through which those whose job it is to serve the boss have to navigate safely every day. The example also reminds us of another of the book's themes: that leadership shapes the system, but the system also shapes leadership. The behaviour of top executives (not just in the banking sector) results from a system that over-rewards short-term success, coupled with political relaxation in the regulatory framework by Thatcher, Reagan and Clinton.

That said, if you are strongly attracted to individual competencies for managers, it is wise to see them at best as a necessary but not sufficient condition for realising improved leadership in a given organisation.[78] This holds true even when those competencies are solely intended to assist individual managers develop their personal professionalism.

But where the company's aim is more ambitious and competencies are intended to benefit the organisation more broadly, directly and fundamentally, and to change the power structure in the organisation, then the point is even more valid: individual manager competencies are nowhere near sufficient, and may prove misleading and foreclose on other options and other ways of thinking about extending leadership.

Bolden and Gosling are critical of the promise offered by leadership competency frameworks: that of solving organisational problems (e.g. the NHS's culture change). They claim that simply restating these organisational problems as [individual] 'management responsibilities' constitutes a sleight of hand. It does feel like 'over to you' with an impossible brief.

To achieve wider organisational benefit requires that competencies are complemented with something that speaks directly to what is happening in the organisation to facilitate change.

---

77   Connon, H. (2009) 'New boss earns credit as he sets out on his mission to save RBS'. London: *The Observer*, 25 January.

78   For more on the leadership competencies argument, see Alimo-Metcalfe and Alban-Metcalfe (2008), pp 14-17.

APPLYING LEADERSHIP COMPETENCE

Please lead, but we don't know what!

Leadership is arguably an organisation's most valuable resource. It drives management and is the means by which the organisation achieves its ends. Yet many organisations are content to let individual managers identify what their personal leadership is needed for. While organisations help managers with the means (specifying competencies and making inputs to their personal leadership development), they leave the ends (organisational outcomes) mainly to the managers themselves to determine.

This may be the worst of all worlds. On the one hand, the organisation might be taking too much interest in its managers' leadership competencies. On the other hand, it may be taking too little interest in what managers should use their leadership competence for.

This begins to take us beyond individual frameworks in the direction of corporate competence. If an organisation is content to limit performance to an individual manager's job, such a lack of direction and degree of trust and delegation to individuals may work. But if the organisation itself needs to change what it does and how it does it (and which organisations don't?) then the looseness presents a risk. The authors of *A Manager's Guide to Leadership* (Pedler *et al*, 2004) reflect this doubt:

> 'Leadership development based on models of individual characteristics or competencies is often helpful for personal development, but does it lead to useful action in the organisation?'

Giving primacy to the organisation

In terms of affecting *organisational* performance, individual competencies struggle to deliver this outcome. One of the central messages articulated in this book is:

> '... When attempting to improve leadership in the organisation, don't focus primarily on individual managers; certainly don't begin your journey there. Instead, put your energy into the spaces and the gaps. Notice the effect of the haze that envelops everyone and everything'.

The conventional view of competencies implies that all will be well with the organisation if only individuals are competent. This overlooks what binds individuals together to produce their collective success and to achieve success for the system. Value is added at the points of connection, in the gaps, and in the milieu that envelops managers. We also made the point that if the company wants to handle leadership more strategically, it has to start with the organisation's needs and not with those of individual managers.

The point was made in Chapter 2 that one cannot isolate any one system variable (such as leadership) as though it can exist independently from its surroundings. The individual and the individual's environment are indivisible. Competencies make no concession to such systemic principles. The relative power of the organisation compared with that of the individual manager – the foundation that underpins this book's rationale – is unrecognised by competency methodology. For these reasons, competencies fail to address directly and explicitly what needs to change for the organisation as a whole.

To avoid these pitfalls, competence must be considered as a property or characteristic of the organisation: i.e. organisational or corporate competence. Such a corporate model raises some strategic questions, among them:

1. How does the organisation integrate individuals' competence so that it manifests 'corporate competence' (think of an orchestra rather than a solo player)?
2. How can the organisation and its managers do the right things, and not just do things right (i.e. competencies)?
3. How should the organisation first be clear about its own leadership needs and use that information to drive individual managers' leadership competencies?

Ceci n'est pas une pipe
(with acknowledgement to Magritte's famous painting of a pipe annotated with 'This is not a pipe'.)

Competencies may emphasise having the *capability* to lead, and having that potential developed, assessed and rewarded. However, like Magritte's famous painting of a pipe, this must always fall short of the real-live *practice* of leading (Bolden and Gosling, 2006). Assessment of competencies in everyday use is supposed to get round this. But this requires supervisors to be competent at assessment and to be able to find the time, which may prove burdensome. Even such live assessment of demonstrated competencies places HR tick-box means ahead of interest in organisational usage, outcomes and ends.

○ **Example: The case of 'Baby P'** The issue of managing competence may shed some light on the case of the tragic death of 'Baby P' in the London Borough of Haringey. My focus, and the inspector's, is on corporate and collective competence and delivered system performance, because that is what the public ultimately requires from child protection services. A particular social worker's (or even departmental director's competence – whether assessed as a capability or as actually performed) is a subset of that, although it is what most people, including the media and government ministers, choose to concentrate on in cases like this.

The case provides a graphic reminder of how measures of competence (both individual and collective) in a Council's Department of Children and Young

Persons Services serve as a simple and simplistic proxy for the complexity of real performance. There are several reasons why these measures can never constitute *actual* performance:

- The measures comprise a limited range of metrics deemed by certain planners to be sufficiently indicative of overall performance.
- The metrics are chosen because they are measurable (e.g. completion of records), while important but immeasurable ones are omitted (e.g. quality of relationships).

> *'The key truths about our child protection system are not told through number flows and bar charts but through narrative.'* [79] (Patrick Butler)

- The measures represent just one party's contribution (i.e. the Council's) in a complex web of interactions within a wider system that includes police, schools and hospitals.
- The measures require an inspection, which is a subjective process that calls for interpretation.
- The managers who are the target of the inspection selectively provide the data to an Ofsted inspector.

> *'Successive governments have persistently signed up to the philosophy that every service provided can be evaluated in the same way as the sale of groceries … wasteful and delusional inspection process … all stick and no carrot.'* [80] (Ross Sutton)

Ofsted's routine inspection of Haringey's Children and Young Persons Services beginning in November 2006 and published in November 2007 (shortly after Baby P's death in August) had ticked all the right boxes and awarded the department '3 Star' status of 'Good'. Yet a year later when Ofsted, the Healthcare Commission and Police conducted an enquiry into the department it found gross systemic failure, at which point Ed Balls, the government's Secretary of State for Children, Schools and Families, removed Haringey's director from her post.

How could Ofsted effectively overturn its judgement? An inquiry into the inquiry showed that Ofsted had originally allowed itself to be hoodwinked. The assessment method was open to manipulation. 'Officials in the Council were able to "hide behind" false data to earn themselves a good rating'.[81] The motives are clear: successfully jumping through the government's hoops brings resources, money and political advantage.

---

79   Butler, P. (2008) 'Star ratings don't tell us the real story.' *The Guardian*, 10 December.

80   Sutton, R. (2008) 'The inspectors call – but fail to arrest the problem' (letter). *The Guardian*, 8 December.

81   Curtis, P. (2008) 'We failed over Haringey – Ofsted head'. London: *The Guardian*, 6 December.

There is an even more fundamental flaw in the quality system. It lies in its concept. Its roots can be traced back to the earlier discussion on extrinsic versus intrinsic models of motivation. The problem lies with the inspectors' question. That question forms a crucial part of managers' environment. Inspectors are interested in the question: 'Is the service up to standard?'. A high rating lets everyone relax, and a low one damns them. This is the wrong question to be asking. They should be asking: 'What are you doing to improve?'. A culture of learning and continual improvement would then replace a culture of cheating. Volition in an improvement mindset is very different from that engendered by a compliance one.

Generalising from the Baby P case, assessed competence of a manager against a competency framework is likewise a mere proxy for performance. It falls well short of real performance – for the individual, not to say for the organisation as a fully functioning system.

> 'In the presence of an incompatible organisational system or culture a leader may remain powerless to achieve what is expected of him/her. Likewise, failure to consider the broader social context of leadership is to miss the significant role played by other factors (including followers, managerial rewards and sanctions, beliefs about legitimate authority, organisational systems, nature of the work and cultural environment) in the leadership process.' (Bolden and Gosling *ibid*, citing the work of Salaman, 2004)

UNLEARNING AND SHEDDING UNWANTED COMPETENCIES

Not all competencies are of equal status. A way of categorising them is shown below:

1. *Emergent competencies*
   Competencies that are of increasing importance to the organisation.
2. *Legacy competencies*
   Dated competencies that have outlived their usefulness.
3. *Enduring competencies*
   Competencies that the organisation will always need and value.
4. *Transitional competencies*
   Competencies that are relevant for the short term, such as privatisation or demerging.

> 'At the beginning of the 1980s a political decision was taken to withdraw British Airways from the state sector. Until then it had been a 'nationalised industry' along with utilities such as coal and gas. The corporation had been run as a bureaucracy, dependent on the government for annual funding. The skills needed to do this were no longer relevant and were counter-productive in the new, entrepreneurial culture.
> *cont. overleaf*

> They had to be abandoned, so the decision was taken to replace the whole board at one stroke. In future BA would need to be led by people who had a successful background in private sector finance, and who would understand the importance of customer service. BA needed privatisation skills within a political climate of deregulation. It needed leadership skilled at major turnarounds and culture change. Organisation psychology would be a key requisite, as would the courage to tread on toes and challenge past norms.
>
> Aspects of the new leadership model were new but would become enduring. Others would last just a few years and were best seen as projects. Leaders could be selected for their competence as measured against the new requirements. This affected the roles of chairman, chief executive, human resource director, finance director, head of customer service, head of management development, and so on.' (Tate, 2003a)

Thinking about competencies in this four-way categorisation calls for considerable in-house research effort. A good starting point is the question asked earlier about management development: What does this organisation need more of and less of at this time?

Eliminating legacy competencies

Before new competencies have a chance to establish themselves, some present ones may need clearing away. Out-of-date 'legacy' competencies need identifying in order to manage their decline. One of the challenges in changing the organisation includes how to enable new competencies to gain a foothold in the desired culture and supplant out-of-date and unwanted ones. This applies to individual and corporate competencies alike. An example is described below.

> 'One business was a start-up operation in optical fibre micro-switches. The other was a long-established optronics company with a legacy of strongly hierarchical, bureaucratic management. Both companies wanted to embrace the latest ideas on how to be innovative. But what innovation meant for one was wholly different from the other.
>
> At this time in its growth the first business depended on a high degree of individual inventiveness. It also needed to concentrate on raising finance and to find new markets. The second business was lumbered with a host of legacy issues and needed to manage change. In terms of moving from state A to state B, the first company could concentrate mostly on achieving state B. The second company, with its strongly dysfunctional culture, had first to unfreeze state A.
>
> The kind of competencies needed, how they are prioritised, how they are applied in practice, and who is spotlighted is different in each of these businesses. For example, if innovation for a given business depends upon breaking out of or crossing the boundaries of domains or functional disciplines (as with the second of these companies), then networking competence comes to the fore. Coping with anxiety would be an appropriate competence in both the cases cited, but the nature of the anxiety, feeling of loss and personal threat would be very different in both.
>
> Unless we know what the company's agenda proposes to target, we cannot judge what individual competencies will assume greater significance in the future. Nor

can we assess which competencies are in decline, which change-management competencies will be helpful during the transition process, and which will endure and remain valid as core competencies.' (Tate, 1997)

Transitioning from a long-standing bureaucratic model, especially where the workforce is heavily unionised, is fertile territory for the consideration of appropriate leadership competencies. In large corporations it was not, and in some cases still is not, uncommon for managers to 'manage by manual'. This suits trade unions, because they negotiate the rules and can better predict managers' day-to-day decisions affecting their members. They can then defend these to those members; this makes life easier for them. And for many managers too; they don't need to think or work as hard because they don't need to manage variation. But for the business, and for managers who want to be more than administrators, the practice is the antithesis of leadership.

The fact that legacy competencies are possessed by the top executives compounds the problem (leaders are effectively talking about themselves). Notwithstanding this anomaly, the present leaders and their present competencies will be required to change. This highlights a well-known paradox: 'You have to work with the present culture if you are to change it'. It explains why major change is so difficult. Inherent vested interest brings in-built resistance to change. (That explains why, in the British Airways transformation, the airline's board was dismissed in July 1983 when the airline's values and aims changed. Board members would be neither able nor credible to pursue these changes themselves.)

A commonplace self-protecting response to this dilemma is for an organisation's top leaders to claim that competencies apply to all levels below them, but not to themselves (after all, they argue, they wouldn't be in their positions if their own competence was in doubt!).

Using performance reviews

Performance reviews are a key time in making the connection with reality that is so often lacking. When goal-setting, there can be an opportunity to strengthen the link between expected results and applied/developed leadership competence. There is invariably scope for sharpening accountability for demonstrating leadership in practice (other than for amassing assessed units of competency). Feedback on applied leadership can be more tightly focused. If this is not done, there is a risk that the organisation will invest heavily in defining and developing individual leadership competencies but will not get its own specific and timely needs met for usefully applied leadership.

The desired outcomes can remain hit-or-miss unless the organisation clarifies what it wants leadership exercised on and then makes it possible. These additional elements call for suitable organisation 'structures', including:

- Space, permission and safety for managers to step to one side of their operational role and ask awkward and challenging questions about what the organisation is doing (why, whether and how).
- Freedom from constraints, such as who people are allowed to talk to.
- A good plot. In other words, providing managers with a compelling narrative of the journey that the organisation needs to go on and which all managers are part of. This helps to describe the business and organisational context that justifies and requires the application of leadership.

Competencies concentrate on what people <u>can</u> do. If they are to be applied, then it is equally important that managers <u>want</u> to do, and that they are <u>enabled</u> to do. (See 'Can do. But want to do? Enabled to do?' in Chapter 8, *Leadership and Learning.*)

ADAPTING COMPETENCIES
AND LOOKING AHEAD

Leadership style

When a new leader needs to be replaced, even if he or she has possessed unquestioned competencies, the prescription for the sought competencies of the new candidate are likely to owe more to the need to switch, complement or overturn the old rather than to build on the previous incumbent's competencies. There is a good reason for this, as the change in the BBC's choice of director general in 2004 illustrates.

In 2004 the comings and goings at the top of the BBC in the wake of the Hutton Enquiry reminded us that leadership style needs to be attuned to where an organisation currently lies in an oscillating cycle of change. An organisation needs the right kind of leader at the right time.

After the era of John Birt, Greg Dyke was arguably a good choice as a very different kind of leader. Yet, by the same token, the right replacement for Dyke might need to be more like Birt than Dyke. The theory that underpins this seemingly odd conclusion is that there is no happy medium. An organisation must either be moving towards greater freedom, creativity and decentralisation, or towards greater control and budgetary discipline. The strength of each state is countered by the weakness reflected in the absence of the alternative state.

When the downside of one extreme becomes unbearable, it is time to seek the benefits of the alternative. This may entail suppressing the knowledge that, in due course, the weaknesses in that new state will become apparent and there will be a call for its opposite.

So why not seek the middle ground and split the difference? Answer – an organisation that seeks neither state will lack excellence and dynamism. Hence the

---

> centralising/controlling/managerial Birt needed to be followed by the decentralising/loose/creative Dyke. Of course, neither leader will see it this way. Unable to see their alter ego, they would like to be replaced in their own image.

If the Birt/Dyke argument is accepted (see Chapter 3 for a discussion of the tendency for organisations to oscillate between centralising and decentralising agendas), then it casts doubt on the ability of competencies to capture best practice other than in broad generalisations. These will omit key questions of focus, timing, capitalising on unique personal strengths, wishing to make a mark, and needing to make changes to how the organisation works.

MANAGING THE COMPANY'S REPUTATION FOR COMPETENT LEADERSHIP

What does the organisation as a whole want to excel in as a leader (sector, industry, brand, etc.)? Companies may be known as leaders (sector leaders, market leaders, brand leaders, etc.). Such leadership reflects their prominence, reputation, what they stand for, and how they represent their sector. Any organisation has to ask itself how it wants to be recognised for giving leadership. Examples include:

- high-quality products
- value for money
- safety of the public and employees
- good care of the environment
- honest governance
- inclusive relationships
- product innovation
- customer service

Hewlett-Packard was long respected for its leadership in printer technology. Canon led the way in the design and manufacture of the internal printer engines.

Industry sector leadership often combines with other human or social values that extend beyond the boundaries of the firm. The drinks firm Diageo claims:

> 'We are not content just to comply with high standards of behaviour; we want to provide leadership and involve our corporate partners in good citizenship activities. … Diageo has been a prime mover in the drinks industry in establishing social aspects organisations (SAOs) … promoting sensible drinking and helping to prevent alcohol misuse.' (Tate, 2003a)

Some companies' reputations, values, preoccupations and commitments become synonymous with particularly dominant individuals. For a long time Dixons [now DSG International plc.] was indelibly associated with Sir Stanley Kalms. Some companies approach their leadership with a dominant stakeholder in mind; e.g. Rentokil/Initial and for a long time Sir Clive Thompson ('increases in profits every year'). Others parade their leadership with a wider group of stakeholders, with customers or society (e.g. BP and 'beyond petroleum'). Marks & Spencer promotes its superior green credentials. Tesco claims price leadership. Ryanair cost leadership. Johnson & Johnson superior ethics.

Besides their market image, these stances have an internal relevance. They can form a key input to the process of defining the leadership expected of individuals in the culture. And they can shape the purpose and content of leadership development programmes.

The positions adopted by companies that wish to be recognised in such a way are a reflection of their leaders' and organisations' values. An explicit set of values and principles grounds desired executive behaviour and places boundaries around it. Values serve as a continual source of reference against which leaders may test their decisions and determine appropriate action when faced with tough choices. The values, more than the managers, 'tell' employees what is right and wrong, as the well-publicised Tylenol contamination scare reminds us.

'When Johnson & Johnson was faced with its Tylenol contamination scare [in 1982] local store staff knew to withdraw the product from shelves without waiting to be told. Though costing millions of dollars, the company's credo (as leaders in ethical practice) left them in no doubt that this would be the right thing to do. Making values explicit helps to meet the needs of organisations looking for ways of empowering employees and increasing their self-managing capability.' (Tate, 1999)

Doing right things and doing things right

There are times when the act of taking a decision and getting on with it is more important than agonising over what is the best decision. The difference between options may be small, but timing may be everything. In a similar vein, some people argue that what you do matters less than how well you do it. They focus on the means and neglect to question the ends. They see little difference between 'doing right things' (ends) and 'doing things right' (means).

It is sometimes claimed that a key difference between leadership and management is the difference between doing right things (leading) and doing things right (managing).

If the distinction between *right things* and *things right* is not made, inappropriate things get done. In *Roads to Success*, Robert Heller (2001) examines the decline of Lord Weinstock's GEC: 'His companies did many things right: but were they truly the right things?'

Both *doing right things* and *doing things right* need to be thought about carefully, especially where the ethical conduct of business is concerned. Prizing individual competence without thinking properly about where that competence will be applied, can lead to ethical disasters. Equally, concentrating on results without specifying the 'how' can be risky. Take the case of hacking into competitors' computers:

> Managers at Princeton University in the United States were discovered hacking into the students' database at rival Yale University. The unethical practice had enabled Princeton to offer discounts to students to switch courses. But the revelation was immensely damaging to its reputation, one of its prime assets.

The managers who were involved in Princeton's computer hacking scandal may have been highly skilled at what they were doing, but they were not doing appropriate things. Another way of looking at this is to say that the university's specification for the managers' required results failed to place limits on the means of their achievement.

Why so many organisations choose to put so most energy into means (especially defining lists of desirable competencies) is unclear, when it still leaves much to chance. It says *how* managers are expected to lead, but not *what* they should apply their leadership ability to. It appears to assume that once managers know *how* ('doing things right'), they'll make sound choices about *what* ('doing right things'). But organisations are full of people doing wrong things, however competently.

> *'Both roles are crucial, but they differ profoundly. I often observe people in top positions doing the wrong thing well.'* (Warren Bennis, 1989)

The same is true for departments and whole organisations. Sometimes competence that served them well in the past is no longer needed. Sometimes it's simply poor judgement. Here is an example where the question 'Are we doing the right thing?' appeared to be overlooked:

> Norwich City Council discovers that a hairdresser is offering a glass of mulled wine to customers at Christmas time. It writes to all hairdressers telling then that its officers will visit hairdressers incognito to put a stop to this practice where hairdressers do not have a licence to serve alcohol, pointing out that hairdressers could be fined £20,000 or be sent to jail for six months.[82]

The council exists to serve the needs of the public who pay its staff for the services they 'enjoy'. While the law may be being breached, the question arises: is deploying enforcement inspectors in this threatening way a service that the public is keen to pay its council tax for? Has the council got its ethos, values and priorities right? Many would say No, and would question the council's judgement.

---

82 Copping, J. (2008) 'Hairdressers face jail for offering customers mulled wine.' *Telegraph Online*, 29 November www.telegraph.co.uk [accessed 30 November 2008].

Balancing results and competencies

When British Airways launched its performance-related reward scheme for managers, it weighted results and competencies (which it called 'management practices') equally. It later changed this to favour results (60%) at the expense of competencies (40%), believing and signalling that what ultimately matters is results. Such a change carries dangers. Companies need to be aware of the risks they take in over-emphasising results and the messages conveyed to employees and other stakeholders by this tactical switch. BA subsequently suffered unethical and costly experiences similar to those of Princeton.

However, a focus on competencies is not enough. Talent and intelligence do not necessarily equate with high principles, or indeed commonsense or sound judgement. Nor, as this chapter argues, do they guarantee that the values of the organisation and its employees will be aligned.

Moreover, the leadership culture may be corrupt. Even ethical and well-intentioned individuals can lose sight of their values and principles and find themselves swayed and caught up in unethical decisions in fulfilment of their organisation's financial success – even without the lure of high personal reward.

The scandal of Enron is a case in point; here some potentially good leaders turned bad, influenced by a dangerous culture. Failing to understand the 'fundamental attribution error' (see page 31), the American consultancy McKinsey designed Enron's leadership culture, and has been much criticised for it:

> 'The failing of McKinsey and its acolytes at Enron is their assumption that an organisation's intelligence is simply a function of its employees. They believe in stars, because they don't believe in systems. …But companies … don't just create; they execute and compete and co-ordinate the efforts of many different people, and the organisations that are most successful at that task are the ones where the system is the star. …The talent myth assumes that people make organisations smart. More often than not it's the other way around.' (Gladwell, 2002)

Jack Welch, ex-boss of GE, used to claim that the most dangerous combination in his organisation was competence and unalignment (i.e. with his goals for GE). If people were unaligned, better they were incompetent.

Alignment comes through values and clarity about desired results and outcomes. Equally, specifying results alone is not enough; they need coupling with acceptable managerial and leadership practices and behaviour. Both are needed. The organisation's values (assuming that they are ethical and can be communicated publicly) should drive both the sought-after results and the competencies. This is true for the leaders themselves, for the organisational entities they lead, and for the people they are responsible for. It also brings competency approaches out of universal and archetypal realms and back into the context of their organisation, where they can contribute to a collective and systemic end.

SUMMARY OF CHAPTER KEY POINTS

1. Leadership competencies may make a contribution to a manager's personal professionalism. The sum of all such managers' personal professionalism does not, however, equate to leadership competence for the organisation as a whole. Further elements that only the organisation can bring are needed.

2. While managers should, of course, be personally competent as leaders, the use of leadership competency frameworks for individual managers does not take account of the aim or principles of systemic leadership. The relative power of the organisation (its dynamics, culture, policies, etc.) to affect and effect leadership compared with that of the individual manager is unrecognised by competency methodology.

3. Substantial scope for improving the organisation's overall leadership competence and performance is generally found in the gaps between managers, and in what the organisation surrounds managers with (e.g. hierarchy, power structure, protocols, climate, policies, objectives) more than in the gaps within individual managers' competence.

4. Competencies concentrate on what managers can do. If they are to be applied, then it is equally important that managers want to do, and that they are enabled to do. The organisation can help to shape both of these contributing factors.

5. Why organisations choose to put most energy into means (especially defining lists of desirable competencies) is unclear, as it leaves much to chance. Frameworks says how managers are expected to lead, but not what they should apply their leadership ability to.

6. Competency frameworks assume that once managers know how ('doing things right'), they'll make sound choices about what ('doing right things'). But organisations are full of people doing the wrong things competently.

7. Competency frameworks offer a company's senior leaders an imagined hope of stability, that what works today will work tomorrow, that what works for one will work for another, that what works for the individual will work for the organisation, and that managers and the organisation can master universal truths. This makes people and organisations easier to manage. If only! They hope to avoid the messy reality of wide variation in the patterns of human strengths among successful leaders, and the inconvenience of changing needs.

Where a company already makes use of leadership competencies:

8. Competencies for managers should recognise the difference between the act of managing/management and the act of leading/leadership. This difference should then be reflected in the performance management system.

9. Competencies can be categorised in four ways; for example, legacy competencies can be identified and managed out of the system.

CHAPTER 10:

LEADERSHIP AND CULTURE

- ☐ *Understanding the leadership culture*
- ☐ *Measuring the culture and climate*
- ☐ *Challenging the leadership norms*
- ☐ *Critical followership*

A company's reception desk or call centre provides visitors and customers with a litmus test for that company's culture. You quickly notice clues to: what lies beyond the public image, what the company's values are, where it places its priorities, and what it thinks of its employees, to say nothing of its customers.

Managers and consultants develop an ability to gain insights into an organisation through the illuminating lens of corporate culture – especially in cases of high-profile failures. One cannot read a story of how, say, a nursing home has failed in its duty of care to an elderly resident, without automatically thinking 'What does this tell us about the culture of this place?' and 'What does it tell us about the organisation's leadership?'. Understanding, acknowledging, changing and stewarding the culture is a leadership responsibility.

> *'The queen bee does not make decisions; she just emits a chemical substance that holds the whole social system together. In human hives that is called culture.'* (Henry Mintzberg, 1999)

The behaviour that Mintzberg ascribes to the queen bee probably most closely approximates to what Bennis (1989) labels being a *conceptualist* – being a leader with entrepreneurial vision and the time to spend thinking about the forces that will affect the destiny of the institution.

Intimately bound up with the corporate culture and leadership are two closely related issues:

- First, can the overall culture be described as a 'culture of leadership', where leadership is one of the company's core values, permeating its everyday behaviour at all levels of the organisation?
- Secondly, what is the specific *leadership* culture – the way leadership among the senior executive cadre is round here?

The practical question I would ask you to reflect on is this:

Is your organisation's culture (corporate and leadership) functional or is it dysfunctional? That is, is the culture currently serving the needs of your business and wider stakeholders that your organisation is designed to serve, and is it fit for the future? If not, what is leadership's role in changing it?

If the answer is that the culture is dysfunctional, then there is a need to consider leadership's role in changing it. If the leadership (sub)culture at the top of the organisation itself is dysfunctional, how can leaders change the general culture and install and instil a culture of leadership? How realistic is it to expect the formal leaders (in any company) to change themselves and their own leadership culture? The latter presents leaders with the tougher challenge because it is 'in here', whereas they can argue that the general culture is 'out there'.

> 'Credit Suisse [UK] have been fined £5.6m [by the Financial Services Authority] after a scandal in which rogue traders deliberately mis-priced securities. "The fine was dwarfed by the £1.5bn loss on the trades to shareholders, but the reason for the fine was that the management systems, or if you like the culture within the firm – which the FSA is very keen on, the probity of the culture – meant that when doubts were raised by the back office that the traders were up to something, they were effectively ignored because of deference to the money makers." ' [83]

The banking crisis and disclosures about the way the finance sector works reveals severe 'breakage' in the culture at all levels: the sector, company and the specific leadership culture. In the case above, the subsequent enquiry found that the bank's supervision of traders' work in the Structured Credit Division was so lax that it took five months for it to spot that the positions were wrongly priced. This is somewhat reminiscent of the collapse of Barings Bank in 1995, where London head office supervisors did not understand the technical work of their traders, and took the view that so long as traders in the Singapore office were making money for the bank, there was nothing to understand and monitor.

To ascertain and begin to question the existing leadership culture, you first need to make it explicit. Here are just a few of the key questions that help to define an organisation's leadership culture:

UNDERSTANDING THE LEADERSHIP CULTURE

☐ What are the criteria for becoming a member of the leadership cadre?
☐ How visible are the symbols of hierarchical power and authority?
☐ How widely is leadership distributed throughout the organisation?
☐ What are the flows of power and influence?
☐ How much tension and inhibition surrounds leaders?
☐ Are top managers typically home grown or externally hired?
☐ Is there a tradition of long or short tenure in top jobs?

Table 22: Understanding the leadership culture (Tate, 2003a)

---

83   Bell, A (2008) 'Today: Corporate News', BBC Radio 4, 14 August.

Stereotypes and variations in culture

There are, of course, variations in corporate culture between hospitals, between universities, between regiments, prisons, schools, and so on, but there is a broad sector culture and leadership culture that can be discerned and predicted for hospitals, universities, army regiments, prisons, and schools, for example, and between public, private and voluntary sectors.

The same point can be made about and within the private sector. Retail clothing, high-street banks or newspapers, for example, have different cultures. But to improve the culture means working with a particular organisation and its managers. Those organisations will enjoy a particular reputation in the mind of the general public, customers and with media, as well as internally with the employees.

Variation in culture is compounded by a further factor. Any large and complex organisation will contain professional sub-cultures, for marketing, engineering, finance, etc. On top of this, everyone's expectations, hopes and needs, experiences, perceptions, frustration threshold, and comfort level is unique. They will tell different stories about their organisation's culture as they perceive it, and of which they are a part. They will have different views about its specific *leadership* culture, of which they may also be a part (though quite possibly will not see it that way). If they have been around for a long time they may take the culture for granted and have difficulty in seeing it at all, let alone objectively or critically. They may think of leadership culture simply as something about those 'higher up'.

Leadership culture and climate

There is a dividing line between culture and climate. Culture is deep seated and long term. It is likely to be slowly evolving, representing a shift or developing trend. It is difficult to change an organisation's culture; it may be best to think of how to shift or nudge the culture in the desired direction.

Climate, by comparison, is more akin to the local weather conditions, what the temperature feels like at the moment. Climate is expressed in the quality of relationships and transactions. Climate is likely to reflect a particular leader's values, beliefs or style. When key players change, climate is more amenable to change than is culture. Climate is especially affected by any decision to change working arrangements. Take this example of how changes in a social services team's workspace (introducing hot-desking) adversely affected their climate:

'Management consultants had been into her department and her working life had been turned upside down. She and her fellow team members supported each other very effectively and such support was very important to them when they returned to the office from a difficult day in court, from a challenging visit or when writing a demanding statement. Their office was open plan but their individual workstations were personalised with photographs on their desks and prints on the walls and so

cont. overleaf

> forth. Each knew where everyone was. No more. They had been "hot-desked".
> Someone had decided that they would work more efficiently if their workplaces were
> anonymised so that any member of the department could just sit at whichever desk
> were available. The spirit and coherence of the team had been undermined and its
> members felt devalued. ... no wonder many of the best walk away.' (Edward Lloyd-
> Jones, 2008)

One way of appreciating 'climate' is to see it as resembling the fishtank. It is everything that is in people's environment – what surrounds them – that shapes their mood, spirit, energy and ability to apply their talents.

However we label them, people experience things as they are, which is a combination of culture and climate. People may not be overly bothered which of these two factors accounts for what it is they feel. Whatever the explanation – culture or climate – people and the media will probably call it 'culture' anyway. But it may actually be the climate that makes the more powerful impact, and this is more open to influence by managers.

Getting a measure of the climate

UNDERSTANDING THE CLIMATE

☐ How much freedom is there? Are people tightly controlled?

☐ Do people feel that they are recognised and rewarded for their efforts?

☐ Is there a feeling of belonging, warmth, mutual support and cooperation?

☐ Are people prepared to take risks? What happens when they do?

Table 23: Understanding the climate

Managers experience the climate that surrounds them. They are also responsible for the climate that surrounds their own team. The two are likely to be related.

There is a well-known hierarchical effect: what people experience in their working climate shapes what they pass on. Specifically, if they experience the way they are supervised as being unsupportive, and especially if it is hostile, then two behavioural consequences may flow from this. The first is that front-line staff may work out their anger and frustration on customers; Benjamin Schneider's research in banks revealed this disturbing phenomenon in 1980. The second is that staff may bond or otherwise seek from their customers the warmth that they need in their work; the consultant child and adolescent psychotherapist Louise Emanuel reports the evident risks in the field of social work.

'In the absence of adequate management support, social workers may
unconsciously turn to their clients for feelings of worth. This can interfere with
their ability to act appropriately.' [84]

---

84   Emanuel, L. (2008) 'I have seen close up how social workers can be seized by paralysis'.
      London: The Guardian, 4 December.

Leadership and changing power differentials

Both culture and climate bear a relationship to leadership style. Ex-Prime Minister Tony Blair's presidential style (see page 121) was personal, but was said to echo a general trend in prime ministerial style and the nature of cabinet leadership. Witness the practice of Blair, and then his successor Brown, to take the limelight, making announcements on departmental issues at the expense of cabinet members. And beyond: the trend in the power of the Executive has seen a gradual increase at the expense of Parliament.

It would be a welcome and courageous move for US President Barack Obama to forswear using the president's constitutional power later upon leaving office to grant pardons to anyone (especially cronies) convicted during his presidency. Such constitutional power is a throwback to times when rulers held court unencumbered by a professional legal system. Obama might do the same for the notorious loophole under which the president can pass laws in the last two months of the presidency in a way that escapes scrutiny by Congress:

> 'George W. Bush is ending his presidency in characteristically aggressive fashion, with a swath of controversial measures designed to reward supporters and enrage opponents. By the time he vacates the White House, he will have issued a record number of so-called "midnight regulations" – so called because of the stealthy way they appear on the rule books – to undermine the administration of Barack Obama, many of which could take years to undo.' [85]

Obama's first act on taking up office was to try to halt the egregious last-minute acts of his predecessor. The irony is that the act of relinquishing conspicuous power is a sign of strength, whereas exploiting such power is a sign of weakness.

In the UK, the centralising shift in power is mirrored in local authorities, where the majority party's leadership has been switching to the cabinet model at the expense of the party's backbenchers. Directly elected mayors, in cases where this change has been implemented, also hold more power than old-style council leaders. Political power is gradually being concentrated in fewer hands. A similar concentration of power is happening in many businesses too, but it appears to happen in a somewhat individualistic fashion rather than a concerted or conspiratorial one designed to reshape leadership culture in general, where its effect is noticed more than pre-planned.

In writing about schools' target culture, a past Secretary of State for Education, Estelle Morris, observed that the school system is giving 'more and more power to headteachers'.[86] This shift echoes a recent government pattern of behaviour and apparent belief in strong individual leaders as a solution to societal problems.

---

85   Harris, P. (2008) 'Bush sneaks through host of laws to undermine Obama'. London: *The Observer*, 14 December.

86   Morris, E. (2008) 'Genuine engagement on this testing issue'. London: *Education Guardian*, 27 May.

'... "superheads" to be rewarded with
£200,000 for taking charge of failing schools.'
(Daily Mail headline, 18 April, following
announcement by Ed Balls, the Schools
Secretary.)

Witness new 'superheads' in schools and the accompanying widening pay differentials to emphasise the widening power differentials. While this may make attracting candidates to top jobs a little easier, it makes the leap from the deputy level less plausible.

'We published one report called *The Leadership Effect on the Role of Headteachers in Schools* that we thought getting a new headteacher into schools would radically change a school – and that is certainly the basis of government policy – so we commissioned some researchers to look at how changing the headteachers actually changed the performance of schools ... and actually found that changing the headteachers had very little effect.' [87]

Faith in superheads finds its place in the well-worn and persisting search for heroic leaders, using extrinsic motivators. As long ago as 1990, James Krantz observed:

'Trying to solve our institutional malaise and leadership vacuum by looking for leaders constitutes a flight from confronting the deeper issues of institutional transformation and equally a flight from creating a context in which leaders can lead. ... Efforts to shore up the heroic leader myth persist, despite the nearly overwhelming evidence that it is ill-suited to emerging post-industrial conditions.'

Of course there are some exceptional leaders who are successful, but there is no evidence that the policy of big top jobs with big top pay works, wherever it is applied. Remuneration consultants continue to insist that huge pay packages are needed to attract top talent, but the lesson from the banking crisis suggests that these powerful figures with their inflated egos have no better judgement than the rest of us. The idea of a powerful leader linked with command-and-control leadership is long out of date as a universal strategy.

Appointments such as that of a 'bureaucracy czar', a 'respect czar', or putting Sir Richard Branson in charge of clearing up the nation's litter problem, have a feel of desperation and naivety about them. They conjure up memories of how to get trains to run on time. They fly in the face of modern theories of more distributed leadership, empowered staff, more consensual styles, reflection, learning and humility.

The economic collapse may have a silver lining:

'An economist floats the prospect of a maximum wage, pointing out that JP Morgan, the founder of the company, believed that no firm should pay its

---

87   Browne, A. (outgoing director of Policy Exchange) (2008) 'Westminster Hour, Think Tanks', BBC Radio 4, 21 September.

highest earner more than 10 times the wage of the lowest – and that the Royal Navy runs on a ratio of eight. … Some ministers are very conscious that this could be a turning point. At the Fabian conference this weekend, the climate change secretary, Ed Miliband [UK Government's Secretary of State for Energy and Climate Change], told his audience that this was an opportunity to write the future. He called for bold ideas, a different kind of state where power was dispersed rather than concentrated …' [88]

Generally, in the context of this chapter, I am not making sharp distinctions between leadership culture, climate and style. I am more interested in exploring 'the way leadership is round here' (i.e. the aspects of organisational life that are deep seated, affect many people and are a function of more than one leader) and considering what, to me, is a key question not only for this chapter but for the whole book: 'Is the way leadership is round here functional or dysfunctional and what needs to be done about it?

Loose and tight culture

Some cultures are tight, uniform and controlling. Others are looser, more varied and trusting. In the case of the former, the imposition may come from head office or commonly from government. The concept of employees having discretion is central to their ability to exercise leadership.

> 'The focus on economy and efficiency has led to the 15-minute visit by a home carer to an older person … or the requirement for the community occupational therapist to visit 12 people … no time to talk or listen. Thank heavens there are still a lot of rule benders and breakers who remember what it was that brought them in to the work.' [89]

In one way or another, most people have experienced externally imposed arbitrary targets and time limits. They have endured those annoying scripts which employees are required to follow regardless of their appropriateness: after queuing at tills and with others waiting ('Is there anything else you would like to buy today?'), and call centres at the end of a failed attempt trying to get satisfaction ('Is there anything else I can help you with today?'). The examples below reveal issues and opportunities:

> 'A senior police officer has criticised some of the targets set by the Home Office, saying that they had a damaging effect on policing in England and Wales. The Chief Constable of Staffordshire, Chris Sims, welcomed the Government's ideas for cutting red tape and for simplifying the objectives set for police forces. Staffordshire is one of four constabularies participating in a pilot aimed at giving officers greater freedom to use their own discretion, instead of having to make arrests to meet Home Office targets. Chris Sims said that in recent years a policing-to-targets culture has been
> *cont. overleaf*

88   Russell, J. (2009) 'How can Labour still fear to act for a fairer, greener land?' London: *The Guardian*, 19 January.

89   Jones, R. (2009) 'In our constipated care culture, thank heavens for the rule benders'. *The Guardian*, 10 February.

> encouraged rather than one that tackled public concerns about crime. He described
> one target aimed at improving detection of crimes including thousands of relatively
> minor offences as particularly pernicious, but said that the Government's recent
> green paper indicated a willingness to address an imbalance between a need to
> monitor police officers' performance and the importance of allowing them to use
> their own common sense.' [90]

This case highlights the importance of allowing discretion, but the controlling
instinct of leaders and of governments is to minimise this, as it means ceding
control and relinquishing power. The irony is that there can be no leadership
without discretion. Norman Dixon's initiative is illustrative:

> 'Norman Dixon, a policeman in Scotland, ... introduced a new hand-held device for
> front-line officers, and went about it with a systems approach – understand the work
> as a system, improve it without IT and then 'pull' the IT into the new (improved)
> design. Other police forces have struggled with introducing such technology because
> they adopted the traditional, government-inspired 'design, build and promulgate
> approach.' [91]

If an organisation wants its people to show more leadership, it needs to give them
freedom from over-regulated rules and procedures and allow them to interpret
situations and apply their common sense, initiative and humanity. In sharp
contrast to the lone policeman example, Boots offers a very different picture:

> '... a report about Boots' treatment of a 12-year-old schoolgirl ... detained for trying
> out a dab of nail polish from a bottle that wasn't a tester. The minute the polish
> touched Hannah Gilbert's nail she was stopped by a security guard, told she had
> committed a crime, and marched into an office. Three policemen were called to the
> scene. The policemen checked to see whether she had a criminal record. Boots then
> summoned Hannah's parents, who were told that unless they paid the full (£6.29)
> cost of the nail polish, Hannah would be charged with theft. After more than an hour
> of detention, the shocked child was released.
>
> 'What I wanted to know was how Boots would apologise for this ludicrous, heavy-
> handed overreaction by junior staff. Why had they called the police when a tap on
> the shoulder and a 30-second lecture on the difference between testers and pristine
> bottles would have been enough? Why indeed had a permanently overstretched
> police force decided that this was one of its priorities? How would a company that
> needs to keep the custom of teenage girls in these credit-crunchy times redeem itself?
>
> 'Boots's head office was quite clear. There was no apology. Their statement was
> prim and self-congratulatory: "Our staff were following set procedures." This isn't
> a defence, but a monstrous smoke screen. It's an increasingly common and chilling
> variation of the old defence of the indefensible, "I'm just doing my job". Too many
> organisations seem to imagine that sticking to procedures is in itself a virtue. That's
> not how it feels to those of us at the receiving end of this inflexible, wooden

---

90   Hoskin, A. (2008) 'Today', BBC Radio 4, 15 August.

91   Seddon, J. (2008) *Vanguard News*, 3 September. Buckingham: Vanguard Consulting.

approach. Too often it feels as if we're being corralled into a cage made by madmen, pleading for some kind of intelligence or humanity from the person in front of us or on the end of the phone.' [92]

Similarly, in 1992, Alistair Cooke, that percipient and eloquent observer of society, described in his *Letter from America* the Roman Catholic Church's leadership culture in these terms:

An example of an organisation's leadership culture:

The Vatican Model

□ Role of the organisation's head:

The Pope's role is to issue the terms of the strategy, leaving the doing of it to the cardinals and bishops.

□ Leadership cadre:

A small group of around a dozen advisers at the centre. They look out for breaches of orthodox doctrine.

□ Decisions:

The heart is doctrine. The source is back reference to previous encyclicals and other declarations.

□ Way of dealing with scandals:

Use money to hush things up. Rely on the doctrine of penitence and redemption.

□ Key constituency:

The focus for compassion is fellow clergy.

Table 24: Extracts from Alistair Cooke, *Letter from America*, BBC Radio 4, 29 April 2002

The broad principles of leadership culture cross sectors, as this example illustrates:

Some years ago the multi-national Swiss engineering conglomerate Sulzer was regarded by its foreign-national, local country heads as putting an obstacle in the way of their getting senior management jobs in the Winterhur head office. These positions were, it was said, the preserve of a middle-aged male class, who jealously guarded their comfortable and closely-knit national sovereignty. Long tenure in senior posts went unchallenged. Technical expertise was valued above managerial expertise and strategic thinking. Such attitudes are by no means unusual.

In the instance sited, the senior management tier was an obstacle to a shake up. A lack of diversity is bad for business because it inhibits challenge and ideas. I made a distinction earlier between business factors and organisational ones. For years, Sulzer Corporation searched for a successful business model, whereas perhaps it should have questioned its organisation model.

92 Russell, J. (2008) 'Just following procedure – that's the mantra of cost-cutting Britain'. London: *The Guardian*, 14 August.

Many years ago managers at a well-known British glass manufacturer had to sit down in the same place for lunch every day using a chair marked with their name, eating in one of nine hierarchically differentiated canteens. The company's values of consistency, predictability, gentle pace, and know-your-place, were conveyed through the culture's everyday norms and artefacts. In more ways than one, managers' habits were difficult to budge and the culture was deep seated.

A company's culture is influenced to a degree by its national culture. This can lead to clashes of style, methods and expectations when crossing national boundaries in international and multi-national boundaries. A clash of cultures is often given as a reason for the failure of mergers and takeovers – whether at the planning stage or after the event when operations don't turn out as planned. Prior to its takeover by French-owned Lafarge in 1997, Redland Plc. had extensive international manufacturing interests. Research revealed that differences in culture lay behind some failures to work in a unified manner.

'In 1992, following rumblings of discontent, Redland plc's top management were concerned about perceptions of the company's leaders. So they formally asked operational management what they thought of the company and its leadership. Managers responded that top leadership:
- was too financial and in the pocket of the City
- was not really involved in the 'guts' of the business
- provided no wider sense of vision beyond financial goals
- placed little value on people
- was very UK orientated

Among other things, this feedback led to important changes in the focus given to operational matters.

Important cultural differences became apparent between UK and continental European leadership. American-British leaders were considered to be 'unprincipled chancers', who valued speed, decisiveness, pragmatism and action. Continental Europeans were in turn called 'bureaucratic plodders', concerned with careful research, precision of planning, completeness of preparation and thoroughness of consultation.' (Tate, 2003b)

Issues of power

In any organisation there are always issues of power. Power can be one of the prime causes of toxicity in the fishtank. Power can be an obstacle to managers managing and leading. Negatively used, power can play a significant part in OD programmes, though rarely an explicit one.

'A visit to a recent employment tribunal hearing transported me back in time to an era when Her Majesty's Prisons were, it seemed, not run by the prison service, but were the fiefdom of the Prison Officers Association (POA); when it was the POA's writ that ran.

'The hearing was to decide the amount of damages to be awarded to Emma Howie, an officer at Wakefield Prison. ...

'Howie was a highly-rated officer. In 2003, she was nominated for the National Prison Officer of the Year award. But because she had blown the whistle at her previous jail, Howie was labelled a "grass" by many of her colleagues. Grass clippings and a wreath were sent to her by post. In 2004, when it became known that she was to give evidence in the Lingard hearing [another case], the level of hostility against her was such that for nine months she had to be escorted in and out of the prison.

'... just when Howie was set to return to work after maternity leave she expressed fears for her safety to the new governor at Wakefield, David Thompson. That governor, a self-professed "new broom", told her that her perception of the situation was "grossly exaggerated" and that she should "turn the other cheek".

'She complained ... that the Wakefield branch secretary of the POA had leaked confidential information to a fellow officer, with the intention of drumming up hostility against her as a whistleblower. The tribunal concluded that his only possible motive for this was to "undermine and harm her". The tribunal also found that this officer "deliberately lied" to managers investigating Howie's claims.

'Yet neither he, nor the officer who received the document, were disciplined – though managers had conclusive proof that both had lied. Instead, the union official had received a letter from the governor expressing the hope that the investigation had not caused him "undue stress or concern".

'The tribunal declared itself "astonished" at the way in which Howie's complaint had been handled. The governor admitted in evidence that, if he challenged the POA, it could "make life difficult" for him.' [93]

The power structure is a major factor at work in prison service culture, as it is in all military and quasi-military institutions. Power issues dominated the above case, which all-too-horribly revealed where real power lay, and where, sadly, it was absent in the formal hierarchy. The situation described vividly highlights what was required of formal power (i.e. power vested in positional authority), and Emma Howie's and the public's needs and expectations of authority.

The case showed how power was actually used, and how people gave away their power, sometimes out of fear of punishment – which may come from unexpected quarters (i.e. from above). Higher authorities may also be the source of pressure on managers to hold back on the exercise of their formal power.

Power (and its abnegation) does not arise simply from office, but resides in the situation, in hierarchical differences, in personality and character. Power holds a place both within the official and the unofficial 'shadow' organisation. (See Chapter 13: *Leadership and the Shadow*.) In a prison system there are at least two shadow systems: the case described above shows the shadow cast on the formal management of the prison by the Prison Officers Association (POA). The body of inmates can also be seen as constituting a parallel organisation with typical features such as a hierarchy; this system too has its own shadow system in the form of prisoners' gangs who ruthlessly exert their own power and control over fellow inmates.

Collusion will take place across any official/unofficial divide to find an accommodation on a safe level of power that seeks to avoid unpleasant confrontation and the risk of humiliation and failure. Powerful prisoners

---

93   Allison, E. (2008) 'The head of the prison service must go'. London: *The Guardian*, 9 April.

negotiate with prison officers to obtain favours in exchange for peace (see Tate 1995a for a case study of Whitemoor Prison, where officers agreed to turn off perimeter spotlights and close the doors of cells when powerful prisoners had visitors with them, following a request for extra privacy).

Whether and how power is used can be a function of factors such as culture, history, and a weighing of likely consequences and risks and estimated chance of succeeding.

While power corrupts, so does a complete absence of power. Power can be highly positive and is necessary to get things done. Power has a place when considering the organisation's leadership culture and may be explicit in an intervention's purpose, especially in so-called empowerment programmes.

■ Empowerment

Henry Mintzberg (1999) offers the view that real empowerment is the most natural state of affairs: people know what they have to do and simply get on with it. If an organisation exhibits real empowerment, it doesn't need to talk about it.

> '[Organisations] that make a lot of noise about [empowerment] generally lack it: they have been spending too much of their past disempowering everybody.' (Henry Mintzberg)

There may be something to learn from Frederick Hertzberg, one of the 20th century's best-known psychologists. His Two-Factor Theory says that factors that demotivate (if absent) are different from factors that satisfy or motivate (if present). Workers have what he calls 'hygiene' (or maintenance) needs as well as motivational needs. The workers cannot be motivated by good hygiene factors (e.g. good pay), but they are dissatisfied by poor hygiene factors (e.g. poor pay). Detractors of empowerment discussion and programmes claim that a well-designed job and system provides people with a feeling of having the power they need to do their job. People do not need initiatives to make them feel empowered, but rather an absence of disempowerment.

There are three issues to consider:

1. How is the system designed to operate? Is it optimised to favour empowerment?
2. What is people's actual experience of the system when they take action? Does it deliver? Does it frustrate?
3. As a result of such experience, what are people's *perceptions* of what will happen if they take action, especially if they take a risk, decide something bold, or try something new when told 'you are empowered' to take action?

When those BBC managers were told 'You are the organisation. If it needs changing, it's up to you to change it', what was going on in their thought bubbles? ('Oh, yes?', 'Have you ever tried?', 'You must be joking!', 'You don't know what it's like', etc.)

It is managers' perceptions that hold the key. Victor Vroom's (1964) Expectancy Theory maintains that people will be motivated to behave in certain ways if they believe that doing so will bring them the rewards they seek and value. In essence: 'Is the goal worthwhile, is it within reach, will I benefit?' To this one can add the question: 'Am I in control?', or strictly speaking: 'Do I *perceive* that I am in control, or that others are in control?' (For more on this, see the discussion on 'Shaping perceptions and beliefs' on pages 134-136 in Chapter 8, *Leadership and Learning*.)

Power issues – hierarchical and commercial – even find a place in the relationships between the parties engaged in planning, designing, conducting and evaluating interventions. For example, how much can developers and consultants speak their mind to clients, and how much do they need to keep their lips buttoned?

If you don't recognise the issues of power, or if you try to skirt around them, they may catch you in the tail. If your organisation's culture will permit an honest dialogue, some points for discussion are highlighted below:

SAMPLE QUESTIONS ABOUT POWER AND LEADERSHIP
☐ How is power currently used in the organisation? What is the mix between power over, power with, and power within?
☐ Is the power that is needed to bring about change well distributed through the hierarchy? Is too much power concentrated at the top or the bottom, in the formal/official system, or in the informal/unofficial system?
☐ How tolerant is the organisation of wide differences between those who have and those who do not have power?

Table 25: Sample questions about power and leadership

The key issue is whether the organisation claims to want to change the distribution of power. This is quite an undertaking. If this is desired, how will it be brought about? Where will the power come from to make that change? Who will be expected to have less power? Indeed, is power a zero-sum game, where one group's gain can come only at another group's expense? In the case mentioned below, some senior executives had too much power over people's lives; i.e. to end their employment. Sometimes additional bureaucracy is the price paid for curbing executives' abuse of power:

> 'Post-privatisation of a previously nationalised industry, the strong hierarchy meant that senior managers were entrusted with the power to make severance arrangements for managers reporting to them with very few checks and balances in the system on the reasons for their seeking that termination. Poor inter-personal 'chemistry' led to many careers ending unfairly and abruptly.' (Tate, 2003a)

Challenging the leadership norms

One way of tackling the challenge of change is to think in terms of an organisation's norms. Norms capture the everyday expression of the values, beliefs and traditions embedded in the organisation's leadership culture. They are a practical way of checking 'what leadership is like round here'. Below are some examples of typical leadership norms:

TYPICAL AREAS TO FIND THE LEADERSHIP NORMS
☐   Whether excellence is sought, or a lower standard is considered good enough
☐   What kind of performance earns a promotion
☐   How incompetent you have to be to get fired
☐   How much work is done through committees
☐   What happens to those who display considerable ambition

Table 26: Typical areas to find the leadership norms (Tate, 1995a)

You will find that some of your organisation's norms will be dysfunctional; i.e. you will consider them to be detrimental to the organisation's future wellbeing. Shifting the leadership culture is difficult, for reasons discussed earlier. But a starting process for doing something about this state of affairs is as follows:

1. Identify current norms concerning leadership in your organisation.
2. Label which of these are dysfunctional or detrimental to the organisation's future aspirations.
3. Specify what you would like the norms to be in each of these areas.
4. Produce a *force-field analysis* to show what forces are holding the norms in their present state of equilibrium: the enabling forces pressing for change, and the restraining forces opposing change.
5. To bring about change, try weakening the restraining forces…
6. …and/or strengthening the enabling forces.

Critical followership

Finally, there are no leaders without followers. Followers can either implement or frustrate leaders' intentions. There is benefit to be gained by developers and leaders considering the nature and quality of followership at the same time as leadership itself.

- What kind of followership does the organisation want and need?
- How and how well do leaders get challenged?
- What licenses the followers to challenge?
- What makes it safe for followers to challenge without risking their jobs?
- How is good followership rewarded?

'We might consider a failure of leadership and followership in the form of Rodney Ledward, the gynaecologist from William Harvey hospital in Ashford, Kent, who was "able to severely maim hundreds of women patients because of a hospital culture in which consultants were treated as 'gods' and junior staff were afraid of telling tales".' [94]

ETHOS

An organisation's leaders are guardians over what should be one of its most cherished assets, its ethos ('the characteristic spirit, prevalent tone of sentiment, of a people or community ...' – Oxford English Dictionary). Ethos is more than corporate culture. While sharing the importance of clear ethical values, ethos is projected more externally; culture's effect is reflected more internally and is more transactional in nature. Ethos springs from heritage, another prime responsibility of top leaders. It may be irresponsible and dangerous to meddle with it.

Ethos is less talked about in the world of business than it is in the public sector, though the excesses and collapse of listed banks has brought ethos under the general spotlight. Those who work in local government frequently cite their ethos as a source of pride:

'We're seeing more and more staff recognising they need to serve customers, even if they are not front-line facing ... that they are delivering to the community.' [95] (Pamela Parkes, Director of Human Resources and Organisation Development, London Borough of Croydon)

■ Ethos in schools

In a competitive climate, school headteachers vie for parents' custom by promoting a school's ethos:

Ethos is the ghost in the machine in education. Everyone recognises it when they see it; parents want it; politicians regard it with awe, but how do you produce it? Most would agree that it's the result of a common set of values articulated by the head and shared by staff, governors, pupils and parents. Get that communal consensus motivated around high aspirations, mutual respect and self-discipline, and you have a successful, well-ordered school. [96]

---

94 Performance and Innovation Unit (2000) *Strengthening Leadership in the Public Sector* (report), Cabinet Office, UK Government.

95 Parkes, P. (2008) quoted in *Making Successful Change Happen* (report). London: Improvement & Development Agency.

96 Bunting, M. (2008) 'Faith schools can best generate the common purpose that pupils need'. London: *The Guardian*, 8 September.

■ Ethos in local government

The public sector comes under pressure to adapt its ethos to the commercial world. Local authorities are given new powers to raise revenues from car parking; the London Borough of Hounslow has been accused of sharp commercial practice over this. Darlington Borough Council has been criticised in the press for fining householders over refuse collection infringements, such as a £50 fine for putting their rubbish containers out onto the pavement six hours too early. Such examples of over-zealous commercial behaviour overlook ethos-related questions: 'Why are we in business?', 'Who are we here to serve?' and 'Who is paying our wages?'. Like legislators' thoughtless manipulation of GPs' morality (discussed on pages 111-112), this is a further example of confusing the guardian and commercial syndromes (Jacobs, 1992).

Senior leaders need to be able to think clearly and ethically about this subject. Chapter 6 cited the example of a local authority aspiring to become 'more businesslike'. *'Becoming more businesslike'* affects the organisation model; in other words, how the organisation works. In contrast, an aspiration or invocation to *'become more like a business'* affects the business model, raising questions of whom the business works for. There is a fine dividing line here, which should not be lightly crossed, as can happen when guardian organisations are given commercial freedoms and targets. It is a job of leadership to be highly conscious of the boundary and alert to the risks.

■ Ethos in the justice system

Public service ethos is quickly weakened but slow to regain. The aim of becoming more like business holds risks, now encroaching into the criminal justice system.

> 'So Her Majesty's courts service is "a business" which is in crisis "because of a sharp fall in fee income for the courts" … This is partly due, apparently, because "HM Revenue & Customs, who were our biggest customer, have reduced their use of magistrates courts". In consequence, directors are "reviewing all parts of the business to see where savings can be made"; asking the justice ministry or the Treasury to meet the shortfall "is not an option".
>
> 'I always thought that one of the fundamental requirements of a civilised society was the provision by the state of a system of courts in which disputes between citizens, or between citizens and the state, could be settled, and in which wrongdoers could be tried and, if guilty, punished. I was taught that this system, which we call justice, was the bedrock of a democratic society, and that access to the courts must be protected at all costs. But now it seems that justice has its price, and the system can only work if it pays for itself. …' [97]

---

97   Marder, B., QC (2008) 'The courts are for justice, not profits' (Letter to the Editor). London: *The Guardian*, 8 September.

■ Ethos in banking

Ethos was much to the fore in the minds of building society leaders in the heady days of the late 1990s when societies were converting into mortgage banks. With origins dating from 1851, Bradford & Bingley met its demise in the banking crisis of September 2008. Ironically, in 1999 its directors long held out against demututalisation, spending £5m on publicity to their shareholders in arguing the case to remain a building society, until forced to capitulate to shareholder pressure to convert. In the mid-1980s, the British government had removed the legal constraints that had kept apart the role of building societies and banks, in hindsight opening the floodgates to executive risk-taking, greed and ultimately casting doubt in the public's mind that their money was safe.

> 'At the time a welter of opinion, most of it from carpetbaggers and City pundits, presented conversion of the UK's larger building societies as ushering in a new era of competition among Britain's conservative banks. But the benefits to former members now appear trifling compared to the benefits to the City and the executives who presided over the conversions. The £1bn fees and commission bonanza related to the conversion of building societies and mutual insurers compare unfavourably with the losses faced by the army of small investors who kept their shares. In B&B's case board directors tripled their pay between 1999 and 2004. B&B shareholders, like their Northern Rock counterparts, are likely to lose almost all the value of their shares, and other building societies have been sold cheaply.' [98]

Following demutualisation, B&B's chief executive, Christopher Rodrigues, switched sides, becoming an enthusiastic convert. He experimented with niche strategies including buy-to-let lending, which was ultimately B&B's undoing.

> 'The Bradford bard, Justin Sullivan, described London as "the land of gold and poison that beckons to us all". Once that might have sounded like northern bigotry; this morning it resonates. For the fast-buck culture of the City of London is what brought Bradford & Bingley to its knees. Once a proud mutual, which brought together local savers and local homebuyers, it transformed itself into a bank and has now gone the same way as the other former building societies – all of which have either folded or been bought out. Their commercialisation once seemed to promise a more competitive mortgage market – and a chance for the regions to taste London's financial prosperity.
> 'But now market mayhem in the Square Mile is starting to translate into lost jobs in Halifax, in Newcastle and, indeed, in Bradford and in Bingley. Once it became a bank, Bradford & Bingley dabbled in the dodgy derivatives that last year did for the former building society, Northern Rock.' [99]

As a final word on leadership and culture:

> *'Corporations can and should have a redemptive purpose. We need to weigh the pragmatic in the clarifying light of the moral.'*
> (Max De Pree, 1989)

---

98   Inman, P. (2008) 'How turning into banks led to ruins'. London: *The Guardian*, 29 September.

99   Editorial (2008) 'Home truths'. London: *The Guardian*, 29 September.

SUMMARY OF CHAPTER KEY POINTS

1. Consider if the organisation's corporate culture as it affects leadership, and within that the specific leadership subculture of those at the top of the organisation, is functional or dysfunctional. Is the culture serving the leadership needs of the business and wider stakeholders that the organisation is designed to serve, and is it fit for the future?'

2. Compared with corporate culture, leadership subculture receives less attention, but the latter determines the mood for change and contains the wherewithal to carry it through or hold onto the status quo.

3. A job of top leadership is to act as guardian of an organisation's ethos, especially in the public sector when under pressure to behave more like a business, or when undergoing a change of status or structure.

4. The notion of a more distributed leadership culture throughout the organisation is fundamental if organisations are to tap into front-line experience and generate energy for change. This requires wider distribution of power away from a centralised and hierarchical model.

5. Empowerment programmes are much talked about and popular, but they can be problematical for managers and raise more questions than they answer. Often what is needed is an absence of disempowerment.

6. Power issues are a prime source of toxicity in organisations. Both an excess and an absence of power are corrupting.

7. Giving people discretion in their jobs is a means of granting them scope to exercise leadership to suit the situation.

CHAPTER 11:

LEADERSHIP AND DECLINE

- ☐ *Suppression in organisations*
- ☐ *Dark leaders and leadership*
- ☐ *The slippery slope towards unethical behaviour*
- ☐ *Entropy, decline and renewal*
- ☐ *Reduced openness, discussibility, and taboos*

Decline, decay, disorganisation, disease, destruction, damage, deceive and denial. These D words capture the darker side of organisational life. Such issues are often hushed up or swept under the carpet until a scandal breaks. They are rarely managed. This chapter brings these sometimes painful, sometimes shameful, sometimes simply human and natural features of organisations into the open for discussion, understanding and management and leadership action.

Organisation cultures, hierarchies, rules and routines, and some bosses and their styles of leadership, have an unwelcome habit of limiting people, sometimes squashing them altogether. Most people at some time or another have suffered at the hands of particular leaders who abused their personal or positional power. Many – both on the inside and outside – have experienced the destructive nature of an organisation's culture and the leadership that permits it. Such leaders and their cultures can destroy shareholder value, deceive customers, damage employees, exploit suppliers, and harm the environment.

The scale of the potential damage that can result from bad and corrupt leadership is wide and can range from small numbers of employees to thousands of members of the public. The damage inflicted may be intentional, the result of negligence, cowardice, denial, bullying or turning a blind eye to others' bad behaviour. For extreme cases think Enron and Union Carbide in Bhopal (8000 died). Think Conrad Black and Robert Maxwell. Replace adjectives ethical, light, open, straightforward and enabling with murky, political, frenzied, polluted, and fearful.

> *'What is caged with orders and contained by hierarchy is what can become most cruel. The corporation is one of the ugliest forms of organisation that we have ... can enact their international cruelties for two reasons. First, that evaporation of responsibility through hierarchy. And second, the inculcation of obedience ...'* [100] (Jay Griffiths)

---

100 Jay Griffiths (2009), author of *Wild: An Elemental Journey*, speaking on BBC Radio 4's *Off the Page*, 19 February. Used by permission of The Marsh Agency.

Griffiths mentions the social psychology experiments begun in 1961 by Yale University psychologist Stanley Milgram, on the perils of obedience (Milgram, 1974). The studies demonstrated the shocking willingness of participants to obey an authority figure who instructed them to perform acts that conflicted with their personal conscience. 'In a hierarchy, that's when it's too easy for conscience to play truant', warns Griffiths. But Milgram's work and other research in connection with the Holocaust Nazi trial defence ('amtssprache') suggests that a bureaucratic defence of 'I was just doing my job' holds as much force as 'I was just following orders'. Soldiers who refused to shoot Jews were moved to other 'work' without punishment. Other social elements in the design of a system of employment can exert control and compliance; for example, artificially stimulated internal competition and rivalry, as in Enron's 'rank and yank' rating of employees' performance and automatic termination of the bottom 10%. The design of such systems is as much a leadership responsibility as the giving of orders.

The levers behind mis-selling

In the business world, few organisations come close to delivering the best possible result for the businesses they are designed to facilitate, for their managers and all employees, and for other stakeholders they are there to serve. Some are misleading, or their whole industry is dishonest. Charges of mis-selling and claims for compensation never go away.

> '... there were the insurance companies' mis-selling scandals: selling inferior personal pension plans to people already in secure occupational pension schemes. I talked to an insurance salesman once. At his induction he was told: 'Get yourself a Porche and plenty of debt. That will give you an incentive to sell the policies. And don't worry: you'll do so well you'll be able to pay it off in no time at all.' (Tate, 2004b)

In such cases it is important to recognise that these payments are not simply 'thank-you' rewards for successful performance *after the event* (like John Lewis's scheme for its employee partners); their purpose is to encourage – 'incentivise' – salespeople to do something for their company that they would not otherwise do. True incentives are intended to manipulate people's behaviour in some way *before the event*. They succeed only to the extent that the incentives are large enough for greed to triumph over self-respect, autonomy and individuals' congruence with who they really are. This is the game being played; this is what companies are messing with; and this is a measure of the companies' own lack of self-respect and their respect for others.

As an example of the psychological minefield of incentives, a chief constable was told by his police authority that they were setting him crime reduction targets, for which, if he hit them, he would receive a bonus. He interpreted the authority's action as an attempt to influence his performance with an incentive, and replied in disgust that he was already doing everything he could and was not going to be bought. He resigned.

The slippery slope from grey to dark

'I had to sell things to customers that they didn't need or want, such as warranties, and I got a bonus.' (Ex-Comet employee)

Most of those who do their company's commercial bidding probably see themselves just doing a job. They may themselves have been on the receiving end of manipulative practices of supermarkets or financial advisers.

We are becoming inured to reading headlines like these:

'Egg fined £721,000 over insurance mis-selling' (*The Independent*)

'Lawyers made millions from sick miners' (*The Guardian*)

'Top plastic surgeons round on 'anatomically impossible' adverts' (*The Times*)

'Supermarkets fined £116m for price fixing by Office of Fair Trading' (*Country Life*)

There is a risk that dubious ethical and legal practices may cease to be noticed or may be excused as 'normal'; i.e. part of what makes us human and what makes organisations human. Others may claim that they are what helps a company to compete in a tough market.

Sometimes ethical malpractice may be disguised, in the hope of slipping it past unobservant eyes or where stakeholders face a conflict of interest, as in this example of a carefully crafted (or crafty) resolution at a company's Annual General Meeting:

> 'Construction group Tarmac faces a revolt over its demerger plans from shareholders incensed at the firm's determination to install Sir Neville Sims in the joint role of chairman and chief executive and give senior executives potentially unlimited bonus packages.
>
> 'Tarmac's determination to breach conventional corporate governance standards and deprive shareholders of the chance to vote on some of the most controversial aspects of boardroom remuneration has angered senior investors.
>
> 'Clerical Medical, known for its robust stance on corporate governance issues, has told Tarmac's chairman, Sir John Banham, that it will vote against the whole demerger plan at the extraordinary meeting next Thursday. William Claxton-Smith, Clerical Medical's director of UK equities, said: "It is our view that investors should be given the opportunity to vote separately on substantive and potentially controversial issues ... but the single resolution only allows us to express our opposition by voting against the totality of the demerger. Despite our commercial support for this, we will be doing so".' [101]

The darker aspects of an organisation can be likened to the shadow side of human personality.

---

[101] Buckingham, L. (1999) 'Tarmac investors threaten revolt'. London: *The Guardian*, 2 July.

'The shadow is the "bag" we each drag along behind us where we put all the "stuff" that doesn't fit with being a good boy/employee/ citizen … Dragging this bag around takes a lot of energy. The more that's in it, the more energy it takes.' (Robert Bly, American poet and writer)

■ Dark reputations

Unattractive features may not be proudly on public display but may 'leak' and reveal themselves at times. The worst excesses (greed, bullying, cheating, etc.) – whether organisational or personal – may be kept private and hidden from view because they pose a threat to self-image and self-understanding. But some sectors and some occupations attract notoriety.

'It is easier to rob by setting up a bank than by holding up a bank clerk.' (Bertolt Brecht)

The banking crisis which broke in September 2008 brought into painfully sharp relief the darkness prevalent in that industry.

Attitudes towards such behaviour – by perpetrators and observers alike – vary according to personality. Some are critical or ashamed about dubious behavioural aspects; yet others parade them as virtues.

'[New Labour] is intensely relaxed about people getting filthy rich.' [102] Lord Mandelson, UK Labour Government Secretary of State for Business, Enterprise and Regulatory Reform

'I think there is an element of the bonus system that is unacceptable.' [103] Gordon Brown, UK Labour Government Prime Minister

Richard Aitken-Davies, President of the Association of Chartered Certified Accountants, wants to see action: 'If directors ignored bad habits, if they accepted complacency after a prolonged bull market then they should be held accountable. If they have allowed greed to flourish then they are accountable for this too.' [104]

Yet powerful leaders whose ethics are borderline are often valued by investors because they deliver the numbers. Their commercial success is attributed to their not being sidetracked by sensitivity, relationships or scruples. Some of these executives have a squeaky clean public image, but behind the scenes bend the rules; for example, breaching anti-trust laws, employing corporate lawyers to cover their tracks.

---

102 Mandelson, P. (1998) Speech in United States. London: *Financial Times*, 23 October.

103 Brown, G. (2008) Speech to Labour Party Conference, 22 September.

104 Aitken-Davies, R. (2008) 'Accountable crises'. London: *The Guardian*, 6 October.

Leadership Quarterly (2007) devoted a special issue to papers relating to aspects of 'destructive leadership' because, as the editors state, '… we are increasingly faced with the reality that those in leadership positions sometimes have the capacity, and motivation, to be destructive'. They might have added 'self-serving':

> 'This mercenary model of management (greed is good, only numbers count, people are human 'resources' who must be paid less so that executives can be paid more, etc.) is so antisocial that it will doom us if we don't doom it first.' (Henry Mintzberg, 1999)

Writing about the 'dark side of charisma', Beverly Alimo-Metcalfe and John Alban-Metcalfe (2008) observe it frequently and say how hard it may be to spot:

> 'Most individuals will have encountered or worked with some individuals in leadership positions who, although charismatic and inspiring in public, might be overwhelmingly arrogant in private. They are people who 'take all the glory', or who show no concern for the impact of their behaviour or ambition on others.'

The authors point out that 'certain individuals who appear charismatic and highly attractive might hide less appealing characteristics below the surface … the discovery of their dark side might come too late to save colleagues and organisations from the damage and destruction they have wrought along the way'.

> *'Robert has the techniques: a prolonged, firm handshake, prolonged eye contact, simulated sincerity, and so forth. He was also not averse to a subtle touch of hidden and undetectable character assassination when this could injure a potential rival.'* [105]

THE SCOURGE OF HUBRIS

Hubris existed long before 22 June 1633 when the Vatican Inquisition (itself a model of hubris) found the Italian scientist Galileo Galilei guilty of supporting the Copernicus Theory when he exposed the fallacy that claimed that the sun and stars rotate around planet Earth. Hubris didn't cease at that point. Many CEOs are prone to it. So are Government ministers; consider this example from a UK Labour minister:

> In an 11-page document, *Working with Liam Byrne,* issued to his civil servants, the minister spells out exactly how he expects to be treated.
> 'The room should be cleared before I arrive in the morning. I like the papers set out in the office before I get in.' For briefings, officials should tell him 'not what you think I should know, but you expect I will get asked. … Never put anything to me
> *cont. overleaf*

---

105 Birchmore, T. (2003) 'Psychodynamcis of Scapegoating, Persecution, Bullying' (paper). www.birchmore.org [accessed 11 March 2009].

unless you understand it and can explain it to me in 60 seconds'. He adds: 'If I see things that are not of acceptable quality, I will blame you'.

Byrne reveals a fervent desire to control the news agenda. 'We need to produce a grid ... outlining [the] story of the week. Once something has been slotted into a grid, my expectation is it will be delivered.' [106]

'That's the difference between a proper leader, who knows that you inspire your staff by restraint and humility, and a little Hitler, who doesn't. The new cabinet enforcer shows spectacularly how to get it wrong. "Working with Liam Byrne" should be a set text in junior Home Office circles: an awful warning about the primrose path to pomposity.' [107]

Apart from Byrne's tragic-comical belief in his self-importance and his leadership model of command-and-control, plus his preoccupation with story management, and his not wishing to be told things he may need to know, just reflect on this question: What is the climate with which the minister surrounds his civil servants? The chances are that they become wary, defensive, reactive and cynical; and, as research has shown, it is likely that they mirror similarly dominant, negative and untrusting behaviour down their own chains of hierarchy.

In all walks of life, the tendency of leaders to personalise positions and announcements increases after long periods in office. Power becomes increasingly associated with the person rather than with the office. Leaders believe their own press. They attribute success to their own brilliance. They blame failure on the incompetence of others. They don't seek critical feedback.

'This is the paradox of success: The very traits that launch people to the top – supreme self-confidence and unabashed salesmanship – can also send them tumbling to the bottom.' (Mathew Hayward, 2007)

In *Ego Check: Why Executive Hubris is Wrecking Companies and Careers and How to Avoid the Trap*, Hayward shows how the hubristic leadership culture can extend to the company. He describes how Merck mishandled allegations regarding the safety of arthritis drug Vioxx, ignoring feedback that could have prevented billions in claims.

▪ Pride before a fall

Nemesis (the Greek goddess of retribution) keeps a watchful eye out for those who succumb to the temptation of Hubris (the god of arrogance). Hubris is responsible for many failed companies and takeovers, where leaders have

---

106 Topping, A. (2008) 'Leaked demands portray minister as an eager diva'. London: *The Guardian*, 17 November.

107 Walsh, J. (2008) 'Cabinet enforcers have to throw their weight around – but not like this'. London: *The Independent*, 18 November.

grandiose expansion plans. The finance sector has been particularly afflicted. Such was the case with the demise of Royal Bank of Scotland and its chief executive, Sir Fred Goodwin. Such leaders need a means of being held accountable for their hubris and resulting misjudgement. This aspect of the RBS case is discussed in Chapter 14, *Leadership and Accountability*.

John Seddon (2004) proposes a systems solution to the problem of overly-strong hierarchical leadership: turn the company through 180 degrees to face the customer rather than the boss. Making the organisation demand-led instantly changes the CEO's role, which becomes one of supporting front-line employees in serving customers. The perception of who matters and to whom you owe responsibility – whether CEO or front-line staff – changes dramatically.

> 'Hierarchy is an organisation with its face toward the CEO and its ass toward the customer.' (Jack Welch)

A more commonly claimed solution is to seek alignment between directors and the company's shareholders. But Gary Hamel criticises CEOs who boast of their alignment with shareholders, pointing out that it is customers who create shareholder value. The most progressive companies put employees first (as they are the all-important contact point with customers), customers second, and shareholders third. To put shareholders first runs the danger of mistaking the scorecard for the game. In any case, being aligned with shareholders' interests (in the design of remuneration packages) in practice doesn't appear to be successful at controlling some leaders' self-interested behaviour and excess.

Whether manifested in leaders, organisations or societies, there is a natural pattern of decline followed by renewal (including replacement) that can be observed and managed. The economic business cycle of 'boom and bust' is one such example. In the next section I study the phenomenon and use it to explain the role of leadership in this cycle.

ENTROPY, DECLINE AND RENEWAL

Most development activity aims to improve individual competence and performance. Only occasionally is the word 'renewal' heard. Relatively little interest is shown in understanding just what is breaking down inside the organisation that gives impetus to the need to take improvement action. Solutions (such as training interventions) frequently come unattached to organisational weaknesses.

The important subject of how organisations inexorably degenerate and how they need practical and moral regeneration receives little recognition and discussion compared with competence. Yet understanding, recognising and responding to signs of entropy are key leadership skills.

All organisations suffer from the natural process of entropy – disorder, disintegration, disorganisation, decline, degeneration, disease and decay. An organisation on the slide feels like a lost community. Managers pull in multiple directions, following their own agendas. Individual interest is pursued more than the team's, and factions' interests take priority over the wider good (consider extreme partisan politics). Managers blame each other and blame things on 'the management'. Bureaucracy is rampant; the company blames government for this (the problem is 'out there'), but it is often self-inflicted (the problem is really 'in here'). (See 'Projecting the group shadow' in Chapter 13, *Leadership and the Shadow*.)

> 'A group that is threatened by internal competition constantly focuses on issues of internal competition in other groups while denying it within itself.' (Gemmill, 1986)

Armed with a fuller understanding of entropy, managers and developers can better apply its antidote: renewal. Renewal has both structural and psychological components.

But just what is it that breaks down? How can we identify the symptoms? How can we diagnose the root causes? And importantly, what strategies can we evolve for restoring the organisation to full health? When the organisation shows signs of falling down, how can we help it rise again?

Order and chaos

There is a view that the natural state is order, and that order will naturally emerge out of chaos. This is a central concept in general systems theory, which states that systems have a strong tendency to move toward a state of order and stability, or adapted equilibrium (von Bertalanffy, 1968).

> *'Planned change can sometimes be exceedingly difficult in a large, complex system because of the equilibrium-seeking nature of organizations.'* (Mike Chase, Professor of Psychology, Quincy University)

To others, chaos is the natural state, and managerial intervention is required to tame it and re-create order. Behind this view lies the scientific principle of *entropy*. But these two views are not the polar opposites they appear to be. The Second Law of Thermodynamics, on which the principle of entropy is based, propounds that the outcome of chaos as a by-product of using usable energy for work is ultimately a state of equilibrium – though by then, everything is worn out and there is no more energy left.

The conclusion is that things wear out, even things like human values, energy, intentions, communication and morals, as well as business models, systems and processes. Such things cannot be relied upon to remain in a constant state of good health on their own; they need timely monitoring, replacement or restoration.

Signs of entropy

Decay in organisations takes many forms. It can mean a decline in standards, authority, relationships, efficiency, quality, cooperation, morality, on-the-march bureaucracy, and so on. Nowadays, the ethical aspect attracts considerable interest, as we frequently witness decline in the principled conduct of business. Three cases make the point:

○ **Television companies** The television premium phone-charge scandal, where both public and commercial television broadcasts encouraged members of the public to phone in their views to vote on a contestant or a pet's name, to which the outcome had already been decided, rendering the phone call a waste of money. In some cases the result had been fixed in advance to favour someone living close to the TV studio, for practical reasons, or an insider was briefed to phone in.

○ **Severn Trent Water** The second case concerns the Severn Trent Water falling foul of the regulator, not for the first time:

> 'A judge was urged yesterday to make an example of Severn Trent, the water firm that has admitted providing false data on leaks to the regulator, Ofwat. Severn Trent, which supplies 8 million customers, pleaded guilty to two charges of making false returns to Ofwat earlier this year in a case brought by the Serious Fraud Office. The data was faked during 2001 and 2002 and came to light when a whistleblower accused the company of manipulating its figures.
>
> 'Severn has already been fined £36m by Ofwat for providing false information about its customer service performance and using those figures to justify increases in household bills.' [108]

○ **Management consultants** I briefly worked for a firm of productivity consultants who undertook diagnoses for struggling companies and then proposed remedies. The consultancy had a standard patter following their initial diagnosis that they used regardless of the clients' apparent state of health. The message exaggerated the situation, portraying the client as being on the brink of complete failure. It went on to offer a glimmer of hope, saying that the company might just be capable of rescue if they invested in further work by the consultancy to see if the company could be saved. It was completely dishonest, but a winning formula – at least in the short-term.

It is not difficult to associate these three failings with leadership, and indeed with systemic leadership. In the first case the malpractice had been allowed to become industry wide. In the second, the motive was derived from the business and regulatory model, not from self-aggrandisement. In the third, besides blatant dishonesty by a few top executives, some degree of manipulation of clients one

---

108   Teather, D (2008) 'Severn Trent faces huge further fine for faking leakage data'. London: *The Guardian*, 3 June.

way or another is endemic in much of this sector, and corrodes trust of the profession.

Max De Pree (1989) puts forward his own fascinating list of signs of entropy in *Leadership is an Art*, which includes the gem 'a loss of grace and civility'. He routinely asks his directors:

> *What are three signals of impending entropy you see in the company?*
> *What are you doing about it?*

The case of a company takeover shows some ethical danger signs:

An engineering company bought out the electronics subsidiary of the ailing conglomerate Dowty. The new owners instructed the acquired company's personnel director to carry out their plans to cut costs by removing staff cheaply on pain of her dismissal without anything more for her than statutory redundancy pay.

Most of the directors were removed immediately. Discussion then centred on the standard redundancy terms that would be available for the levels below. It transpired that the acquired company's normal terms were far more generous than the buying company's, and the new owners were not prepared to honour them. All they would offer was the statutory minimum. They then set about publicly humiliating the senior managers, implying that they must have been incompetent to let their business get into such a parlous state. Managers were attacked on a personal basis, irrespective of their performance. One was told he must be a rotten husband. The new bosses seemed to go out of their way to be aggressive, rude and spiteful, demonstrating their absolute power. Several managers couldn't take it and quickly left of their own accord, as the new owners hoped. Others were made redundant on the inferior terms available, happy to be out. By such dubious methods the company saved itself a considerable sum. So how can we be sure 'a loss of grace and civility' doesn't pay off? Why is it bad business?

Morale and commitment in the old company slumped. People worked strictly within the confines of their jobs. Deadlines were missed as staff didn't put in the extra effort they would have done willingly in the past. More telling, when a head-hunter advertised for a Product Manager, he called the (by now ex-) personnel director to tip him off, saying he had never received so many applications from one company, and to ask what was going on. The chickens were coming home to roost.

The effect of entropy on leaders

'The Parliamentary Ombudsman's report into Equitable Life ... found catastrophic failure on the part of the government regulators over a decade ... In the run up to the crisis, the regulators were "passive, reactive and complacent", ... failing to establish how it could afford to pay out bonuses. They also allowed its then boss, Roy Ranson, to run the company as a personal fiefdom.' Ranson was unceremoniously thrown out of the actuaries' professional body for breaching its standards of 'integrity, competence and professional judgment'.[109]

---

109 Sunderland, R. (2008) 'The final judgment: regulators, too, were far from Equitable'. London: *The Guardian*, 20 July.

High-powered leaders at the top of large organisations and politics are especially vulnerable because of the corrupting effect of power that takes hold over after too long a period in office, with all the perks that go with it, and fawning acolytes seeking favour. Confidence leads to arrogance, a sense of infallibility, a narrow concentration of power, and browbeating. With it comes complacency, a loss of a sense of challenge and knowing what to change, which in turn leads to stagnation and a preoccupation with one's legacy. This recipe can prove fatal for a company (and indeed a country) and for all those who have a stake in it. People come to refer to the period as 'wasted years'.

Leadership doesn't start like this. It usually begins life with a strong sense of mission, a determination to sort out certain problems, and with much positive energy. Once new leaders have accomplished their initial agenda, they tend to lose the driving force of their vision and they run out of steam. A series of new challenges may work for a while, perhaps with stimuli like takeovers to liven things up and provide adrenaline. But the high cannot be sustained indefinitely. A different order of change is needed.

The problem is that many leaders become blinkered and can't and don't want to see this new need and face its uncomfortable implications. They have come to enjoy the kudos, familiar comforts and attractions of power. For some, their agenda transforms into one of hanging on and staying there. Instead of continuing to add value of their own, such leaders start to deride competitors, both outside and inside.

It takes only a few years to shift from being part of the solution to being part of the problem. Recognising the tell-tale signs, those around begin to mumble 'It's time for a change.' Entropy has had its way – as we knew all long it would – with the individual and with the organisation.

> 'The definitive study of senior business managers found they were more likely to suffer from several personality disorders, such as narcissism, than inmates at a secure mental hospital.' [110] (Oliver James)

Always remember the system's responsibility in allowing these flaws to develop.

■ Extended power

Organisations decay as leadership decays. Just consider the life cycle of well-known prime ministers, presidents and chief executives. We know that power has a corrupting effect in many ways: on energy, motivation and motives, on self-image, humility, objectivity and ability to envision. As this decaying effect on top executives and other leaders takes hold, the organisation and its stakeholders suffer. Yet factors like weak governance systems, mere custom and practice, traditional deference, fear of a charge of disloyalty or felt impotence often result

---

110 James, O. (2009) 'The psychologist's view: Rich pickings' (commenting on the financial crisis). London: *The Guardian*, 11 February.

in a situation where organisations and near colleagues relinquish influence and control over their leaders' tenure. How often we hear critics pulling their punches, saying 'I think he should go, but of course it's up to him; I hope he will see this for himself and resign'.

Of course, in theory it is possible for, say, a chief executive's long tenure to be characterised by frequent organisational renewal action and distributed leadership. In practice, this is usually difficult to realise: leaders get defensive and cannot admit to the need for renewal arising on their watch, they come to hold power ever more tightly, they believe their own propaganda and succumb to hubris, whether in business or politics.

> '... as Mbeki prepares to leave office prematurely, humiliated and rejected by the party he dedicated half a century of his life to, there are few who do not believe he was the architect of his own downfall. The vision of a new Africa has long since been buried under the years of vilification for fiddling with intellectual debate over the origins of Aids while hundreds of thousands of the people died of the disease. The promise of good administration has given way to accusations that he purged state institutions of critics, interfered with the justice system and protected corrupt officials from investigation, most notably the country's police chief, who was accused of links to organised crime and covering up a murder. Even Mbeki's much vaunted economic policies, which have seen growth and financial stability, are vilified by the people now taking over the country as enriching a new black elite but leaving the mass of poor behind. There's no doubt that he centralised virtually all control. It was almost Leninist. It was based on the pretext that all power should be vested in the leader and there should be no gainsaying of the leader.' [111]

Of course, there is more to soiled leadership than that, and there is more to understanding entropy's bad breath. For individuals who have reached their peak and can only decline, the answer (at least for those on the receiving end) is for the leader to make a timely move (i.e. bow out at the top). But that solution isn't easy when you're the person at the top; it's highly tempting to hang on (and hang onto both the trap and the trappings of power) and hope.

> *'I have no desire to outstay my welcome. Most people stay on their bike and get pushed off. I quite like to get off mine, park it and gently get on with something else.'* [112] (Sir Stuart Rose, *Executive Chairman, Marks and Spencer plc.*)

Excessively long leadership at the top of any organisation usually ends in decline, insanity and tears, as the trappings and temptations of power take their toll, and the inexorability of entropy has its way.

In an 'Afterthought on Paranoia and Politicians' in *Families and How to Survive Them*, Robin Skynner and John Cleese (1984) offer a wonderfully descriptive

---

111 McGreal, C. (2008) 'How did it all go so wrong?'. London: *The Guardian*, 23 September.

112 BBC (2008) *Today*, BBC Radio 4, 20 September.

explanation of leaders' inevitable decline into delusion and paranoia. When the leader can no longer blame his predecessor for creating the problems that he is required to solve, he must continue to find new enemies to avoid having to confront the awful self-truth – the problem is not external; the demons are within.

> *'Never forget the press is our enemy, the establishment is our enemy, the professors are our enemy. Write that on the blackboard 100 times.'* [113] (President Richard Nixon tells advisers Henry Kissinger and Alexander Haig on 14 December, 1972)

Organisational leaders eventually find themselves in a position where they are blaming the problems as 'out there', when they are really 'in here'. They particularly blame government bureaucracy but fail to address their own, of which they have become tired, inured or blind.

'For many American companies, "the enemy" has become Japanese competition, labor unions, government regulators, or customers who "betrayed us" by buying products from someone else. "The enemy is out there," however, is almost always an incomplete story. "Out there" and "in here" are usually part of a single system.' (Peter Senge, 1990)

Whether talking about government at the level of the nation or a business, without renewal the organism will wither and die. Entropy is a process that cannot be prevented. But developers can respond to it, not merely replacing the sick elements, but improving the general fitness of the organisation and moving forward.

■ Things wear out

The concept of entropy is applied to organisations to explain how they work and exhaust themselves. The Second Law of Thermodynamics states that in any system the quality of energy deteriorates gradually over time. Natalie Angier (2007) defines entropy as a measure of unusable energy. As usable energy decreases and unusable energy increases, entropy increases. As usable energy is irretrievably lost, disorganisation, randomness and chaos increase. The Law can be summarised as 'Things wear out. You're always losing useful energy'. The 'arrow of time' only runs in one direction; things become colder, darker and worn out.[114]

> *'Entropy is like a taxi passing you on a rainy night with its NOT IN SERVICE lights ablaze, or a chair in a museum with a rope draped from arm to arm, or a teenager.'* (Natalie Angier)

---

113 The Nixon Presidential Library.

114 Bragg, M. (2004) 'The Second Law of Thermodynamics', BBC Radio 4, 16 December.

According to science writer Boyce Rensberger (1986):

> 'Examples of entropy can be found throughout the everyday world. Desks will get messy. Cars will wear out ... Without librarians, books get scattered and jumbled. Lacking nutrients, organisms die and rot. In each case, a highly organized system will inevitably proceed to a state of disorder and chaos unless energy (which is equivalent to work) is brought into the system to re-establish order.'

In *The Renewal Factor* Robert Waterman (1987) argues that:

> 'A company, even one with a long history of good performance, needs to introduce fresh management energy into its system to stave off the inexorable forces of decay.'

This pattern of decline and intervention applies to all working environments. All organisations become toxic, in a variety of ways and to a greater or lesser degree. All organisations need a detox from time to time. But how do you tell your chief executive that the organisation has become toxic? In what way is the organisation toxic? What if the chief executive has become toxic? Do you notice the toxicity if you are up to your eyes in it every day, if you have come to terms with it and take it for granted? In any case, is there an antidote?

Whistleblowing

Whistleblowing is a bold exercise in personal leadership (or professional suicide). Logic and need suggest that those who bring abuses and malpractice to authorities' attention would be made welcome! This rarely happens. The various parts of the system join forces against the whistleblower. Heads go down. Formal leadership goes missing. Why? Because the high-profile challenge is disturbing and threatens change to comfortable relationships, settled compromises and accommodations. It also threatens reputations – the institution's and its so-called leaders. There would be unwelcome visibility and embarrassment if the word got out. But it usually does, and any attempt to suppress it usually backfires.

In the mid-1990s British Biotech was flying high on the back of favourable publicity about its 'Messiah' drug Marimastat for treating all forms of cancer. The value of the company rocketed, and its chief executive believed the company would shortly rival the giants like GlaxoWellcome. All that changed when Dr Andrew Millar, the company's Director of Clinical Research, exposed dishonesty at the heart of the company. He was sacked.

According to the campaigning organisation *Freedom to Care* ('*promoting public accountability*') Dr Millar was sacked for breaching confidentiality by discussing his concerns about the company's research and commercial development with two fund managers at Perpetual, an investment manager with a significant shareholding. Apart from Dr Millar's own ethical misgivings, the US Securities and Exchange Commission was at the same time investigating the company over allegations that it had issued misleading press releases in 1995 and 1996 about its new cancer drug.

From his examination of the results of clinical trials, Dr Millar had grave misgivings about the likelihood that the 'wonder drug' would turn out to offer

---

only at its effect on the investment community, but also because he was ordered to continue trials with hundreds of new patients who were pinning their hopes on the drug. When he raised his concerns at the highest levels about the obligations he felt towards patients, he was told that 'the company was run to make profits for its shareholders'.

Once the whistle had been blown, the share price collapsed, and a third of the staff lost their jobs. Dr Millar was victimised and harassed. He was sued for professional misconduct. Later revelations vindicated him. The company was forced to admit that the drug was no more effective than a placebo in treating patients with inoperable gastric cancer. It also carried unpleasant side effects, causing severe joint pain. In 1999 Dr Millar received a large financial settlement. A £2billion company lost most of its value, falling to £100m. The chief executive lost his job, and a new management team now runs the board. (Tate, 2002)

Challenging taboos

Reduced openness and discussibility and a growing number of taboo subjects are signs of an organisation's increasing toxicity. Gerard Egan (1994) asks: What is never discussed but you think should be? What is currently beyond discussibility? What is too dangerous even to mention without putting your career on the line? Returning to my fishtank metaphor, these questions are about examining the state of the tank and the nature of its toxicity. A simple test of organisational health is this:

> How much is taboo (i.e. keeping subordinates and their leaders in
> their rightful and respective places, maintaining the social order, and
> safeguarding the status quo)? What issues cannot be raised – at least
> not at an appropriate level – because of fear of stepping over the mark
> and breaching the organisation's norms and the conventions concerning
> hierarchical deference?

Egan offers a continuum:

Not discussed	Not discussible	Not mentionable

Increasing level of inhibition, risk and fear →

Figure 10: Egan's continuum of undiscussibility

These stages represent increasing levels of danger for those who want to push the boundaries. He offers oral strategies for making discussion safer without simply blurting something out and paying a heavy price. As a way of testing the temperature of the water and preparing the ground, he advises beginning by delicately, respectfully and politely expressing personal reservations and asking if it might be possible to have a discussion about the assumed undiscussibility of an issue (that for the moment will remain undisclosed). You can then see what the response is and how much you trust it.

Some of the themes in this chapter are picked up and examined from a systems perspective in Chapter 13, *Leadership and the Shadow*.

SUMMARY OF CHAPTER KEY POINTS

1. Organisation cultures, hierarchies, rules and routines have an unwelcome habit of limiting people, sometimes squashing them altogether.

2. There is a continuum, a slippery slope, of manipulative behaviour that is not the sole preserve of evil people. Many perpetrators are employees who are simply following instructions, believing that they have no choice, and who claim that they are simply doing their job.

3. Views vary widely about controversial behaviour and what is shameful and should be disguised, and what is virtuous and should be paraded. Standards (other than when laid down in regulations) are personal and relative rather than absolute.

4. Aggressively competitive commercial practice can easily tip over into the dark side, where prosecution and a damaged reputation may follow.

5. All organisations are continually engaged in a cycle of decay and increasing disorder, usually followed by rejuvenation and order which may be brought about through the exercise of leadership.

6. It is the job of developers and leaders to know how to spot the warning signs of decay, and to know how to take renewal action.

7. Leaders should recognise and beware their own hubris and the risks it holds for their organisation. Organisations should likewise develop a culture and governance system with checks and balances that constrains leaders' behaviour and the damage they can do if they become too full of themselves.

8. Discussion of entropy (the organisation's and the individual's) should find a place in senior managers' performance review discussions.

9. Reduced openness and discussibility, and a growing number of taboo subjects, are signs of an organisation's increasing toxicity.

10. There are ways of challenging these undiscussibles with bosses without managers needing to take excessive personal risk.

CHAPTER 12:

LEADERSHIP AND SYSTEMS

- ☐ *Systems models*
- ☐ *The organisation as a system*
- ☐ *Leadership as a system*
- ☐ *Systems basics*
- ☐ *Systemic failure*
- ☐ *Change systems*

Expressions such as the 'criminal justice *system*' roll naturally off the average manager's tongue. They don't ask 'What do you mean *system*'? Where a number of organisations are involved (police, courts, prison, probation, crown prosecution, Home Office, etc.), managers accept the notion of a system. But when it comes to discussing a particular organisation, how it works, its failings, and how to improve it, some managers feel awkward talking and thinking about it as a 'system'.

Yet, almost everything can be construed as a system. A car is a system, and within a car is a transmission system, and a lubrication system, and so on. There are systems to help you understand these systems: electronic warning signs on the dashboard, bleeps, handbooks and helplines.

Systems thinking is a management discipline, concept and language that helps understand how things work and relate, and what causes what effect.

> 'Business and human endeavors are ... systems. They ... are bound by invisible fabrics of interrelated actions ... Since we are part of that lacework ourselves, it's double hard to see the whole pattern of change. Instead, we tend to focus on snapshots of isolated parts of the system, and wonder why our deepest problems never seem to get solved. Systems thinking is a conceptual framework, a body of knowledge and tools that has been developed over the past 50 years, to make the full patterns clearer, and help us see how to change them effectively.' (Peter Senge, 1990)

Thinking in a systems way aids diagnosis and improvement of how the work works, how the organisation works, and how change works. This chapter explores the application of the language and concept of systems thinking to leadership itself, its improvement and application.

The organisation is a system

In a systems way of thinking, an organisation is a system, with leadership as one component. The term 'system' captures all the facets, arrangements and norms that are required to work together to deliver a desired outcome.

'System' embraces culture, partnership arrangements, roles, responsibilities, resources, records, reporting arrangements, standing committee structure, policies, processes, standards, hierarchical structure and supervision, IT, codes, protocol, targets, inspections and injunctions. The system also contains 'the unwritten rules of the game' (Scott-Morgan, 1994), various unofficial practices, values and dynamics, and its 'unofficial side'. (See the next chapter on *Leadership and the Shadow*.)

> *'The unwritten rules are what help people survive and thrive.'* (Peter Scott-Morgan)

These elements in the system – official and unofficial – all need to come together successfully if the organisation is to perform well systemically.

Some managers' reluctance to embrace the language and idea of systems is sorely tested when it comes to construing leadership itself as a system. Yet a systems way of thinking about leadership has much to offer by way of insights and routes to improving the relationship between organisations and leadership. Leadership itself can be examined, understood and improved by taking a systems perspective. This is quite apart from the capability, practice, development and accountability of individual managers and their personal leadership.

Managers' interest in the system is twofold. Managers need to understand systems thinking and be able to view the organisation as a system – say, in relation to improving a call centre operation or raising productivity. Managers also need to be able to understand how the system has an impact on their own behaviour and on their attempts at leadership and managing change processes.

The system's own identity, power and influence

A system has a dynamic that is independent of the individuals who work in it. A family is an example: in some cultures a family's honour may be so threatened that the family will turn against a wayward member. Systems can behave like that (and, of course, a family is a system). John Renesch, a San Francisco 'writer and businessman-turned-futurist' explains:

> 'Systems tend to suppress anything perceived as a threat. The more dysfunctional the system, the more likely the distortion of trust and 'dark' the behaviour becomes, including possible illegal activity. … When someone dares to question these dysfunctional cultures, they are branded a troublemaker, a radical, or more politely a whistleblower, and are often ejected from the system or ostracised in some way so the system remains stable.' [115]

---

115 Renesch, J. (2005) *Better Future News No. 83* (Electronic newsletter), 1 June. www.renesch.com [accessed 11 March 2009].

The way the system is designed, and how it operates in practice (whether as it is intended to work, or in spite of it) has an influence that can be positive and facilitative (such as giving authority) and negative (such as imposing obstacles). The story of Bede College (page 72) showed how the educational system's checks, inspections, reports and plans thwarted the principal's role in providing leadership to the institution.

> *'Either I can't manage this place, or it's unmanageable.' (Warren Bennis, 1989)*

When he was ten months into a new post as president of the University of Cincinnati, Warren Bennis (1989), 'bone and soul weary' and mired in a mass of paper on his desk, admitted to a discovery:

> 'I had become the victim of a vast, amorphous, unwitting, unconscious conspiracy to prevent me from doing anything whatsoever to change the university's status quo. Even those of my associates who fully shared my hopes to set new goals, new directions, and to work toward creative change were unconsciously often doing the most to make sure that I would never find the time to begin.'

The system's contribution to leadership

> *'You can only develop leaders; you can't develop a system. In any case, people are responsible for the system. It's not separate.'* (Participant in Annual Windsor leadership dialogue, 2008) [116]

While a system cannot be developed to 'lead' as such, it can be developed and improved to be more supportive of managers' individual and collective leadership, and less vulnerable to systemic weakness and failure.

The system's contribution to how well the organisation is led, and how well it supports individual leaders and teams, is amenable to improvement through organisation development methods. In contrast to management development, OD means that people are involved in diagnosing, recommending and improving:

> *how the system contributes to leadership being applied (or obstructed), and how leadership in turn contributes to the way the system can be improved.*

Think systems thinking

■ The EFQM Excellence Model

This model, from the European Foundation for Quality Management, is an example showing the relationship between leadership and the system. While portraying leadership as the driver, the system usefully contains a feedback and learning loop returning to leadership. But, arguably, 'feedback and learning'

---

116 www.windsorleadership.com [accessed 11 March 2009].

understates the power of the system to affect leadership, which is pointed at policy and strategy, and then to processes.

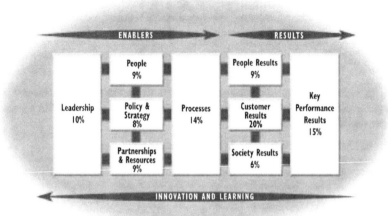

Figure 11: EFQM Excellence Model [117] (copyright and trademark © EFQM)

EFQM offers this definition:

> *Excellent Leaders develop and facilitate the achievement of the mission and vision. They develop organisational values and systems required for sustainable success and implement those via their actions and behaviours. During periods of change they retain a constancy of purpose. Where required, such leaders are able to change the direction of the organisation and inspire others to follow.*

1. *Leaders develop the mission, vision and values and ethics and are role models of a culture of Excellence.*
2. *Leaders are personally involved in ensuring the organisation's management system is developed, implemented and continuously improved.*
3. *Leaders interact with customers, partners and representatives of society.*
4. *Leaders reinforce a culture of excellence with the organisation's people.*
5. *Leaders identify and champion organisational change.*

Note that EFQM's definitions simply equate leadership with leaders, a link which this book challenges in its espousal of systemic leadership.

Excellence models such as the above one are put forward as a basis against which senior executives and organisation developers can self-assess and score their own organisation. But there is a question as to whether this is the best place to start. John Seddon argues that:

---

117 EFQM. (2008) Excellence Model, European Foundation for Quality Management. www.efqm.org [accessed 11 March 2009].

'... the best starting place is a thorough understanding of the 'what' and 'why' of current performance – to understand their current organisation as a system, warts and all. When managers start in this way, they have more confidence in actions for improvement-producing results.' [118]

■ Burke-Litwin Causal Model of Organizational Performance and Change

Another depiction of the organisation as a system is the Burke-Litwin Model. This model carries a greater focus on change. It distinguishes between 'transactional factors' and 'transformational factors'. The former are concerned with everyday interactions and exchanges that create the climate. They include such items as structure, tasks, policies and skills. But fundamental change, the authors argue, can be brought about only by changes in the external environment or by working on the elements of mission and strategy, organisation culture and, crucially, leadership.

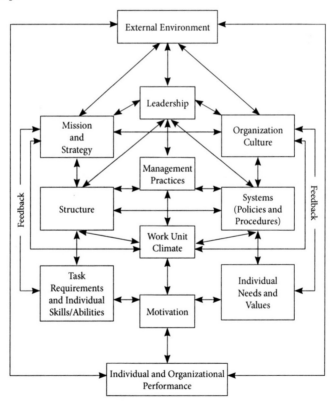

Figure 12: Burke-Litwin Causal Model of Organizational Performance and Change (Reproduced by courtesy of W. Warner Burke and Pfeiffer & Co.)

118 Seddon, J. (2009) 'Systems thinking & business excellence'. www.systemsthinking.co.uk [accessed 11 March 2009]

In this model the box marked 'leadership' addresses four questions:

- Who provides overall direction for the organisation?
- Who are the role models?
- What is the style of leadership?
- What are the perspectives of employees?

The Burke-Litwin Causal Model depicts an *open* system, one that includes the organisation's environment as a key ingredient in consideration of the system and the vital two-way interactions and interdependencies. The relationship with external stakeholders is a key part of the overall system and how it works.

In contrast to the perspective offered in *The Search for Leadership*, both models strongly identify leadership with leaders, rather than the book's 'systemic leadership' approach. The models emphasise leadership *within* the system, whereas systemic leadership also has 'of, by and for' dimensions (as explained in Chapter 4, *New Conceptions of Leadership*).

Systems thinking basics

The basic principles of systems thinking are shown in the table below:

BASIC PRINCIPLES OF SYSTEMS THINKING AFFECTING MANAGEMENT AND LEADERSHIP
□ *Systems thinking* is a management discipline that concerns an understanding of a system by examining the linkages, interactions and causal links between the components that comprise the entirety of that defined system.
□ The *whole system* is a systems thinking view of the complete organisation in relation to its environment. It provides a means of understanding, analysing and talking about the design and construction of the organisation as an integrated, complex composition of many interconnected systems (human and non-human) that need to work together for the whole to function successfully.
□ Whole systems are composed of *systems*, the basic unit, which comprise several entities (e.g. policies, processes, practices and people) and may be broken down into further sub-systems.
□ Systems may be thought about as having clear external boundaries (*closed*) or having links with their environment (*open*). An open systems perspective is the more common and realistic.
□ The *boundaries* of a whole system may be chosen and defined at a level suitable for the particular purpose under consideration, e.g. the education system or a complete school system.
□ Similarly, *systems* can be chosen and defined at different levels and can operate alongside each other as well as hierarchically; e.g. the finance system, the decision-making system, the accountability system.
□ An organisation as an entity can suffer *systemic failure*. This occurs in the whole system or high-level system, where there is a failure between and within the system elements that need to work together for overall success.

□ Factors in systemic failure may include confused goals, weak system-wide understanding, flawed design, individual incentives that encourage loyalty to sub-ordinate (rather than super-ordinate) goals, inadequate feedback, poor cooperation, lack of accountability, etc.

□ Whole system success requires a *performance management system* that is pitched above the level of individual systems and their functional leadership. Features may include group or team-level goal-setting, development, incentives, communication, reviews, rewards, accountability. The aim is to focus on what binds individuals together and what binds systems together rather than on functional silo, local or individual performance.

□ Whole system failure may coexist alongside functional success. The leadership of *silos* may individually be successful but not be sufficiently integrated into the whole system owing to a shortcoming of systems design, management or understanding.

□ A whole system can succeed only through managers collaborating in and across a number of functional systems. The whole system can fail only if leadership at the level of the whole system fails, and where several senior managers are involved. Hence, such failure may be labelled a *systemic failure of leadership.*

□ In cases of systemic failure, individual leaders who operate at a lower sub-system level may be free of responsibility and blame. They may argue (correctly) that it was the wider system that failed. They may claim that particular systems that integrate with their own work let them down. However, responsibility and accountability for the successful design and running of the (integrated) 'whole system' should rest somewhere.

□ Understanding and anticipating how the whole system is intended to work, actually works, and how it may buckle under pressure, can practically elude and defeat most leaders. To avoid censure for this tough challenge, they sometimes seek recourse to the often hollow mantra 'lessons will be/have been learned'. They also try to divert attention and reassure investors by referring to a single *bad apple* (e.g. a 'rogue trader'), behind which usually lurks a systemic failure.

□ The leadership challenge is accentuated by the realisation that for every legitimate, official or consciously designed system (which is intended to be and is supposedly rational) there is a *shadow system*. The shadow system is where all the non-rational issues reside; e.g. politics, trust, hopes, ambitions, greed, favours, power struggles, etc.

□ The system can confuse, overpower, block, and fail leadership. But leadership can fail the system. A major failure of leadership within, across or down an organisation is referred to as 'systemic'.

Table 27: Basic principles of systems thinking affecting management and leadership

Systemic leadership failure

Failings in large and complex organisations cannot and should not simplistically be blamed on individual leaders, and are increasingly spoken of as 'systemic'. When an organisation fails systemically, there has been a systemic *leadership* failure, as the following examples show.

■ Stephen Lawrence

A landmark case arose following the fatal stabbing of Stephen Lawrence in 1993. An inquiry headed by Sir William Macpherson concluded that the police force was 'institutionally racist'. This form of racism is distinguished from the racial bias of individuals by the existence of policies and practices within the institution and its culture that have the effect of disadvantaging certain racial or ethnic groups.

■ Victoria Climbié

Another high-profile case occurred in local government: the murder of eight-years-old Victoria Climbié in the London Borough of Haringey in 2000. In June 2005 Lisa Arthurworrey, the disgraced social worker at the heart of the series of mistakes that failed to prevent Climbié's murder, launched a legal attempt to win back her good name. She argued that she had been made a scapegoat to protect senior officers in Haringey Council. Her appeal was successful. Reported systems deficiencies in Haringey included the following:

- an unreasonably high caseload
- lengthy investigation of cases lasting months and even years
- a culture that was hostile to cooperating with the police (there was a sign pinned on the wall 'No Police')
- flawed local procedures at odds with national guidance
- an absence of supervision
- a lack of people for social workers to share case worries with
- and an unclear structure of accountability.

■ Baby P

Just two years later, in 2007, something similar happened again in the London Borough of Haringey, only a few streets away from Climbié's murder. This time 'Baby P' was killed by his mother and accomplices. In Chapter 9, I discussed the corporate competence aspects. Here, I return to the case to explore it from a systemic perspective.

Instinctively, we look for an individual in authority to blame: if not a social worker, then the pediatrician who examined Baby P and failed to notice the child's back had been broken. In a tragic case like this, we assume that it's a matter of someone's professional incompetence, carelessness or neglect. There may be an element of that, but systemic issues always begin to surface after a few days, such as professional agencies who didn't share information. Even the pediatrician is able to describe her environment as problematic.

In this tragic case, systemic failures that were reported included:

- Insufficient strategic leadership and management across the board
- Failure to comply with recommendations about written records

- Failure by the local safeguarding children board to question the agencies that reported to it
- Lack of independence in its approach
- Lack of communication and collaboration between agencies
- Failure to identify and address the needs of children at immediate risk of harm
- Inconsistent quality of frontline practice among all those involved in child protection

Looking at how the service operates we find 'the government has now centralised the system and, crucially, split it between a front-end referral and assessment function that filters incoming cases, and a back end that handles demand for ongoing care'.[119] Baby P saw 60 Haringey officials, the police and hospitals, yet very few professionals twice. The new working system replaced local teams which had responsibility for handling cases from start to finish. At its heart is the Integrated Children's System (ICS), a computerised recording, performance management and data-sharing system, which relentlessly chivvies officials to complete their on-screen documents:

> 'Workers report being more worried about missed deadlines than missed visits … The computer system regularly takes up 80% of their day. … use of tick boxes was criticised because of a lack of precision that could lead to inaccuracy. … If you go into a social work office today there is no chatter, it is just people tapping at computers.' [120]

Work by Sue White from Lancaster University highlights the role of the ICS in her explanation:

> 'ICS's onerous workflows and forms compound difficulties in meeting government-imposed timescales and targets. Social workers are acutely concerned with performance targets, such as moving the cases flashing in red on their screens into the next phase of the workflow within the timescale. … social workers report spending between 60% and 80% of their time at the computer screen.' [121]

> *'Switching off the flashing red light bears no relationship to protecting a child … but slippages carry sanctions.'* (Sue White)

John Seddon explains why children get seen by lots of different people: every time a child is referred, it is treated by the IT system as a 'new' case. Those who visit will be predisposed to avoid taking the child on. Why? If you take a child on, the computer system will allocate 'workflow' activity targets, hard-wired to a status that gets managers hovering if anything is 'going red'. It is better to

---

119 Caulkin, S. (2009) 'Blame bureaucrats and systems for Baby P's fate'. London: The *Guardian*, 23 November.

120 Booth, R. and Stratton, A. (2008) 'Child protection stifled by £30m computer system – report'. London: The *Guardian*, 19 November.

121 White, S. (2008) 'Drop the deadline'. London: The *Guardian*, 19 November.

discount relatives' or neighbours' reports and/or find any reason not to take the child on.[122]

Some systemic questions about leadership arise:

- Who has clear responsibility for social workers' environment (for what surrounds them, separately from their competence and daily performance; i.e. for the fishtank rather than the fish)?
- Who has responsibility for the design, functioning, monitoring and improvement of the system within which social workers are required to perform their jobs, and for how this responsibility is divided between the local authority and the government's Department for Children, Schools and Families?
- How is the accountability for these aspects of officials' performance managed in the ordinary course of events; i.e. before things go wrong (including the roles of elected councillors, since they were deemed to have failed too and were removed)?
- When serious cases are reviewed (as they are regularly), how do they guard against unconsciously noticing only evidence that supports their earlier decision? Do they, for example, use a Devil's Advocate? Do they use different chairpersons to avoid defensive behaviour?

The danger is that, in place of clear answers to such tough questions, the public will yet again be offered the balm of 'lessons will be learned'.

Almost as shocking as Baby P's death is the naivety shown by Ed Balls, the UK government's Secretary of State for Children, Schools and Families, who insists that 'there is nothing wrong with the system and Haringey was a special case'.[123] Has he not read Ofsted's report? Instead Balls has ordered council children's services chiefs to undergo intensive training programmes, a point discussed in Chapter 6: *Leadership and Management Development*. Without wishing to discount training, it should be recognised that it has less leverage in situations like this than other systemic interventions. He went on: 'We must do more to value good leadership across the whole of children's services'.

> *'I want to make sure all directors have the skills they need.'* (Ed Balls)

Balls makes the common mistake of equating training with improved leadership (see 'Separating leadership from development' on pages 7-8). If ever evidence was needed of the importance of understanding and taking a systemic leadership perspective and the uphill battle of awakening influential figures to it, the minister's woeful response provides it. But remember that a call for training is an OD opportunity. So the challenge for the trainers is to switch the minister's brief into one based on OD principles.

---

122   Seddon, J. (2008) *Vanguard News*. Buckingham: Vanguard Consulting, December.

123   Lipsett, A. (2009) 'Balls orders intensive training for children's services directors in wake of Baby P tragedy'. London: *The Guardian*, 9 January.

■ Jonathan Ross/Russell Brand

In October 2008 two controversial media stars made lewd jokes at the expense of Andrew Sachs, a popular, 78-years-old comedian and his grand-daughter on a pre-recorded BBC Radio 2 broadcast. Over 27,000 members of the public complained at the presenters' behaviour and the BBC's editorial decision to allow the broadcast to go ahead.

In instances of this kind, an employer's instinctive response is to look at people: who knew what, who didn't do what, whose job was it to do such and such, who should be sacked, etc.? In the case cited, Russell Brand resigned, Jonathan Ross was suspended for three months, and Lesley Douglas, the Controller of Radio 2, resigned.

But an alternative way of investigating, understanding and responding in such cases is to filter the data through a systems lens. The outcome will usually result in a systemic explanation for what went wrong. A systemic analysis looks like this:

The power structure: Fairly lowly and young producers are typically appointed to manage programmes – in the Brand/Ross incident, a 25-year old. Some highly paid and egotistical celebrities resent the producers' decisions and advice, and sometimes berate them and disregard their judgements. Artists can appeal over the heads of their producers and get their way. Producers' bosses usually cave into the artists' wishes. Producers who stand their ground can find themselves being moved to appease the artists. So, for practical purposes, producers lack the editorial quality control that they are nominally responsible for, while, formally, the buck stops with them. There is a mismatch between power and responsibility.

Conflict of interest: In line with the vogue for outsourcing, the producer was employed directly by the artist Russell Brand and not by the BBC. (NB: this practice has since been stopped.)

Competitive market pressure: Ferocious competition in the new media market has exacerbated the power gulf between editorial and talent. Some stars are bigger than programmes, or even a channel.[124] Pay differentials between stars and executives are huge.

Pressures and targets: Executives are charged with grabbing audiences and are required to take risks.

Organisation model: The director general and top executives drive a ratings-based, competition-obsessed model, which signs up stars and then expects people lower down to deal with any fallout. An ex-producer complained that their systems devolve all the risk and none of the reward.

Remote policy: Policy is set down in guidelines by senior executives who are remote from the realities of the front line and the painful business each day of deciding where to draw the line.

---

124   Russell, J. (2008) 'Killed by the Radio Star'. London: *The Guardian*, 31 October.

Other well-publicised instances of systemic failure include:

- The MoD was accused by an enquiry of providing inadequate resources, equipment and intelligence, which led to the wholly avoidable death of a soldier in Afghanistan.
- The United States Army threw out the conviction of the only officer court martialled in the Abu Ghraib scandal, amid criticism that the faults were instead systemic.
- When the Child Benefit Agency (part of HM Revenue & Customs) lost two CDs containing private data, the Chancellor of the Exchequer initially sought to blame a junior official for a failure to follow proper security procedures. But systemic failure ('institutional and corporate') was confirmed by an investigation by the Independent Police Complaints Commission.[125]
- The collapse of Northern Rock, and the negligent Financial Services Authority in its failed oversight and regulation of banks' risks.
- A rogue trader, 31-year-old Jérôme Kerviel, cost French bank Société Générale €4.9bn (£3.7bn) in the biggest fraud in financial history. Later it was admitted that there had been a systemic failure in the bank. It was discovered that the bank had twice been told by outside organisations that there were unauthorised transactions by this individual.

> 'The banking industry used to have a reputation for honesty, trust and prudence. This latest scandal, on top of the massive losses in credit markets, and the ongoing incidence of mis-selling to retail customers, indicates that there is a systemic deficit in ethical values within the banking industry.' [126] (Roger Steare, Professor of Organisational Ethics at Cass Business School in London)

Defending or blaming the system

Usually, the institution tries to protect its reputation by refuting the charge of 'systemic failure' since this would point the figure at those responsible at the apex of the organisation for its governance – themselves. The label of systemic failure might also signal to shareholders and other stakeholders (such as the public) that it might happen again. Instead, managements seek to blame individuals and claim they were acting alone; for example, labelling them 'rogue traders'.

But sometimes admissions go the other way. The 2007 inquiry into the tragic shooting of the innocent Brazilian Jean Charles de Menezes at Stockwell tube station unsurprisingly (given the evidence) found a 'systemic leadership failure' by the Metropolitan Police, but not by individual officers. This conclusion suited the police, who wanted the individual officers exonerated.

---

125   BBC (2008) 'The World at One', BBC Radio 4, 25 June.

126   Steare, R. (2008) in Walsh, F. and Gow, D. 'Société Générale uncovers £3.7bn fraud by rogue trader'. London: *The Guardian*, 24 January.

The public – conveyed via the media – wants it both ways. They will not be reassured by the 'one-bad-apple' explanation, believing the system is at fault. But they may also want to see individuals named and punished.

MANAGING THE PROCESS OF CHANGE

In Chapter 3, I introduced the idea that all managers have two roles; one is a management role concerned with today's operational requirements. The second is their leadership role and its aim to bring about change and improvement, with tomorrow's success in mind. This section expands on the second of these roles, and places it in a systems thinking framework.

The problem and power of the status quo, the discipline of systems thinking, and the need to manage accountability all coalesce when trying to bring about change. Where major change is required that affects a number of managers, there needs to be action from above that makes clear to managers that the status quo is untenable, and that they will be held to account for leading and delivering an improvement process that will have failed if it doesn't change the status quo.

In systems terms there are always at least two parallel systems at work that govern managers' roles. These systems exist conceptually and help our understanding by contributing to organisation design and human resource management. In organisations these are not usually talked about or formalised as systems, let alone two separate ones, though it could help if they were. I describe these systems and refer to them as System 1 and System 2.

System 1: Delivering today (a management system)

This is the operational system focused on *delivering today*. This system is concerned with how the *work* works. Or more precisely, this is how the work is expected to work, intended to work, believed to be working and perceived to be actually working. 'Today' consists of things like delivery production deadlines, urgent orders, waiting customers, excessive costs. 'Today' is more likely to concern problems than opportunities.

This is a maintenance system. It calls for *management* action. It is about managing what we think we know we know.

Understanding such a system and introducing remedies can become confused with and overpowered by concerns about how the *people* work. This leads to blame, explanations of 'bad apples', workers' low productivity, etc. But usually it is the system that is flawed, not the people. The system needs improving, not the people. In instances of systemic failure, it is this management system that has failed.

System 2: Securing tomorrow (a leadership system)

The purpose of System 2 is to look ahead and *secure tomorrow* – to make sure that the future is better than today. This system works in parallel to System 1 and is the means by which it is improved. By comparison with today, tomorrow is relatively unknown. Externally, 'tomorrow' consists of options, possibilities, changing markets, new products, fresh sources of income and changes to the business model. Internally, 'tomorrow' includes rectifying and improving the current system and way of working. It concerns what we know we don't know, and what we don't know we don't know, and calls for innovation. System 2 is a strategic system requiring *leadership* action.

In practice, System 2 is often absent or spasmodic, unrecognised and not formalised in managers' jobs. This state of affairs happens where organisations give too little thought to the question 'What do managers need to be doing to take care of tomorrow as well as today?'. Anne Owers, chair of the charity Christian Aid and Chief Inspector of Her Majesty's Prisons, appears to recognise the twin roles:

> *'You need to look at the systems which have led to the problems that you are dealing with. ... Do something practical, but also look at the systemic issues.'* [127] (Anne Owers)

The more senior a manager's position, the more time they should be devoting to System 2 work; in other words, concentrating on managing and improving the system for tomorrow rather than managing the people within today's system.

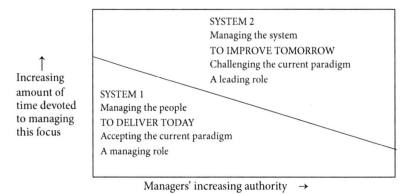

Figure 13: How time and authority impact on System 2

The case of inviting tenders (see page 43) perfectly illustrates the choices that managers have either to repeat the same old process or to stop for a moment and ask the question posed earlier: 'Why am I continuing to do what I am continuing to do the way I am continuing to do it?'.

---

127 Owers, A. (2008) Interview on 'Sunday', BBC Radio 4, 16 November.

System 3: A super-leadership system (an initiating, overseeing and holding-to-account system)

Superimposed onto System 2 is a third system, one that is responsible for the action referred to earlier, whose job it is to kick off change. The managers exercising leadership in a significant manner in System 2 won't take action without there first being another system to launch it. This system sits above the System 2 leadership system and for this reason is sometimes referred to by systems thinkers as a *super-leadership system* (System 3). A clear case for System 3 (as well as System 2) becomes clear in the NHS case cited below:

> Alan Milburn MP, when Secretary of State for Health, was a deeply frustrated man when the NHS did not respond sufficiently to his calls for improvement. So he announced that he would take hands-on control of the NHS reins by donning the hat of chief executive in addition to his political, non-executive hat. Predictably, his naive action simply added to his woes and sleepless nights. It subsequently led him to resign 'to spend more time with his family'.
>
> What Milburn lacked (as do many non-execs and indeed top execs too) was an understanding of the organisation as a system. He needed to realise that the design of the system means that it has a limited capacity to deliver, which makes it resistant to just turning up the volume knob. A leader will fail if he resorts to the bully's techniques: edicts, targets and other forms of pressure, because the system cannot respond. What's more, if you play the parent's game, you will trigger a child-like response in people.

■ How to launch and oversee major change

It is not the top executive's job (or politician's or non-executive's job) to think of solutions. The boss's role is to agree an overall minimum standard and to manage a process by which executives are held to account for how they propose to meet that standard. This is a model of leadership by pulling change upwards rather than pushing change downwards, and the principles, process and values are then mirrored down the hierarchy. [128]

The boss's role is, first, to get the team to agree that change is needed. He/she has then to charge them to discuss and work together and consult with their own direct reports in turn – to make proposals and to convince the executive team member of how they plan to achieve that change or improvement. This is *systemic leadership* at work.[129]

In detail, this super-leadership system:

1. provides a context, reason and challenge;
2. gives permission for the process and events to happen;
3. provides funds, time and other resources;

---

128 Robson, I. (2006) Perception Dynamics. www.perceptiondynamics.com [accessed 11 March 2009].

129 Robson, I. (2006) *ibid.*

4. defines a standard of what success or 'good enough' looks like;

5. ensures readiness for change: a point of possibility between excessive stability and anarchy (In complexity theory this point is known as the *edge of chaos*. Managers who have grown up believing that their job is to create order may find this expression intimidating.);

6. disturbs or shakes up the status quo for relevant aspects of how the organisation works and moves forward, making clear that the status quo is not an option. In parallel, it maintains stability of appropriate business interests (e.g. safeguarding customers' confidence during the change);

7. loosens the system, to weaken strictly hierarchical management of change;

8. licenses more widely distributed power for managers to engage in system-wide improvement activity;

9. gives managers a collective and cross-departmental identity;

10. makes people's fate rely on interdependence, which leads to cooperation, warmth in relationships, and people taking a fair share of responsibility;[130]

11. makes clear how the relevant people will be held to account, individually and collectively, setting a tight timescale to instil urgency, agrees this system of accountability (asking them, say, 'is it reasonable for me to ask you to report back to me on this as a team in a week's time?'), then conducts a process by which directors and senior managers are formally held to account for the required improvements to the organisation.

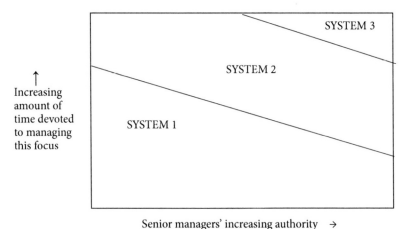

Figure 14: How time and authority impact on System 3

---

130   (2008) *Kurt Lewin: Groups, Experiential Learning and Action.*
      www.infed.org/thinkers/et-lewin.htm [accessed 11 March 2009]

Lacking a System 3 mental model or the confidence to trust others, government ministers suffer from role confusion and take over the change action that professional managers should undertake. In particular they make the mistake of equating heavy-handed *management* of change with leadership. At the other end of the spectrum is an absence from above of pressure on managers to change.

Applying this systems thinking model of change to particular cases

○   **Example: Invitation to tender**   Returning to the case of the routine invitation to tender (discussed on page 43), somewhere in the system is someone sufficiently senior whose job it is to provide a System 3 challenge to the manager responsible for issuing tenders. If System 3 supervision is absent, it is unreasonable to expect ITT managers to stick their neck out and perform a System 2 role by challenging the normal routine procedure.

○   **Example: Baby P**   Returning to the Baby P case, Sharon Shoesmith, the dismissed Director of Children and Young Persons Services in the London Borough of Haringey, was criticised for providing insufficient strategic oversight to her department. As with Lisa Arthurworrey in the Climbié case, Shoesmith became a scapegoat, conveniently protecting the minister Ed Balls, Ofsted and others who had a share in the responsibility for the design and running of the failed child protection system.

This raises the question of how clearly Shoesmith saw her role and involvement in Systems 1, 2 and 3? How did she allocate her time – between delivering today under the present system and improving the system to secure tomorrow (1 versus 2), and between a hands-on role leading change and an overseeing one where others seek and propose solutions and make the change (2 versus 3)?

For senior executives there is a risk of becoming reactive to the needs and demands of others, as Warren Bennis explained earlier in this Chapter, of confusing the three role systems, of ending up responding to the urgent and tactical short term ahead of the important and strategic longer term, and of addressing the people rather than the system. This is a difficult enough balancing act if undertaken consciously. It is almost impossible without the help of a mental model like that above, a coach to prompt reflection, and a superior to ensure accountability.

This raises another important question in the Baby P case: what role in this scenario was being played by the person to whom Shoesmith had to account for her performance? Was it clear to her? Was it clear to them?

In seeking improvement the starting point is to change senior executives' perceptions of their various roles and involvement in these three systems. Such a discussion should be part of a performance review. But bear in mind that a performance management system designed for delivering today's agenda (for example, executive bonuses tied to short-term results) may at best be irrelevant and at worst counter-productive in terms of safeguarding tomorrow's.

Risks if there is no System 2 or System 3

Without a mental model of the kind described above, there is a risk that incidents will be 'solved' by finding someone to blame, an explanation ('staff member sick'), by someone being asked to make a procedural fix, and then by offering customers, the public and media a reassurance that 'lessons have been learnt'. What is usually missing is a process of developing and culturally embedding the permanent systemic leadership capability that the organisation needs.

System 4: The shadow system

That is not the end of the (systems) story. Overlaying Systems 1-3 is the unofficial or shadow system. This shadow system includes the political context and behaviour such as the urge to find someone to blame. (To understand this system, see Chapter 13, *Leadership and the Shadow*.)

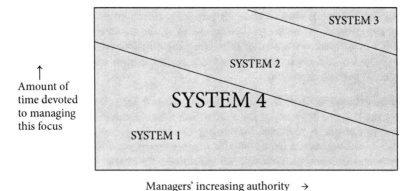

Figure 15: System 4's shadow overlaying the other systems

SUMMARY OF CHAPTER KEY POINTS

1. In order to better understand and improve organisations, work and leadership, it helps to adopt a systems way of thinking about how the various aspects of the organisation come together, interact and work as one.

2. When a leadership problem arises, ask 'Might we be overlooking a systems dimension?'.

3. While being a creation of man, systems behave as if they have a dynamic and mind of their own.

4. Where there is a systemic failure in an organisation there is a systemic failure of responsible leadership behind it in some form, that needs to be understood, acknowledged and acted upon.

5. Institutions find it in their interest to refute charges of systemic failure in order to protect the organisation's reputation, especially with investors. But they may also sometimes find it convenient to blame systemic failure in order to take the spotlight off particular individuals.

6. There are managerial/operational systems concerned with delivering today. There are leadership/strategic systems concerned with safeguarding tomorrow. There are also super-leadership systems concerned with initiating, overseeing change, and holding managers to account for their leadership in terms of leading change and improvement – in their own local jobs and more widely in the organisation.

7. It is helpful to managers and to their performance to understand their separate roles in systems terms for managing, leading and overseeing leadership, and holding such a mental model in their mind.

8. A performance review system which is focused on 'delivering today' may not be productive when it comes to 'safeguarding tomorrow', and may need redesigning.

9. Performance review discussions can be used to educate and reshape managers' perceptions of their leadership role in systems terms.

CHAPTER 13:

LEADERSHIP AND THE SHADOW

- ☐ *The nature of the organisation's shadow*
- ☐ *The unwritten rules*
- ☐ *The two halves of organisational life*
- ☐ *Shadow networks*
- ☐ *Managing the shadow system*

This chapter discusses the false assumptions that organisations are rational places, that decisions are logically and rationally taken, and that logic and rationality are the proper purpose and focus for management. MBA programmes perpetuate this myth.

The truth is that humans, and the organisations they inhabit, are far from rational in their behaviour. Managers need a way of taking account of this in order to understand and manage their organisation's behaviour. That includes its unwritten rules, bullying, departmental rivalries, nepotism, etc.

To accept that rationality is neither the reality nor attainable and that, at times, it is not even the correct goal for organisations and managers requires the ability to recognise, understand and manage the nature and psychology of an organisation, especially those parts of it that relate to its shadow nature.

This chapter considers the complex, multi-faceted nature of the organisation's shadow. This informal and unofficial 'shadow system' complements the organisation's more formal, legitimate, rational system. I will explore to what extent the systems' shadow elements are shameful and negative, how communication in the organisation is affected, the impact on group relationships, and the implications for leadership.

THE ORGANISATION'S SHADOW

You will have gathered from this that an organisation's shadow side is important, and cannot and should not be ignored. The shadow and how it works as a system must be understood, and it needs managing. Here is a short theoretical background:

'The concept of shadow was elaborated by [Carl] Jung and describes the attempt by an individual to repress those characteristics and aspects which do not fit with the self-image. Every human carries a shadow. It represents the 'other side', the 'dark brother', who is an inseparable part of our psychic totality. In other words, the individual is much more than the persona or mask which is erected to contend with the surrounding social forces.' (Sievers, 1999)

The individual's shadow holds ramifications beyond those of intra- and even inter-personal conflict. Shadow behaviour – especially that of a leader – is obviously important to organisations and needs managing (discussed later in this chapter). But there is another level: this book's prime interest in the shadow is that the concept has been lifted from individual personality and adapted to help understand the collective personality and behaviour of organisations. Organisations, like people, seek to convey a favourable image: one of caring, respectability, probity, rationality, order and efficiency, for example.

We can sometimes glimpse past this façade and note that the organisation has a side that is disagreeable, messy, crazy, opaque, inefficient, callous and disreputable, which it may hope to keep hidden and pretend doesn't exist.

Such facets in the shadow side may be dark and bad, as we saw earlier when discussing the dark face of leadership, but are not automatically so. For example, craziness and disorder, even if repressed, may provide a creative spur. Grapevines can be a valuable source of information. Whether positive or negative, what these features have in common is that they are somewhat slippery, may be denied, and are not normally up for formal discussion, agreement and action. They don't appear on the agendas of management meetings in the way that, say, a new organisation chart might, or a new policy statement.

THE REAL NATURE OF ORGANISATIONS

Many organisations suffer from being disempowering, bureaucratic, hierarchical, secretive, costly, wasteful, exclusive, and inefficient. Some people – some of them inspiring leaders – reach the conclusion that they will never again work in and for the organisation, or even *any* organisation. For some, there is too much infighting, back biting and bad blood. For others, the problem may be the organisation's politicking, inefficiency, inhibition and obstacles.

'Organisations waste thousands, and in some cases millions of pounds every year ... by creating cultures in which even the most potentially effective leaders are frustrated daily in their efforts to have a positive impact...'[131] (Linda Holbeche, Director of Policy and Research, Chartered Institute of Personnel and Development)

131 Holbeche, L. (2008) Foreword in Alimo-Metcalfe and Alban-Metcalfe, 2008.

Inefficiency and waste

The BBC is probably no better and no worse than other large organisations, but receives more media exposure so it is easy to find examples of its inefficiency. Did it really need 50 newspeople to go to Falmouth to cover the homecoming of Ellen MacArthur's record-breaking, round-the-world, single-handed yachting achievement in 2005? What's going on? Why do such things happen? Can we find the answer by delving into the organisation's shadow system?

'David Liddament, the outgoing ITV boss at the time (August 2002), questioned what the BBC was for. Eddie Mair, a BBC broadcaster, replied as follows:

"The BBC is there to do what it has always done. Take on the common enemy. Each other. You may hear *Today*, and *The World at One* and *PM* all coming out of the radio on the same channel, Radio 4. But make no mistake. Although we all work for the same network, we are in different departments within BBC News – quite deliberately so – to ensure that we have to compete and to keep our journalism sharp.

"Because our rivals on *Today* and *The World Tonight* can read *PM*'s running order on the communal computer system, we go out of our way to make the stories look as incomprehensible as possible. Editors often give stories joke names. A brutal assault on a pensioner might become 'Bashed Up Granny' in the running order. A particularly inept policy initiative might become 'Hopeless'. It could be argued that this is merely part of the dark humour that lurks in all newsrooms. It could also be the product of very sick minds. I really don't care. We don't even put names of guests in the running order any more. If we've secured a Peter Mandelson interview, he simply appears as 'P'. Similarly, Theresa May is 'T', and Dame Judi Dench is 'M'.

"When new producers arrive with us from *Today* or *The World Tonight*, they are asked, informally, if they still have computer access to their old contact lists. If they say yes, they are taken to a windowless eight-foot-square room with a table, two chairs and a light bulb and debriefed until they're whimpering. And that's just the job interview.

"The point is, though, that rivalry between different departments within the BBC is far greater than that directed towards different broadcasters. We at *World at One* and *PM* are far more interested in what the *Today* programme is doing than what commercial radio is up to." ' (Tate, 2005)

Intensely competitive internal departmental behaviour is an example of the organisation's shadow nature. It may be seen by some people as rational and virtuous; others may consider it to have negative qualities and be at the expense of the business's overall performance. By definition, optimising a departmental silo's performance carries a cost to the overall company performance. But a degree of rivalry – not tipping over into antipathy – may be positive.

The National Freight Corporation were concerned that their staff lacked sufficient competitive instinct to do battle with their external competitors. The company believed that staff could not distinguish between different targets to which to apply their competitive instincts. Controversially, it decided that the route to competing externally was via first competing internally; it would not be able to get one without the other, and would therefore need first to artificially stimulate internal competition.

Another company reorganised its structure with what appeared to staff to be similar departments, only with different names. The consultant advising the chief executive explained that he wanted them to compete, and the better one would come through.

We can laugh at these examples of internal rivalries. And, it must be admitted, where there are negatives there are also positives (for example, competition can keep people on their mettle).

But, when the BBC's Head of News announced she was clamping down on 'stupid duplication', this was easier said than done. The roots of dysfunction are located deep in an organisation's psyche, in its shadow system, well below the surface of its public persona or façade. Pronouncements, policies and design are part of an organisation's rational side. They have less potency than the shadow side, most of which is hidden below the surface like an iceberg.

Physical and psychological abuse

Instances of physical and psychological abuse are prevalent in strongly hierarchical organisations such as prisons and the military. In March 2000, Zahid Mubarek was beaten to death by Robert Stewart, his cell mate, in HM Young Offender Institution and Remand Centre Feltham. An inquiry four years later, after a prolonged legal battle by Mubarek's family, asked why Mubarek was sharing a cell with Stewart when there was information within the Prison Service that Stewart was a violent and racist psychopath. As part of his evidence into racism at the prison and the appalling conditions there, one former Feltham governor revealed that three white officers were given a written warning but not sacked after handcuffing an ethnic minority inmate to his cell bars, removing his trousers and smearing black boot polish on his buttocks. The inquiry looked into the claim of the so-called 'Coliseum' gladiator games at Feltham, during which some officers allegedly put together prisoners they believed likely to fight. The allegation was first made by a prison officer in an anonymous call to the Commission for Racial Equality. The police were unable to substantiate the claim. However, in the inquiry's later seminar sessions, evidence emerged from some officers that such gladiatorial betting had taken place in some prisons.

Wide power differentials, macho cultures, tough training methods, and a racial mix make physical and psychological abuse more likely in prisons and the military. But abuse is not confined to these sectors; it is found in care homes, families and schools, for example. Abuse takes many forms, including bullying.

All it takes for a bully's actions to go unchecked in an organisation is easy availability and access to victims, spaces, methods, confidants and colleagues who can be persuaded to join in or be coerced and suppressed, plus incentives and threats.

Where there is abuse, there is a strong shadow system at work, explaining, facilitating and manifesting the abuse. To tackle such abuse calls for both management and leadership. See Table 28 for systems-related questions:

TACKLING ABUSE: SYSTEMS-RELATED QUESTIONS

- ☐ Who in authority inside the organisation knows what is going on and is in a position to do something about it?

- ☐ Who in authority inside the organisation *should* know what is going on and is failing in their duty if they don't know?

- ☐ Is it clear who is in a position of authority, and can be held to account?

- ☐ How does the system by which they are held to account <u>actually</u> work?

- ☐ Who in authority believes the system will defeat them if they try to stop abuse? How can they be helped to overcome fear and resistance and to successfully and confidently take action?

- ☐ What do those in authority perceive their job to be in this area? How do they see their leadership role in comparison to their administrative role?

- ☐ What part is being played by the super-leadership system (see previous chapter)?

- ☐ What messages cascade down the hierarchy concerning tackling abuse? Do these ever say 'Don't rock the boat', 'You'll never stop it', 'There will be a backlash if you try', 'You'll get no thanks', 'It's always been like this'?

- ☐ Who in authority is choosing to 'turn a blind eye'?

- ☐ Who in authority knows what to do, and where to begin? Do they know how to use an understanding of system dynamics to bring about improvement (as opposed to pointlessly sending people on anti-bullying training courses)?

Table 28: Tackling abuse: Systems-related questions

Bullying is a property of organisations, not just of individuals. It is especially endemic in the retail sector in the way companies squeeze their suppliers. It may appear more respectable, disguised as simple commerciality, yet can constitute an abuse of power nevertheless.

'... store groups "are abusing their power at the expense of their suppliers" by imposing changes to payment terms to boost their profit margins. "Suppliers are left with little option but to accept the changes for fear of losing orders if they don't." The Forum for Private Business has produced a "Hall of Shame", listing 26 retailers it claims use their size to "intimidate and frighten" their way to bigger profit margins. The list includes Bhs, B&Q, Homebase, Halfords, Matalan and New Look.' [132]

Unwritten rules

'Every organization is a creature of its unwritten rules.' (Scott-Morgan, 1995)

The shadow aspect of organisational life receives little formal acknowledgement; indeed, its very nature is informality. The shadow system's 'rules', such as they are, remain unwritten.

---

132 Finch, J. (2006) 'Suppliers cite 26 bullying retailers in their hall of shame'. London: *The Guardian*, 2 November.

'All the various written rules, together with the behaviour and actions of top management, send signals into the body of an organisation. But then various factors go to work on the signals – factors that no managers can control or even measure: things like national and local culture, the economic climate, … people's private agendas … All these factors transform the signals … – reinforcing them, undermining them, twisting them – until the original management actions and written rules have a complete set of parallel unwritten rules that actually drive people's day-to-day behaviour.' (Scott-Morgan, 1995)

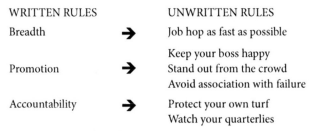

WRITTEN RULES		UNWRITTEN RULES
Breadth	→	Job hop as fast as possible
Promotion	→	Keep your boss happy Stand out from the crowd Avoid association with failure
Accountability	→	Protect your own turf Watch your quarterlies

Figure 16: Examples of Scott-Morgan's written and unwritten rules

Being streetwise

There is much that managers can gain from being better informed about the organisation's shadow and finding ways of talking about it and taking it into account, recognising choices they may have, being more open, even directly intervening in the shadow system. They can then be more successful in leading and managing, especially concerning change; it helps them to:

- become aware of how the shadow system can stop planned change in its tracks and obstruct managers from making rational change;
- directly target dysfunctional features of the shadow system when making organisational change or improvement interventions;
- recognise the interconnectedness of the rational/legitimate system and the informal/shadow system when intervening to make improvements.

THE TWO HALVES OF ORGANISATIONAL LIFE

Gerard Egan (1994), a leading authority on the shadow side in business, offers this definition:

'All the important activities and arrangements that do not get identified, discussed and managed in decision-making forums that can make a difference… The shadow side deals with the covert, the undiscussed, the undiscussible, and the unmentionable. It includes arrangements not found in organizational manuals and company documents or on organization charts.'

Described like this, all aspects of organisational life seem to fit an equation, neatly dividing between the rational and non-rational.

The rational half of organisational life

This is concerned with how managers prefer to think and talk about the organisation; for example, how job roles fit together, and therefore how (at least on paper) work is assumed to get done. Decision making is taught as a logical process. Centralisation of functions (such as 'back-office *factories*', purchasing, HR, etc.) is pursued on the assumption that it will produce economies. The levers to pull on to bring about improvement and change are rational – for example, new organisation structures, appointments, targets, announcements and edicts. Little thought is given to unintended consequences, which may have their origins in the shadow side, and may undermine rational intentions.

The non-rational half of organisational life

Here reside those unwritten rules of the game. Here we find what really makes the organisation tick. To get a fuller and more honest picture of the organisation we need to become aware of the non-rational half of the organisational equation, the more powerful half. This is a small sample of what comprises each half.

RATIONAL ELEMENTS	NON-RATIONAL ELEMENTS
□ Directives	□ Trust
□ Strategic plans	□ Friendships
□ Organisation charts	□ Jealousy
□ Job titles	□ Fear and insecurity
□ Policies	□ Power
□ Training courses	□ Ambition
□ Budgets, etc.	□ Grapevine, etc.

Table 29: Sample elements of the two sides (Tate, 2003b)

The assumed dominance of the coldly rational model is slowly changing. Acceptance of 'emotional intelligence' and its importance in workplace leadership has played a key part in this shift:

> 'The world's most effective leaders are alike in one crucial way: they all have a high degree of emotional intelligence (EQ). Research by Daniel Goleman, psychologist and author of the book Emotional Intelligence, suggests that EQ levels determine up to 85 per cent of leadership success. Some of the characteristics of high EQ include the ability to cope successfully and proactively with life's demands and pressures, and to build and make use of rewarding relationships with others, while not being afraid to make tough decisions.' [133]

For items in the right-hand column in Table 29, Gerard Egan uses the term 'arational' or non-rational, distinguishing it from *irrational*. He regards the effect that these factors have on the health of the organisation as a mix of positive, negative and neutral. Thus, friendships, for example, are not rational features of

---

133 Goleman, D. (2008) 'How to develop emotional intelligence'. London: *People Management* magazine, 1 May.

an organisation, but neither are they negative or irrational; they can have a variety of effects. For example, friendships between people at work can be the means of getting round obstructions and bureaucracy, yet they can also make people feel excluded or undervalued.

The nature of the two halves

The two halves of organisational life bear some similarities to the two halves of the brain, though the connection is not scientific. It is commonly accepted that the two hemispheres perform different functions, though the precise division is disputed. The left hemisphere favours rational thinking, numbers, etc., while the right hemisphere is more concerned with colour, music, intuition, and so on. Based on this analogy, and as a way of gaining understanding of the rational/non-rational concept, I liken the two sides of the brain to the broadly differentiated organisational characteristics, as shown below:

RATIONAL CHARACTERISTICS (left brain)	NON-RATIONAL CHARACTERISTICS (right brain)
□ Designed to happen	□ What really happens
□ Things	□ People
□ What	□ Who
□ Logical/thinking	□ Emotional/feeling
□ Overt	□ Covert
□ Discussed	□ Undiscussed

Table 30: The character of the two sides of organisational life (Tate, 1999)

The rational factors are generally more explicit and find more ready acceptance for legitimate discussion in formal management meetings. They are usually written down somewhere and captured in policies. They tend to deal with 'what' issues. By contrast, non-rational factors generally remain implicit and are more likely to concern 'who' issues. Here is an example of someone's experience of the two sides taken from the 2008 UK Labour Party Conference:

> 'We have all been living in two parallel universes for the last few days. ... There really are two worlds here. The one that we're in now, that Harriet (Harman) and you have been in for the last few minutes where the microphones and cameras are and journalists with notepads and with pens. And there's another where private conversations are going on. And they are happening everywhere. I don't just mean in the bars late at night when people have had a few drinks, and they start speculating wildly about things, but I mean everywhere at this conference, in hotels, in corridors...' [134]

A fuller list of the two sides is shown in Table 31:

---

134 Kuenssberg, L., political correspondent. (2008) 'Woman's Hour – at the Labour Party Conference', BBC Radio 4, 23 September.

RATIONAL FACTORS (LEGITIMATE OR OFFICIAL SYSTEM)	NON-RATIONAL FACTORS (SHADOW SYSTEM OR UNOFFICIAL SYSTEM)
☐ announcements	☐ culture
☐ edicts	☐ climate
☐ directives	☐ values and beliefs
☐ exhortation	☐ ethics
☐ mission	☐ norms, custom and practice
☐ goals	☐ myths
☐ objectives	☐ personal rivalries
☐ targets	☐ departmental rivalries
☐ strategies	☐ territorial ('turf') disputes
☐ policies	☐ power struggles
☐ systems	☐ empire-building
☐ statistics	☐ competition/collaboration
☐ databases	☐ personal jealousies and envy
☐ plans	☐ biases and prejudices
☐ standing instructions	☐ office politics
☐ company rules and regulations	☐ ambition
☐ codes of practice/ethics	☐ greed
☐ statements of business principles	☐ self-interest
☐ credos	☐ trust
☐ organisation charts/structure	☐ respect
☐ budgets	☐ fear and insecurity
☐ sign-off authority levels	☐ turning a blind eye
☐ contracts	☐ personal friendships
☐ laws and statutes	☐ sexual relationships and attraction
☐ job descriptions	☐ socialising
☐ job titles	☐ networking
☐ published policies	☐ short cuts
☐ committee structures	☐ expediency
☐ qualifications	☐ groupthink
☐ skills, knowledge	☐ bosses not on speaking terms
☐ lists of competencies	☐ in-groups and out-groups
☐ appraisal procedures	☐ grapevine
☐ pay structure	☐ bullying and intimidation
☐ training courses	☐ personal appearance
☐ office standards (e.g. dress codes)	☐ favours
	☐ bribes and backhanders
	☐ horse-trading
	☐ surveillance
	☐ sabotage
	☐ ploys

Table 31: Extended list of elements in the two halves of organisational life (Tate, 1999)

Note how seldom items in the right-hand column of Table 31 find a place on the boardroom agenda, despite their potency. Note how most shadow elements are the kind of behaviour and characteristics that we associate most naturally with individuals, but a few are direct organisational manifestations: for example, the organisation's culture, customs and norms, and departmental rivalries. Note too that some of the items in the non-rational column are vital for the organisation to function effectively; for example, trust and relationships.

Note too how most development and educational activity, including that of business schools, is located in the rational half. They conduct themselves on the basis that what is learned can be applied. But this book shows how much of what the organisation (and colleagues) surround people with frustrates potential. Developers and educators are in a state of ignorance or denial about these shadow forces in so far as these forces affect what they teach and how they teach it.

> 'Management education privileges decisiveness over reflection. We need to correct this to encourage deeper, more multi-dimensional thinking embracing systems, values and the right as well as the left side of the brain.'[135] (The Management Innovation Agenda)

The twin list does not attempt to capture all possible explanations of behaviour in organisational life and culture. While the list goes beyond items contained in Egan's model by containing some attributes of individuals on the non-rational side that have organisation-level manifestations and implications, it does not attempt to capture all human foibles, quirks and weaknesses. For example, people's perceptions, while vitally important in determining how they work and behave, is not listed, though their biases and prejudices are. The list is neither exhaustive nor definitive. It paints a picture and helps draw a distinction between the two sides.

■ Crossover items

Some of the aspects listed are crossover items, on a journey from right to left as they gain legitimacy. A good example is networking, once labelled 'skiving'; now it is important to spend time away from your desk talking to a wide variety of people. IBM's fabled white shirt practice had official sanction, though could not be described as rational. 'Dress-down Fridays' legitimise the informal and try to make a corporate standard out of what might otherwise stand out as excessively individualistic, rebellious and challenging.

■ Separate or connected halves

One can think of the two halves of organisational life as comprising separate and competing sides, with the personal features in the shadow side as likely either to constrain or to assist the organisation when attempting to bring about change. In particular, the organisation's culture (Egan's over-riding shadow-side component) may be generally supportive or obstructive in facilitating change.

---

135 London Business School (2008), 'The management innovation agenda', *Labnotes 'Renegade Thinking'*, Issue No 9. London: Management Laboratory, London Business School, September.

Trevor Bentley (2001) takes a more 'holistic' view that sees the organisation as a whole. For him the legitimate and shadow systems act in partnership, connected and overlapping. In the context of managing change, the two systems need to be considered together so that a positive balance can exist between them. Ralph Stacey (1996) says something rather similar:

> 'The basic dynamics of an organization are determined by the manner in which the legitimate system and the shadow system' interact within an organization.'

IRRATIONAL PURSUIT OF THE RATIONAL

Stacey, a well-known writer on complexity and chaos theory, puts forward this definition of the shadow system:

> 'The set of interactions among members of a legitimate system that fall outside that legitimate system. It comprises all social and political interactions that are outside the rules strictly prescribed by the legitimate system. It is the arena in which members of an organisation pursue their own gain ...' (Xin-An Lu, 2000)

Stacey and his colleagues Douglas Griffin and Patricia Shaw (Stacey *et al*, 2000) go further than other management theorists in critiquing managers' belief in the cause of pursuing the rational, arguing:

> 'Most managers continue to believe that their role is essentially one of designing an organization and controlling its activities. The capacity to design and control depends significantly on the possibility of making reasonable enough predictions of the internal and external consequences of one design rather than another and of one action rather than another. Question predictability and you question all of these management beliefs. Furthermore, most managers believe that it is the role of organizational leaders to choose strategic directions and persuade others to follow them. This too is questioned by the claims of management complexity writers about the limits to predictability. Most equate success with states of equilibrium, consensus and conformity. Again, this assumption is called into question by the complexity sciences. Most managers still believe that there will be no coherent patterns in the development of an organization in the absence of a blueprint or plan. The complexity sciences suggest otherwise.'

These authors' depiction of how managers see their role and how they spend their time may be true of only a minority of senior managers. That said, if Stacey *et al* are right about the claims by complexity writers, many management and leadership activities are based on illusory ideas about what these planning activities achieve and thus constitute a serious misdirection of attention and energy.

> 'To the extent that images of the organizational machine and the rational manager still persist, it can be argued that the assumption of rational action itself is tantamount to a 'psychic inflation' which leads to hubris which, eventually, will carry ill-fated consequences.' (Yiannis Gabriel in Sievers, 1999)

The illusion of control

Illusory control is a problem for managers. They think their job is to control and to be in control. Many think, naively, that they actually *are* in control. Those who don't think that believe that their reputation depends on the illusion of control. And they think that the psychological wellbeing of those they (don't) control depends on maintaining that illusion (i.e. 'it's good for them to believe it') – or so they tell themselves.

As far as wellbeing is concerned, for both individuals and organisations, that may depend more on personal freedom and autonomy. According to Kauffman (1996), 'the optimisation of activity within groups and within the organisations as a whole depends upon allowing people the freedom to strive for their own personal fulfilment and that of the community/group to which they belong'.

> 'All organisational functioning lies within the relationships that exist between the individuals who choose to operate within the organisational system in order to satisfy some personal need. All communication and interaction have the single endeavour of personal satisfaction. The desire to conform and the desire to differentiate both have this ultimate focus of attention. ... no organisation can legislate for what might happen in individual relationships. The consequence of this is that it is the ebb and flow of human relationships that determines organisational success and not the visions of leaders ...' (Bentley, 2008).

Complexity science implies that managers must give up control – or rather, the illusion of control – when they are trying to lead their organisation to some goal. But they do need to create the environment in which creativity can emerge (Lewin, 1999).

Leaders can influence the environment in which people work, they can impact on 'what matters to the business', they can cause disturbance, generate energy, all of which might influence the relationships that people have and the choices that they make. But, argues Bentley, it is primarily the relationships and choices of individuals and small work groups that determine the destiny of the business and/or community. All attempts to design, control, direct and lead from the top have the potential to fail to move the organisation in any direction that individuals and their work groups, particularly their shadow groups, don't perceive to be beneficial for them (Bentley, 2008).

Gabriel (1996) considers that the image of leaders and leadership sits alongside that of highly managed and controlled individuals, organisations and societies. This self-serving falsehood needs puncturing. Managers depend on the illusion of control for their reputation, living and high earnings, he claims, which is the source of management hubris.

> Lord King of Wartnaby, chairman of British Airways from 1981 until 1993, instructed the editor of *British Airways News* to run a story and show a picture of him in each fortnightly issue. King argued: 'This is not for me. It's for them. They need to believe in me'. Perhaps they did, but there are ample grounds for remaining

distrustful of power, or of over-exaggerating positional power's importance. Sir Frank MacFadzean, an earlier BA chairman, claimed that he found it impossible to get anything done in the airline: he announced what he wanted, yet nothing happened.

■ Risks of personalising the illusion

Lord King might claim that he satisfied a deep psychological need that people have for certainty. The same might be argued for prime ministers' fondness for the presidential style of appearing to take charge and be in (almost sole) control of events, which may be better explained by a combination of ego and insecurity. Such behaviour, claims Gabriel, is unhealthy and prevents such leaders and their followers from maturing. There is a risk of a leadership personality cult developing inside the organisation.

'All hierarchies, public or private, have the potential to become cults. If the men and women at the top decide that the argument is a species of treason, then everyone who values their career shuts up and knuckles down.' [136]

'I would see some of the most senior people in the bank trembling before Sir Fred Goodwin and saying "I hope it's not my turn to be carpeted". If you raised doubts, you were accused of belonging to the "business prevention unit" and told to shut up or get out.' (Manager at Royal Bank of Scotland)

This internal cult is often mirrored externally with a celebrity cult. Knighthoods and peerages follow. Sir Fred Goodwin was given his knighthood for services to banking and awarded the accolade of 'Businessman of the Year' by Forbes Global 2002 for the takeover of NatWest. Mintzberg (1999) abhors media's conspiracy to portray an organisation's performance as a leader's single-handed achievement.

'Canadian scholar Henry Mintzberg (1999) has expressed his distaste for the 'celebrity-like' focus on those in the most senior leadership positions. He chastises the common practice of business journals to display on their front cover a photo of the latest CEO to single-handedly 'save' his or her company by, for example, enabling a new and highly lucrative product to come to market. He states that they are not only making a ludicrous assertion, they are dismissing the contributions of the many hundreds or thousands of employees in the company. Moreover, they are in danger of contributing to the creation of a culture of emasculation and submission ...' (Alimo-Metcalfe and Alban-Metcalfe, 2008)

The model of success by celebrity leaders, cynically eulogised by the media, not to say politicians, is demeaning all round and, of course, bunkum. The same may be said for an institute's failure; this owes too much to the system, within and beyond the organisation.

---

136   Cohen, N. (2009) 'A club that refuses to accept its failures.' *The Observer*, 15 February.

■ Chaos theory makes control an illusion

The explanation for the aspiration of control being nothing more than an illusion is to be found in chaos theory:

> 'Chaos, in its scientific sense, is not utter confusion. It is constrained instability: a combination of order and disorder in which patterns of behaviour continually unfold in unpredictable but yet similar, familiar, yet irregular forms.' (Stacey, 1992)

Gabriel makes three points in rendering management's professional foundation unstable:

1. Human cognitive capabilities, the unpredictable nature of organisations and the complex link between learning and action preclude full understanding, and therefore control of organisations.
2. Non-rational features of organisations, such as emotions, humour or fantasies, can never be fully controlled through managerial processes, and will always therefore introduce chaotic features in organisations.
3. Organisations entail a bewildering variety of processes of resistance to management controls; these may at times be silenced but can never be overcome, nor can their manifestations be anticipated.

> *'Instead of seeking to contain and control chaos, an alternative strategy might be to try to understand it, and then learn to live with it.'*
> (Yiannis Gabriel, 1996)

According to the garbage can theory of decision-making (Cohen, March and Olsen, 1972), no one in an organisation is in overall control or knows clearly what is going on. According to Gabriel (1996), problems and solutions emerge and collide with each other in an almost accidental manner, producing unintentional or unpredictable effects:

> 'Like the rest of us, managers are most of the time confused, erratic and irrational; they deserve neither exorbitant praise for success nor total vilification for failure.'

Thus leadership of the system means being honest, curious and savvy about unintended consequences and the non-rational and messy shadow-side of organisational dynamics that exist alongside assumed rational decision-making. In an open systems model, the shadow system extends beyond the boundaries of the company's organisation, as in this example:

> In the US House of Representatives' inquiry into the Bernard Madoff Ponzi scheme scandal, Harry Markopolus (a Massachusetts financial analyst) presented 60 pages of evidence showing how he had been trying for nine years to convince the US Securities and Exchange Commission (SEC) that Madoff's financial results were mathematically impossible and fraudulent. SEC officials behaved in a lofty manner, phone calls weren't returned, leads were not followed up, and internal SEC rivalries stopped sympathetic officials from working with Markopolus.[137]

---

137 Pratley, N. (2009) 'Financial Viewpoint: Whistle in the wind'. London: *The Guardian*, 5 February.

The extreme seriousness of many examples is relieved only by their humorous aspect:

> 'It was 9.30 in the evening. The crew of three air force members decided to rest a little and within 15 minutes they were fast asleep. They awoke several hours later. The only problem was that the room in which they were snoozing was the missile alert facility at Minot air force base in North Dakota. Directly beneath them was the control centre containing the keys that can launch ballistic missiles, and in their care were boxes containing codes that allow the nuclear button to be pressed. The incident is the latest in a series of foul-ups and poor ratings that is turning Minot into the Fawlty Towers of the air force.' [138]

While this story raises a chuckle, it also makes a deadly serious point. Huge sums are spent on designing rational systems (such as the 'star wars' missile defence shield) on the basis that when they are required to work they will work. That takes no account of the human factor. Even on a small scale the principle holds.

Consider the case of the Metropolitan police killing of Jean Charles de Menezes. A police surveillance officer missed seeing a suspect because he took a toilet break, and officers following the suspect lost touch when they needed to stop to fill their car with petrol. Plans, designs and intentions can be shot down by realities on the ground. Besides asking the question: 'What is the best possible system we could design, managers need to ask 'What could go wrong?, Where are the possible weaknesses in its operation?'.

Gabriel concludes that:

- Most organisations operate in a chaotic environment, for which they are themselves partly responsible.
- Neither long-term planning nor central control is possible. Simple cause-effect chains do not apply.
- A measure of stability in organisations is not the product of control or rational procedures, but rather the result of spontaneous self-organisation.
- Reverting to rational procedures, routine, cost and waste minimisation, control and linearity undermines creativity and innovation, the very qualities necessary to survive and succeed.
- Strategic plans, mission statements, leadership visions are a total waste of time as instruments of change (though not for overcoming anxiety).

There could be no better illustration of chaos theory's triumph over control, cause-and-effect, good order, planned management and logical decision-making than the global economic crisis beginning in 2008. It was not predictable. Each development caught people unawares. There was no logical path, only a series of loosely connected events that kept emerging.

---

138 Pilkington, E. (2008) 'Sleeping crew held codes for nuclear missiles'. London: *The Guardian*, 26 July.

A growing awareness of complexity and chaos, of the limits of rationality and managerial infallibility may be where some modern management practices, forms of intervention, and new leadership styles stem from. Awareness, combined with humility and other human values, supports the model of more widely distributed leadership, talk of the 'wisdom of crowds', workplace experimentation, and official support for positive shadow-side activity (see the Halfords case study on pages 244-245).

SHADOW NETWORKS

The grapevine (mentioned earlier) is an aspect of the shadow system; its messages are conveyed along shadow networks, rather than the official networks that reflect the formal organisation structure. These unofficial networks are formed out of friendships, social relationships, past colleagues, sympathetic and like-minded thinkers. They extend beyond the boundaries of the firm, and are increasingly electronic and use the internet. Such shadow networks have a significance in organisational life beyond the grapevine.

In the context of this book, what is the role of leadership in understanding and 'managing' these networks? What is the nature of the communities that comprise these networks?

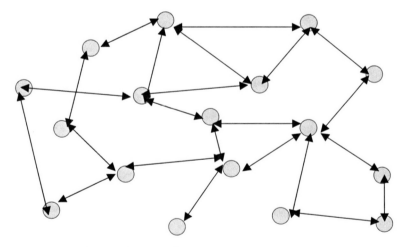

Figure 17: Formal network in a small and simple organisation

Figure 17 represents a simple organisation of seventeen people showing the connections that are required by the organisation for it to achieve its purpose, a form of network hierarchy, according to Bentley (2008). We can call this the formal system. Though some people seem isolated, or only having one or two connections, they are in fact interconnected to everyone in the organisation.

We can superimpose on this the unofficial, shadow network (see Figure 18). Some of the one-to-one connections are duplicated. Others are new. And yet others (not shown) reach outside the organisation yet have a bearing on the organisation's direction, life, creativity and wellbeing.

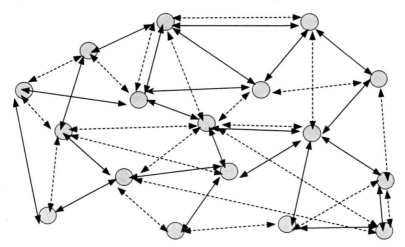

Figure 18: Network in a small and simple organisation overlaid with the shadow network

Bentley explains that where individuals have both a formal and a shadow connection with another individual there is the potential for an effective and influential relationship to develop. The main reason for this is the nature of choice inherent in the shadow connection, usually through a strong mutual resonance. At the same time there is also plenty of space for dissonance, and this is what creates a high degree of creativity and potential for growth.

Resonance and dissonance need to be an acceptable state of balance. (See Figure 19). Excessive dissonance may threaten the survival of the system:

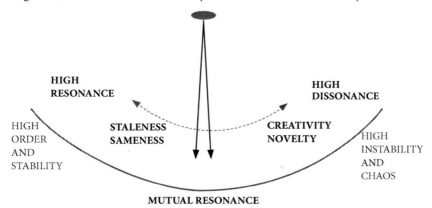

Figure 19: The resonance-dissonance pendulum

INTER-GROUP SHADOW BEHAVIOUR

Projecting one's shadow onto others

According to Carl Jung's work, individuals seek comfort and enhanced self-esteem by casting their less pleasing aspects into their unconscious shadow. They can then pretend – especially to themselves – that these traits don't exist. We all recognise the person who, when having difficulty understanding something, blames the other person for explaining it badly – to make themselves feel better. That way they can claim that the problem is with the other person: '*they* need to change; *I* don't'. The phenomenon has its organisational parallel, which holds ramifications for leadership and group behaviour.

This is how the psychological phenomenon of 'projection' works: unconsciously disowned characteristics in one's shadow that need to be displaced find themselves projected onto someone else (known as a 'screen'). That way the originator can then criticise, blame and find fault in these weaknesses, doing so at the expense of others and not of him/herself.

There is a price to be paid for projection: it is (unconsciously) dishonest and unfair. It can become a source of interpersonal conflict. There is no space or reason for learning and therefore no impetus for self-improvement. It also imposes a burden on leaders, raising unrealistic expectations.

> 'The belief that people on top are "in control" and responsible for everything can be gratifying, partly because it is reassuring to know that at least *somebody* is in control in this world. ... Equating leadership with leaders reflects this kind of dependency, for it locates excessive responsibility at the top. The tendency for groups to believe in the unrealistic power and knowledge of their leaders is what Bion (1959) termed Basic Assumption Dependency, one of the main unconscious strategies employed to bind the troubling anxieties that arise in work situations.' (Krantz, 1990)

Pierre Turquet (1974) observed that leaders are active targets for other members' projection of love, hate, responsibility and blame, and are thus profoundly influenced by their followers. Thus are the seeds of a cult sown.

Projecting the group shadow

The above illustrates the consequence of projection for individuals and their employing organisation. But we can go further: what is true of individuals is also true of groups. Organisations may display dysfunctional behaviour based on group shadows that are conveniently projected onto other groups, whom the first group then loads with an 'enemy image', as, for example, between the marketing and operations departments.

> 'A group may consciously or unconsciously create or focus on an enemy group to avoid openly confronting internal tensions and problems. ... The enemy group functions as a scapegoat for what are experienced as unacceptable negative qualities, impulses, feelings, and thoughts within the group.' (Gemmill, 1986)

The practice operates at a national level too. US President Ronald Reagan thus 'invented' Russia as the 'evil empire', replete with many of the self-same traits that other countries were in turn projecting onto the United States and its government – territorial ambition, military hostility, world domination, etc. In his own eyes Reagan's motives were probably as white as the driven snow. Clearly, politics plays a part here, assisting one's own image and manipulating the electorate. But it may not be fanciful to suggest that international misunderstandings, animosity and hostilities can result from projecting onto the other party what may be one's own suppressed group shame. Recognising, understanding and managing this phenomenon holds implications for leadership, not just at an organisational level but in a global context as well.

■ Integrating the shadow

If managers can develop greater self-awareness and can learn to expect and recognise such behaviour in themselves, then this is a starting point for their taking ownership of the traits that they seek to push into their shadow. They may then be able to reflect upon this and consider the possibility of making personal changes. If they can also learn to expect the same of others, they may be more understanding towards them and temper their temptation to retaliate. This process is called 'integrating the shadow'. For individuals to complete this process is a lifelong calling.

> 'No man ever quite understands his own
> artful dodges to escape from the grim shadow
> of self-knowledge.' (*Lord Jim*, Joseph Conrad)

But how practically does this behaviour and advice apply at an organisational level?

> 'The war to end all wars never works because, although a group might annihilate its enemy, it cannot annihilate its shadow. A new enemy will be invented unless the members of the group learn how to deal more directly with the shadow. Until a group can own its shadow and internally begin work on it, it will be haunted by it, finding it everywhere.' (Gemmill, 1986)

Silo behaviour

The existence of silos in organisations will be familiar to anyone who works in a large and complex structure. Groups and departments erect firm walls around themselves; they defend their territory, role and local goals against other groups at the expense of the wider interests of the organisation, services or customer need as a whole. In the case of Victoria Climbié, the various agencies exhibited silo behaviour, to the extent that the social services department put up a notice against involving the police.

■ What is going on?

As we have seen, groups manage and protect their own identity and favourable image by bolstering their own at the expense of others. Any group has its own dysfunction within itself; for example, it may be inefficient, bureaucratic, excessively competitive or internally rancorous. But such aspects are 'worked out' by projecting these failings onto other groups, which thereby acquires an enemy image, while claiming harmony and other virtues for itself.

Some of these targeted groups may go on to acquire scapegoat status in the organisation (see Birchmore, 2003); this sometimes happens to a Human Resources department. In society and the media it appears to happen to social workers. The impression thus created within the initiating group is that its members are justified in not wanting to communicate and cooperate freely across these departmental boundaries. By such processes are the foundations laid for classic silo behaviour.

■ What can be done?

In some measure the solution is similar to that mentioned above for individuals. If managers can recognise what is going on, and if they can afford to put aside any political advantage in painting other groups as flawed and inferior, they may behave more maturely and see their own groups' shortcomings and choose to address them.

Such solutions lie in the realm of psychodynamics: the psychologically based dynamics within and between individuals and also between groups that focuses on the interplay between conscious and unconscious motivation. At the group level, there is still much to learn, and there is a shortage of expert facilitation skills able to cope with such sensitive group behaviour. But awareness is a good place to start.

There are additional ways of responding to silo behaviour that are based in the rational domain. In Chapter 14, *Leadership and Accountability*, I explain a managerial response that makes use of the accountability structure to bring about increased cooperation. But the foregoing discussion attempts to explain why such an intervention might be needed by showing how the problem might have arisen in the first place.

MANAGING THE SHADOW SYSTEM

Achieving a balanced state

From the list in Table 31 it is easy to see how an organisation in which the shadow-side variables predominate might be chaotic or anarchic. On the other hand, if these are strongly repressed, the organisation might be too restrictive, predictable and unimaginative. Hence, we reach the idea that these two sides of the organisation form an equation, with some kind of balance needing to exist between them, as Bentley (2001) argues.

The balance of power and influence that one side has vis-à-vis the other varies between organisations. Some workplaces are fairly straightforward, predictable, easy to fathom and possible to manage. Others remain a mystery, are 'crazy' and difficult to manage unless you understand the quaint rules and have well-honed political skills.

The legitimate system

The legitimate system embodies the aims, purpose and values of the organisation as espoused and understood by its leaders or authority figures. In the legitimate system people operate in conformity with the established culture. They do things the 'way that things are done around here'.

This is the way the organisation claims to understand its culture and wishes to present it. It's how an induction programme might tell recruits 'this is how we do things round here' (with the implied 'and we expect you to comply'). This might be less than the full picture as seen by those not in authority. When recruits later join their department, they may be told to forget what was said and 'this is what really happens'. This is akin to 'You can forget that' said occasionally to people returning from training courses.

The shadow system

Bentley (2001) points out that this system is more obscure. People participate in ways that serve their own needs rather than those of their organisation, a point echoed by Stacey (1996). This is the system that supports people in being who they are rather than how the organisation needs them to be.

In this view, the canteen is not just for eating. So-called 'canteen culture' gives life and energy to the shadow system. Among other things, it permits the exchange of gossip about the legitimate system and those in authority. Ironically, the legitimate system may be a few yards away, represented by the curtained-off senior managers' dining area!

A healthy organisation finds ways of legitimising discussion of things talked about in the 'canteen culture' of the shadow system. In overly formal systems these issues remain undiscussed and undiscussible, as observed by Egan.

Overlapping systems

'We can perceive an object only if it includes both light and shadow.' (Burkard Sievers, 1999)

The two systems overlap. The nature and the amount of overlap can vary, as can whether the two systems are joined (a healthy condition) or one is eclipsing the other as in a solar eclipse (an unhealthy loss of light).

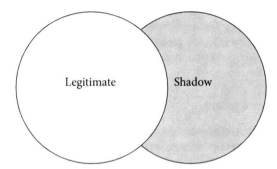

Figure 20: Bentley's overlapping legitimate and shadow system

- If the shadow system is eclipsed by the legitimate system it might mean that people are constrained by an autocratic regime.
- If the shadow system dominates and eclipses the legitimate system, it is more likely that anarchy reigns.
- If the two systems are far apart, the organisation may disintegrate.
- If the two systems are well joined, then the shadow system is supportive of the legitimate system.
- If there is a little overlap, the shadow system may be pressing for change.

Change interventions

The majority of change initiatives in organisations are aimed at the legitimate system. But without the support of the shadow system, it is unlikely that the changes will be successful. Change in Halfords provides a good illustration of the two systems working together.

'In 2000, Halfords was embarking on a period of change. The UK's largest retailer of car parts, cycles and associated leisure products was revamping its 400-plus outlets and introducing new approaches in head office, but staff felt disenfranchised. In the warehouse industrial action had only been narrowly avoided, and the atmosphere was one of control and conformity. ... Instead of getting stuck in the traditional mindset which says that organisations are like machines – so that all that is needed are the right "levers", a plan and a timetable of implementation – Ashridge Consulting prefers an ongoing dialogue. ...

'The technique [known as "appreciative inquiry"] demands that managers abandon the illusion of executive omnipotence. Traditionally, managers like to give the impression that they are able to control, or steer the cultures of their businesses. But with appreciative inquiry everyone gets involved in the process, and both staff and managers must admit that there is no set goal before setting out on their journey. ... In one workshop event the warehouse team acted on a long-standing issue. They got together over tea and called for the removal of the warehouse's most disliked feature – a buzzer that controlled their breaks. One of the guys stood up and said:

"We are going in tomorrow and we are going to rip out the buzzer", [adding a pledge] "we will always be where we need to be when we need to be there".

'... the "pull" approach ... of working with conversation, storytelling and relationship has enabled a new culture to start to develop. It is based on the idea of lighting a few small fires (rather than the usual "big bang" type change initiative). Some of them will go out and you assume that they were not supposed to catch in the first place, but the ones that catch alight will spread faster and soon everything is ablaze.' [139]

Seen like this, there is clear value in the shadow system. It serves as a natural safety valve where people can take care of themselves against the rigours of their formal roles. Streetwise managers will respect this shadow system, understand its nature and maintain it as a kind of semi-legitimate counterweight to the official legitimate system. Like an organisation's overall culture, the shadow system may be dominant and troubling, or more benign, subdued and quiescent. If the shadow system is too powerful and apart, the organisation may disintegrate. Too close to the legitimate system and too controlled by it, the organisation may ossify.

In the Halfords example, the shadow system had enough guts to exert itself but was close enough to the legitimate system to be contained and channelled positively.

The shadow system provides people with a safe place to develop their resistance to the demands of the legitimate system. Because of this, systemic interventions need to be directed at both the legitimate system and the shadow system.

> 'If the needs of the shadow system are ignored, it is likely that the interventions will push the shadow system much closer to anarchy than it currently might be.' (Trevor Bentley, in Tate, 2003b)

The shadow's shadow

When the shadow system acquires a degree of official sanction it may encounter shadow aspects of its own. A recent example is the case of the social worker turned whistleblower in the Haringey 'Baby P' murder. Having blown the whistle, she was herself subjected to disciplinary proceedings (on page 204 John Renesch described how systems close ranks against whistleblowers in an attempt to restore stability). She responded by taking legal action (using an official shadow system of human rights enshrined in law to counter her employer's official hierarchical system). But she then encountered the crazy nature of that system: her application arrived as the law was switching responsibilities between government departments, and her papers were mislaid and shuffled. Months

---

139 Abridged from (2003) 'A little more conversation,' Management Consultancy Association Awards. *The Guardian*, 6 February.

were lost while the case was transferred between two police officers and other mistakes were made. The result was that Baby P's death was not prevented, although with hindsight it should have been.

Ossification versus disintegration

Everything is constantly changing, a point often not understood, according to Bentley. Order is inevitably followed by disturbance and a period of chaos, which in turn is followed by the creation of a new order. Any attempt to resist this 'dance of life' leads to ossification and/or disintegration.

Ossification occurs when the old order is rigidly maintained using an increasingly doctrinaire legitimate system. The inflexible demand for conformity causes people to contract; creativity dies, and the organisation withers away.

Disintegration occurs when the shadow system is so far removed from the legitimate system that the two cannot he reunited. People become so expanded and diverse in the shadow system that the legitimate system no longer holds any value or purpose for them and so it and the organisation die.

The twin dangers of ossification and disintegration can be avoided by judicious interventions in both the legitimate and shadow systems.

Organisations have a tendency to try to force order out of chaos by focusing their attention on the legitimate system. The effect is to generate resistance.

SUMMARY OF CHAPTER KEY POINTS

1. Organisations are not rational places. Besides their formal/official side, organisations have a more potent non-rational side – messy, crazy and sometimes dark, casting a shadow – which can be, and needs to be, recognised, understood and managed.

2. The shadow aspect of the organisation's nature and dynamic can be depicted as a system which describes, explains, contributes to, and displays the reality, richness and at times dysfunctionality of organisational life and performance.

3. The shadow half of organisational life is tragi-comical. There are times to laugh at it, times to be grateful for it, and times for sadness, horror, disgust, grief … but also challenge and hope.

4. The shadow system is inevitable, and needs to be held in a healthy and balanced relationship with the rational/formal/legitimate system.

5. Awareness of, and respect for, the shadow system's contribution and power is essential for effective leadership, especially in the context of change. A healthy scepticism for the rational system's relative impotence (e.g. the futility of relying on edicts) is also a prerequisite of effective leadership, and avoidance of hubris and naivety.

6. Failure to understand and work with the grain of the shadow side and its network is a major source of failure to achieve efficiency gains, as in centralisation, specialisation, economies of scale, hot-desking, targets, inspection and IT.

7. Besides formal networks, and organisation's relationships, interactions and communications have informal ('shadow') networks within its shadow system.

8. The balance between the two networks affects the degree of resonance and dissonance in the organisation (or department/community/group). This, in turn, influences how creative or unsettled the group is.

9. The ability of leaders to shape the destiny of an organisation and fulfilment of their vision is constrained by the self-interested nature of the shadow network. But leaders can foster an appropriate environment for the shadow network's self-interest.

10. For an organisation to be vital, innovative, flexible and changing, it needs to be held at a point that is just stable – not ossified but not anarchic – at a point known as 'the edge of chaos'.

CHAPTER 14:

LEADERSHIP AND ACCOUNTABILITY

☐ *Being held to account*

☐ *Accountability for leadership*

☐ *Individual and collective accountability*

☐ *Accountability versus responsibility*

☐ *Elements in the accountability process*

☐ *Accountability for the system*

Ask what 'accountability' means in organisations, and several thoughts spring to mind. Responses include the cynical 'no one ever loses their job here however bad their performance'. Some people may mention *'paying for failure'*; i.e. the practice of paying huge sums to top executives who fail and are fired. Such perceptions are – with some justification – indicative of a widespread lack of accountability and a failure to practise oversight with foresight. More precisely, they represent a failure by organisations to manage a practical and formal process for holding senior executives properly to account, preferably before failure or poor performance ensues.

While accountability ought to be a key factor in the management of any organisation, in practice it is unimaginatively conceived, poorly understood, relatively neglected and badly executed. For some organisations, 'Have you returned your appraisal form to HR?' is as good as it gets.

Familiar aspects of accountability, such as lists of principal accountabilities and managers' reporting lines of accountability, contribute little to improving an organisation's leadership effectiveness. The key piece in the performance management jigsaw is usually missing altogether; that is, senior managers' accountability specifically for their leadership.

> *'There is a "governance vacuum" at the top of Whitehall: lines of accountability are confused and leadership structures are weak.'* [140] (Guy Lodge, Research Fellow at the Institute of Public Policy Research)

---

140 Lodge, G. (2006) 'An end to mandarin ducking and diving'. London: *Society Guardian 'Public Manager'*, 6 September.

This chapter explores the many facets of leadership accountability and the part it can play in making an organisation successful if a process is properly designed, respected and conducted.

Holding managers to account

The best-known aspect of accountability is that organisations typically spell out managers' so-called *accountabilities*. The term refers to the most important things that managers are responsible for, sometimes prefaced with 'key' or 'principal'. It is doubtful whether managers or employers who use the term this way actually mean those things for which the manager will directly and formally be held to account in a serious and meaningful way. More often, it simply describes the scope of the job.

Many organisations give little practical thought to how managers should properly be held to account for the most important things in their job. These may not be the most important things in their job *description*. The really important things may arise in, or take the form of, short-term projects, crises, specific objectives and the unexpected.

The main value of the job description may not lie in highlighting the most important things for which the manager should be held to account, but as a longer-term, unchanging, background document, used mainly for job sizing purposes. So the link between a manager's stated accountabilities and being held to account for them is, at best, tenuous.

There is a growing awareness that managing and leading are different, but HR systems rarely acknowledge this. Lists of principal accountabilities don't make this distinction, beyond expressions such as 'leads a team of ...'; but the word 'leads' may merely be the equivalent of 'manages', 'is responsible for', 'heads up', 'in charge of', etc. In most organisations' performance management systems, the two roles of managing and leading are usually conflated and discussed as one. Yet there could be considerable value in bringing out the different facets in such settings. This would make it possible to hold managers to account specifically for their leadership. The core question remains:

> *For what and how should managers be tested, challenged and properly held to account, especially for their exercise of leadership (where it is most important and when it is most needed)?*

○ **Example: Breach of anti-trust legislation**   Four senior British Airways managers (one of them the director of marketing) contravened anti-trust legislation by colluding with Virgin Atlantic in 2004-5 to raise fuel surcharges simultaneously. This raises a number of questions concerning their accountability:

1. Beyond losing their jobs, what was the process by which the managers were held to account, once discovered?

2. How were they being held to account on an ongoing basis before being discovered; i.e. during their normal work in this period?
3. Who, representing the interests of the company and its stakeholders, was holding these managers to account, or should have been?
4. Was it clear what the managers were being held to account for?
5. What was the role of the official to whom they were accountable who himself bore accountability for operating a system by which his direct reports could be held to account?
6. What directions had been given to these managers concerning their activities by the person to whom they were accountable? [141]

A proper system of accountability should be in place before something goes wrong, avoiding the need to hurriedly put one in place afterwards. It may help to prevent transgressions and failure.

> Many years ago a senior director in British Airways said to the chief executive: 'HR say that the company's new performance review system should apply to all managers, and not just the middle and lower-level managers. They say that includes directors. I have accepted their argument. Will you please discuss with me my objectives for the coming year?'
>
> Chief executive replies to the director: 'Don't worry. When you are not getting it right, you'll soon know!'

Performance reviews

Mention of 'accountability' triggers thoughts about a company's regular performance review system. Arguably too much is laid at its door. The procedure rarely delivers well against its purpose of holding managers to account. It is not seen as a vital accountability tool, more a personnel system requiring compliance. The level of managers most in need of being held to account may even be deemed too senior to fall within the scope of the scheme.

Under modern pressure to embrace self-review, and in the spirit of participation and empowerment, the review process nowadays frequently takes on a bottom-up, self-managed flavour. However well-intentioned, this is hardly a solid foundation for holding an official to account.

Accountability as paperwork

There is an attitude that equates demonstrating accountability to the appropriate authority with the completion of 'box-ticking' paperwork. The purpose is to indicate that certain required actions have been completed. This bureaucratic process justifies itself by invoking the name of accountability.

---

141 Once discovered, the issue became a legal matter and therefore *sub judice*.

> '... there is perhaps a more insidious threat than the re-direction of funding away from informal adult education. It lies in the obsessive push for accountability, driven by the government and enforced by the Learning & Skills Council and Ofsted. ... for most students Workers' Educational Association (WEA) courses are not about getting qualifications. This worries a government that likes to measure everything to satisfy Treasury targets. So, as a substitute for the hard currency of qualifications, the tutors of these courses are being inundated with bureaucratic form-filling.
>
> 'In a typical WEA adult education class, tutors must submit a course outline and set out the learning outcomes (LOs). Students must be assessed against each LO at the start and end of each course. Tutors must distribute learning records (LRs) to students at the first class. These must be collected and the courses modified in the light of student responses. At the end of courses, these LRs must be issued again alongside an evaluation form. The tutor must then collect these, read them, and fill out a tutor report. This involves providing extraordinary detail on topics too numerous to mention here, including "how well did you meet the learners' needs and interests" and "how well did you guide and support learners to progress?".' [142]

Not only does the requirement for measurable accountability strangle the freedom necessary in the learning process, it also assumes that the responsibility is one way. But surely learners have responsibilities to their tutors too? The design of evaluation documentation can capture this.

What happens when something goes amiss?

The most familiar aspect of accountability is seen when things go badly wrong in an organisation. When the worst happens, the media, public, institutional investors and shareholders complain that rarely is anyone held accountable (by which they mean found guilty and dismissed).

○ **Example: Collapse of Northern Rock** A topical example is the failure of banks to manage risk. In the case of Northern Rock, the UK government removed the board. The subsequent collapse of some investment banks has resulted in chief executives having no option but to resign. In all these cases there appears to have been an absence of an adequate system of accountability *before* disaster struck. Who was properly holding the chief executive to account, and for what? Was it for his leadership? Was it for securing tomorrow as well as delivering today? Long term as well as short term? Or was it simply a case of 'have you hit the growth targets and earned your bonus'?

Where drastic and dramatic action is taken, the high-profile dismissal of a senior manager seems to happen in the absence of a systematic and mutually respectful process for holding senior managers to account; i.e. one that runs continually as part of the company's ongoing performance management framework, and not just after something has gone wrong.

---

142 Baker, M. (2008) 'Form filling could kill off adult learning'. London: *Education Guardian*, 15 April.

When hubris takes hold

I return to the subject of hubris here (considered more fully in Chapter 11) in order to discuss its implications for accountability.

Once hubris takes hold, a proper sense of responsibility to all one's stakeholders wanes. The office takes on the form of a private fiefdom where employment relationships become personal and open to accusations of cronyism.

> 'There is a certain type of male macho manager who loves the idea of rising to the challenge of betting the company when the established odds are at least even to three against. For them there appears to be an intensely virile appeal to the idea, and you can almost smell the testosterone when you enter their office.'
> (Scott-Morgan, 1995)

■ The case of Sir Fred Goodwin and Royal Bank of Scotland

'Chief author of his bank's demise is Sir Fred Goodwin, who heads Royal Bank of Scotland and whose nickname "Fred the Shred" reflects his approach to businesses he takes over. But "shred" could now equally be applied to the bank itself. RBS has never recovered from Goodwin's ego-driven deal to buy Dutch bank ABN Amro at the top of the market last year. ... he took home £5.4m in salary and bonus, and that was without his long-term incentive plan paying out. But his ambition to be a world leader has almost broken the 281-year-old institution ... He pursued the takeover against dissenting voices among his own shareholders – even after ABN Amro had sold the American assets he prized, and when it became clear the world had changed as the credit crunch took hold. ... It is time to hold bankers to account.' [143]

As CEO, Sir Fred paid for his reckless behaviour with his job and reputation, a blow no doubt softened by his extravagant pension. So did his chairman, Sir Tom McKillop, punished for not controlling his chief executive's excesses – i.e. his ambitions, decisions and manner. But the leadership accountability process failed in two ways:

- First, McKillop was not properly managing the CEO's accountability to the chairman, acting for the company and mindful of the board's responsibilities, not least to shareholders. In the City's corporate governance regulations (the 'combined code') this 'check and balance' is the key reason behind the separation of powers of these two roles.
- Secondly, CEO Goodwin was found to have been accountable (i.e. 'retired') only *after* failure. Shareholders, and other stakeholders including society, need the accountability process to be delivering benefits *before* things go so calamitously wrong.

---

143 Hargreaves, D. 'We should take the axe to these architects of downfall'. *The Guardian*, 10 October.

■ The case of Sir Ian Blair and Ken Livingstone

'After the Stockwell affair [the Metropolitan Police's shooting of Jean Charles De Menezes], when [then] London mayor Ken Livingstone stood four square behind Sir Ian [Blair] as many clamoured for the commissioner's head, Livingstone ceased to be seen as a mayor who would ever hold the police to account.' [144]

When the innocent Brazilian was shot by mistake by armed Metropolitan police at Stockwell tube station in 2005, Ken Livingstone, had a choice – if he had thought about it. His choice was not between whether to speak in support or in criticism of Sir Ian Blair; instead his choice was between, on the one hand, *taking a position* (in support or against), or on the other hand *leading a process* on behalf of Londoners by which Sir Ian Blair would have to account for his force's actions, leaving the judgement to follow from that process. By taking an instant personal position, he was foregoing the opportunity and responsibility afforded by his office for systemic leadership; i.e. in this instance for putting in place and conducting a properly democratic accountability process.

There was a process of a kind, but one that was unsatisfactory. Leaving aside the officers who fired the bullets, and those responsible for coordinating their actions and giving orders, first, Sir Ian Blair was not properly held to account at the time of the killing. In 2007 he lost a vote of confidence of the Metropolitan Police Authority, was insulted by the Conservative members and insulted them in return, taunting them to force him to resign, which they had no power to do. He subsequently chose to resign at the end of 2008 under pressure from the new London mayor, Boris Johnson.

Secondly, of course, Ken Livingstone (the then London mayor) in turn, was not held properly to account by the London Assembly for, among other things, (not) running a proper governance process within which accountability is recognised as an important element. The retort that the public do that every four years is a cop out (sic). The above examples illustrate the bunker syndrome, as leaders eventually fall siege and withdraw.

> '... to go up against Ken ... it was like Apocalypse Now. *He'd holed up in his lair and allowed things to go to his head. ... [I had the] sad obligation of having to dispatch him.'* [145]
> (Boris Johnson, 2008)

Politicians are particularly prone to adopting rapid personal and party political positions. They are less inclined to take a managerial perspective, most of them lacking managerial experience. The public's expectation of the politician offering an immediate view reinforces the behaviour. The lack of a managerial perspective is exacerbated when non-executive mayors become executive mayors.

---

144 Muir, H. (2008) 'Ignoring beacons, Brand Ken sailed into a perfect storm'. London: *The Guardian*, 3 May.

145 Barber, L. (2008) 'Boris Johnson – The Interview'. London: *The Observer*, 19 October.

The focus of accountability

There are numerous cases from politics and big business where the vital management act of holding managers to account as a matter of routine is given little thought or attention. It is a serious muddle. The overarching accountability question of interest to any organisation is:

> *How clear, well developed, understood, respected and observed is the system for regularly and routinely holding top executives and senior managers to account, especially for their leadership?*

The need varies. In some sectors, processes are relatively well understood but are simply not observed and managed. In others they require fresh thought and even reinvention, as with the senior civil service.

> 'Conventions [in the Civil Service] are anachronistic and severely inadequate. This is particularly true of the most important of them, the doctrine of ministerial responsibility, which holds that ministers alone are accountable for everything that happens in their departments. Developed in pre-democratic times, it now needs recasting to take account of 21st century government. Times have changed.' [146]

Key supplementary questions for organisations are:

- How is the accountability system designed to work?
- How well does it actually work?
- Are senior managers held to account for both delivering today as well as securing tomorrow?
- Are senior managers held to account distinctively for their leadership?
- Is it clear what managers are responsible *for*?
- Is it clear who managers have responsibilities *to*?
- Is it clear to whom managers account for fulfilling these responsibilities?
- Are senior managers held to account singly or jointly with colleagues, or a mix of both?
- Where appropriate, how is collective accountability managed?
- How well equipped are top executives to provide oversight for the leadership and management of their senior managers?

Take the case of a CEO with directors reporting to him who have professional and technical responsibilities (e.g. an airline's chief pilot or an HR Director). How does the CEO know what questions to ask in order to be able properly to exercise supervision? How much has to be left to trust and chance? Good reflective questions for the boss to ask the director include the following:

- What are your department's strengths and weaknesses?
- What are its opportunities and threats?

---

146 Lodge, G. (2006) *ibid.*

- What are you achieving?
- What feedback do you receive from your customers?
- What are your managers' perceptions and expectations of what you provide?
- What are the main obstacles to your managers doing a better job?
- What is your department's bottom line?
- What are the important political issues?
- How does your department's culture and climate need to change? [147]

The effect of new structures

Modern management structures are making life increasingly difficult for accountability systems to keep pace. Consider larger spans of control, geographically dispersed teams, home-working patterns, outsourced functions, cross-boundary working arrangements, private finance initiative (PFI) behind public private partnerships (PPPs). All these developments can work against holding managers to account via the chain of command.

A system of 360 degree feedback represents a welcome inroad into the hierarchical system by enabling a variety of stakeholders (to whom a manager has responsibilities) to register their feedback. The approach acknowledges the complexity of today's multiple responsibilities (both to and for others) and reveals the ever-increasing shortcomings of command-and-control methods.

Responsibilities versus accountabilities

John Kay, the eminent economist, explains that someone may be responsible *for* or responsible *to*. They may also be responsible to people to whom they are not accountable. Many people display confusion about these terms, and use them loosely, losing sight of important nuances.

> *'You can be responsible to people to whom you are not accountable. ... I feel a responsibility to the readers of this newspaper to begin the process of unravelling'* [148] (John Kay)

Kay uses the example of borrowing a lawnmower from a neighbour to make the distinctions clear:

> 'When I borrow a lawnmower from you, my neighbour, I am responsible for the lawnmower but responsible to you. I do not have any duty or obligation to the lawnmower, but I do to you. ... Company directors are responsible to shareholders, and perhaps others, for their relations with customers and employees. But they are also responsible to their customers and employees.
> 'We might argue about the extent of that responsibility – that is what the stakeholder

---

147   Tate, W. (1995a) *ibid.*

148   Kay, J. (1999) 'Blurring of responsibility'. London: *Financial Times*, 21 July.

> debate is all about – but that it exists is not seriously open to question. At a minimum, the company should treat its employees and customers with fairness, honesty and decency – not because such treatment is in the interests of shareholders, but because that is how you behave. We have responsibilities to others simply by virtue of living and working in modern Britain.
>
> 'This is a not a theoretical point. The 1985 Companies Act [since superseded] makes explicit provision for directors to recognise the interests of employees. It does so because cases had cast doubt on the propriety of directors approving provision for redundant employees in excess of the legal minimum. They felt responsible to workers they were no longer responsible for.
>
> '... The second confusion is between responsibility and accountability ... You are not necessarily responsible to the people you are accountable to ... The home secretary is responsible for the queues outside the Passport Office. He is responsible to you, me and the people in the queue. He is accountable to parliament for the discharge of these responsibilities.' [149]

Drawing on Kay's model, managers are responsible *to* their staff and to their customers and to other stakeholders. They are also responsible *for* their staff, but not for their customers. They are accountable *to* their line manager for the way they fulfil their various responsibilities to others.

Accounting for the leadership process, not leaders

When accounting for performance, a discussion and a distinct focus on the process of leading is almost always missing. Instead, the centre of attention is the individual, and then on that person's general performance. A focus on the *organisation's* leadership is even more rare. These holes in the reviewing and accounting process are serious gaps in most organisations' performance management of leadership.

The accountability gap

Systemic leadership takes a keen interest in the organisation's many gaps – that is, the cracks that open up between individuals, cracks within and between leadership teams and departmental functions, cracks in the leadership culture, and cracks in leadership-related systems, especially the accountability system. Together they amount to failures in risk management; they may cause the organisation as a whole to fail to manifest high-quality leadership.

 o **Example: Learning and Skills Council** The LSC is being closed in 2010 by the Government after a chequered and expensive history. Nonetheless, the LSC commissioned a consultancy to examine the way it handles the huge amount of knowledge and information it gathers.

---

149 Kay, J. (1999), *ibid.*

> A damning, confidential report into the Learning and Skills Council says ... there is a lack of collaboration between different departments and its nine regions in England. The report concludes that ... the quango "does not operate as a single organisation where knowledge and experience flow instinctively between its teams and functions. It works in silos." ... Some staff told the report's compilers that they felt that the LSC's most recent organisational changes had "specifically discouraged collaboration and knowledge sharing". ... impediment to sharing what works arise from the competition between the quango's nine regions. It recommends ... staff to be taught to collaborate.' [150]

Leaving aside the futility of the final recommendation above ('staff to be taught to collaborate'), which is a system issue not a personal competence one, the LSC case raises several issues specifically concerning accountability:

- What were LSC's top executives being held to account for? Did everyone know?
- Was it clear where accountability lay for how well the LSC organisation was designed and operated?
- Were the LSC's top executives previously unaware of the silo problem? What were they doing about it?
- Where did accountability lie for the earlier redesign? Where did accountability lie for the cost of this latest research?

Possible focuses for accountability

The performance management/accountability issues discussed in this chapter can be brought together in the matrix below:

REVIEWING THE PERFORMANCE OF MANAGEMENT AND LEADERSHIP		
ROLE	MANAGING	LEADING
	Operational management to deliver today. Works within the current paradigm.	Strategic leadership to secure tomorrow. Challenges the current paradigm.
THE FOCUS OF THE PERFORMANCE REVIEW	Tends to emphasise management skills.	Tends to emphasise leadership skills.
1. The individual reviewee's performance as an individual Sole responsibility in the context of: ☐ oneself ☐ one's team members ☐ one's other stakeholders ☐ one's organisation systems.	*Usually the dominant or the only focus.*	*More focus needed here.*

150   Kingston, P. (2008) 'Council now learning to let go'. London: *The Guardian*, 15 July.

2. The individual reviewee's performance as a colleague The same person as above but viewed as a team member (as a member of an executive group), with responsibilities across functions.	*E.g. not screwing things up for a colleague running a parallel function or service. Internal department relationships.*	*Entails standing to one side of the operational role – intellectually and frequently physically – to see things (esp. standards) objectively, both as they are and as they need to become.*
3. The team's performance The organisation's collective team working as a joined-up entity to deliver combined performance against a set of shared goals (where this is the case, as in joint projects, or where widescale coordination is essential).	*May be for a combined activity affecting several departments. (E.g. an airline's passenger arrivals and departures operation. Affects flight and cabin crew, ground operations, engineering, catering, ground handling, etc.)*	*Improving a combined activity. May affect several external stakeholders, e.g. in the example given, Air Traffic Control.*
4. The organisation's performance How well the organisation is working as a system: its structure, values, beliefs, everyday norms of behaviour, purpose and goals, processes, workflows, coordination, internal and external relationships with stakeholders. Review of parties' role and performance in relation to this.	*Review and develop systems and structures etc. to support more effective leadership practice needed to deliver today.*	*Review and develop systems and structures etc. to build leadership capacity and enhance leadership practice needed to secure tomorrow.* *How leaders' methods of 'empowerment' involve and challenge subordinates to propose and deliver change according to goals and terms set by the leader.*
5. The reviewer's own performance Self-review in the same categories.		

Table 32: Reviewing the performance of management and leadership

The purpose of the matrix is to help reviewers make distinctions between:

1. the reviewee's performance as an individual (in the context of oneself, one's managed team, one's other stakeholders, one's organisation systems);
2. the reviewee's performance as a managerial team player with peers (i.e. as a cooperative colleague);
3. the team's performance;
4. the performance of the organisation as a system;
5. the reviewer's own performance (self-review).

It then divides these five levels between the context of delivering today (mostly a managing issue) and that of securing tomorrow (more of a leading issue).

The separation of managing and leading mirrors the distinction drawn earlier between the dual responsibilities that managers have both to 'do the job and change the job'; that is, to achieve what they can within the existing paradigm and also to challenge and improve the paradigm to make it more fit for the future.

The point about changing the paradigm focuses attention on the organisation. The matrix reminds reviewers not just to review the performance of their managers (the fish), but also to review the performance of the system (the fishtank) and their own role as cleaners. A good question to ask is:

> What is it about the organisation's culture, systems and protocols that inhibits your own and your managers' appropriate leadership, and how can these barriers be removed?

Quis custodiet ipsos custodies?

The matrix raises an interesting governance issue. The treatment of the senior managers mentioned earlier who lost their jobs for breaching anti-trust law, was a corporate governance matter, one that is the proper concern of the board of directors, especially the chairman and the non-executive directors. In cases like this, the need for a system of oversight[151] is clear cut. The president of the Association of Chartered Certified Accountants, Richard Aitken-Davies, pinpoints the issue affecting the banking sector:

> 'Something has gone seriously wrong with corporate governance. This catastrophic failure [in the banking sector in September 2008] highlights the need for ethics and professionalism to be at the heart of business. ... Remuneration and incentivisation packages for senior figures within the banking world have become too closely linked to short-term, easy-to-manipulate financial metrics.' [152]

But where in organisations is oversight of the governance *process* itself? Who, for example, is holding the HR Director to account for designing and advising on a clear process by which managers at all levels are held to account – differentially for today and tomorrow, for themselves, for others and for the system? Is it even clear in an organisation who holds accountability for the smooth running of the organisation as a system? Is it each head of department? Or do HR directors regard this as one of their roles? If so, are they equipped to undertake that role?

○ **Example: Accountability for child protection** An increasingly common problem for organisations is that the everyday operational system crosses many boundaries. Take the case of child protection services (see case of Baby P discussed earlier). There are several major parties who collectively deliver that system. These include the local authority, police, schools and hospitals. Added to this list are several other bodies and agencies: the government's Department for Children, Schools and Families, Ofsted, the Healthcare Commission and the

---

151 In the sense of overseeing, not neglecting

152 Aitken-Davies, R. (2008) *ibid.*

Audit Commission. There is also the cross-party Commons Select Committee for Children, Schools and Families, which can summon officials to appear before it and ask them to account for their action, yet which has no formal authority to hold them accountable.

In Baby P's case, Haringey Council's Director of Children and Young Persons Services seemed to be expected to hold the ring and shoulder the blame for the system's failings. But she didn't design the overall system, or the national IT system that supports it.

In complex systems like this the government needs to be more clear about where accountably lies and how a fair accountability process should operate.

Single-point or multiple accountability

Popular advice seems to be to make an individual alone clearly responsible for an activity. Conventional wisdom says this assists that person's motivation. It is also claimed to make it easier to hold them to account when things go wrong; if several people are collectively involved it is more difficult to pinpoint where responsibility for failure rests. This example from the NHS reveals the strains:

> 'The government's chief medical officer, Sir Liam Donaldson, will be reprimanded by MPs today for showing lack of leadership as the NHS system for training junior doctors descended into chaos last year. ... Giving evidence to the committee this year, Donaldson said that he did not have 'sole or overall responsibility' for attempts to restrict applications from non-EU doctors.' But the committee report says it found "this excuse weak and unconvincing".' [153]

The system of governance came in for criticism by the Commons Select Committee on Health. Their report said that:

> '... attempts to limit the number of applications from foreign doctors were badly managed, while governance systems were overcomplicated, with roles ill-defined and lines of accountability irrational and blurred.' [154]

The criticism may be valid, but the advice in favour of having a single person who is responsible and who alone can be held to account may simply not accord with the modern-day realities of complex organisations. As we saw with the Baby P case, this is particularly so where partnership working is built into the structure, where responsibilities may need to be held jointly. In such instances, a system for holding numbers of managers jointly to account would be appropriate and should be used, but this is rarely practised.

The Commons Select Committee's own interrogation process (of individuals like Sir Liam Donaldson) itself invites the question of whether MPs should criticise accountability systems. The unquestioned default here, as in business, is that

---

153　Carvell, J. (2008) 'MPs blame lack of leadership for doctors crisis'. London: *The Guardian*, 8 May.

154　Hawkes, N. (2008) 'Foreign doctors fiasco lambasted by MPs'. London: *The Times*, 8 May.

the system always assumes *individual* accountability, and its cross-questioning processes only serve to reinforce that notion. But at times it is essential to treat accountability as shared, as in this example:

> An airline's operations, engineering and security departments were not communicating with each other. They were locked in their 'silos'. Staff members with problems or needs that required liaison with one of the other departments understood that the strongly hierarchical system required them to pass the issue up the chain of command. At some senior level, the manager would speak to his/her counterpart, who would pass the message down.
>
> In order to break the silo behaviour, the senior manager responsible for overseeing all three departments launched a project to change the behaviour and announced that he would be holding the three departmental heads *jointly* to account for the success of the project. This meant that they needed to plan, agree and manage the project together and then report back as a trio.[155]

■ A duty to cooperate

In connection with the Victoria Climbié case (discussed on pages 112-113) the Audit Commission report identified that Children's Trusts were failing to ensure that the various parties were fulfilling their duty to cooperate. So what did the Government do? It announced that it would hold each of the parties individually to account. At first glance this sounds fine, but it is actually the opposite of what the government should be doing. Individual accountability reinforces each party's perception from their own silo's perspective and encourages them to point the finger elsewhere. If you want the parties to see themselves as a joint service and to be managed as a team, they need to be held to account *collectively*. In practical terms that means two things:

First, they must be brought together and *collectively* charged with proposing *upwards* (to government – effectively the Secretary of State for Health) for how they will themselves collectively manage their duty to cooperate. Secondly, they must be brought together to account to government for how they have cooperated collectively.

Accountability in change programmes

Major change programmes that involve a number of partners raise several issues of accountability. The attraction of concentrating accountability in one person on the client side can have damaging side effects.

> A company manager was making use of two consultancies on a single change programme. The consultancies needed to coordinate their work. The manager instructed the consultancies not to communicate directly, but to work through him; he would provide the necessary linkages. The upshot was that no relationship was able to build between the consultancies. Spontaneity and trust didn't develop. Progress was slow. Communication was filtered, interpreted and politically biased.

---

155 Robson, I. (2006) *ibid.*

But what was the alternative? If the manager had given permission for the two consultancies to sort things out between themselves, he would have given up some of his control. He would not have known what was happening. In his own mind, this left him vulnerable. How could he be held accountable by his boss if he had let go of the reins?

There was an added dimension in the case cited. The purpose of the change project was to promote various new values including and using the principle of distributed leadership. Other stated new values included more risk-taking, greater empowerment, faster decision making, and more partnership working. What behaviour was being modelled in the management of the contract? Was that even recognised as a valid question?

In asking 'Does this organisation need to be tighter or looser?', it is clear that the answer is looser; the new ways of working would mean some letting go of the controlling method of working that was dominant in the organisation.

The project manager's way of working could have been the result of:

- The organisation's culture and a strongly individually centred system of holding managers to account.
- A laudable and acute sense of responsibility for spending the company's funds on consultancy.
- A strong personal need to control.
- Mere habit.

In the context of projects of this nature one can ask:

1. How can the way the project is managed model the organisation's desired new ways of working?
2. How can an appropriate new way of project managing enable the project manager to test out and learn about the stresses for other managers in the organisation that are associated with making the transition to a new style?
3. How well equipped is the project manager's own line manager to hold the project manager accountable appropriately? Is the line manager equally trapped and unable to see the options?
4. Who are the consultants accountable to?
5. What responsibilities does the project manager have to the consultants?
6. Should the client/consultant relationship be viewed as a partnership, with the parties together being accountable to the client's chief executive/top team?

SUMMARY OF CHAPTER KEY POINTS

1. In many organisations the discipline of accountability is unimaginatively conceived, poorly understood, relatively neglected and badly executed.

2. A practical and formal system of accountability needs to be part of the management of executives in every organisation, and their expectation.

3. Using their leadership, senior executives need to provide supervision or 'oversight', including holding their managers to account, and they in turn need to be subject to these disciplines.

4. Holding managers to account is not just a post hoc activity for an organisation to engage in once something has gone wrong. Holding managers to account is an inherent part of managing individual managers' and executive teams' ongoing performance.

5. Managers can be held to account separately for their managing and leading, for taking care of both today and tomorrow, and for particular change projects.

6. Accountability is a powerful lever to use with managers where change needs to happen. To bring about change, it is the boss's job to agree an overall minimum standard and to manage a process by which executives are held to account for how they propose to meet that standard by working with others. This is a model of leadership by pulling change upwards rather than pushing change downwards.

7. Responsibility is not the same as accountability. And responsibility to and for others are different. Instead of thinking just upwards, managers have responsibilities for and to their staff, and to their peers and colleague managers, and should appropriately be held to account for these. The latter process is usually, but not inevitably, to a single person within the executive's hierarchy.

8. Business organisations are accountable to their shareholders for how they discharge their duty to their company, which includes responsibilities to all stakeholders.

9. Managers in their capacity as students and learners have responsibilities to their developers and coaches, and not just the other way round. Evaluation and monitoring processes can capture behaviour against these responsibilities in both directions.

10. The first question for an organisation to ask itself is: 'For what and how should senior managers be tested, challenged and formally held to account, especially regarding their leadership where it is most important and when it is most needed?'.

11. The second question is: 'How clear, well developed, understood, respected and observed is the current system for holding managers to account, and how can it be improved?

Conclusion

When undertaking a research project in 2002 for HM Government's Council for Excellence in Management and Leadership (CEML), I pressed the case to consider a level of leadership beyond the individual leader and beyond collective leadership teams. I described this organisational level as 'systemic'. I was told that such a level was not recognised by the top leadership academics and could not be considered.[156]

To this day, the systemic level of leadership remains a major blind spot among the majority of academics in this field. The same holds true for the independent management colleges and centres, and professional bodies and institutes. Such neglect limits the study of leadership and hampers businesses and their management teams in making progress. A few organisations, a few sectors, and a few consultancies show a dawning interest.

Seven years on from CEML, the case for bringing a systems perspective to leadership remains as relevant and important as ever.

Inventing the future of management

In May 2008 a group of 30 of 'the world's most progressive business thinkers' met at Half Moon Bay in California for two days to contemplate why the practice of management is such a failure and unfit to solve the 21st Century's challenges.[157] Prompted by Professors Gary Hamel and Julian Birkinshaw from London Business School, the approach:

- encouraged the experts to throw off one hundred years' worth of assumptions about how to organize human effort and start with a clean sheet of paper;
- dared them to radically re-imagine the ways in which companies create strategies, make key decisions, allocate resources, mobilise talent, and coordinate activities;
- challenged them to turn the conventional management model upside down with the goal of creating organisations that are as adaptable and innovative as the people who work there.

Styled as 'renegades', those invited were 'individuals who have demonstrated a capacity to imagine bold alternatives to the management status quo, an eclectic mix of visionary executives, provocative authors, renowned business school professors, and bleeding-edge* technologists'.

---

156 For more about this project, see (Tate, 2000).

157 Management Lab (2008) *Management 2.0*™: *Inventing the Future of Management.* London: London Business School, 28 May. www.managementlab.org [accessed 11 March 2009].

[NB: * Adapted from Wikipedia, the *bleeding edge* may be harmful and draw blood since it lies in front of the 'cutting edge'. It exists under the following conditions:

Lack of consensus – there are competing ways of doing some new things and no one knows which way the market will go.

Lack of knowledge – organisations are trying to implement something new that the journals have not yet started talking about, either for or against.

Industry resistance to change – journals and industry leaders have spoken against something, but some organisations are trying to implement it anyway because they are convinced it is superior.]

According to observer Simon Caulkin, 'the very presence of such a group under one roof was eloquent testimony to the urgency of the underlying premise: management is broke (sic) and needs fixing'.[158]

> Most participants agreed that although modern management had achieved much, like all obsolescent paradigms it had itself now ossified into a formidable barrier to progress. The charge sheet against it is long. It does exploitation better than exploration; yet efficiencies are running out of steam. Consumer cynicism leads to increasing marketing budgets for diminishing returns. Employee disengagement is at record levels. Too often, internal change only comes about through crisis or coup.
>
> Even worse than wasting resources, today's zero-sum management imposes ever heavier burdens on society as a whole: witness the credit crunch, colossal inequalities and the pillaging of Earth's resources without provision for the future. Citizens trust neither big companies nor their bosses. In short, a discipline that evolved as a technology of compliance to enable mass production is simply unable to address the much wider issues involved in building organisations fit for the 21st century.[159]

Some of those present have been urging action for many years:

'Unless [American business] gets off its destructive kicks – the mindlessness of managerial groupthink, the mercenary "me" of shareholder value and executive compensation, all the noise and the hype – it will be in deep trouble.' (Henry Mintzberg, 1999)

What emerged from Half Moon Bay was a *crie de coeur* for innovation in management and a licence for experimentation.

'Decouple power and position; allow the led more choice over their leaders; reverse the flow of accountability; broaden the leadership franchise – all with the aim of dissolving (formal) hierarchy, eliminating silos and collapsing the distance between centre and periphery.'[160] (One of the challenges from Management Laboratory.)

---

158 Caulkin, S. (2008) 'It ain't what you change, it's the way that you do it'. London: *The Observer*, 22 June.

159 Caulkin, S. (2008) *ibid.*

160 Management Lab (2008) *Labnotes 'TopCoder'*, No. 8. London: London Business School, 28 May. www.managementlab.org [accessed 11 March 2009].

None of this can come about without leadership. But it is leadership itself that needs to change. In this book we have spoken of this Catch 22 and its in-built resistance to change.

> 'We can't solve problems by using the same kind of thinking we used when we created them.' (Albert Einstein)

A manifesto for improving leadership

Leadership is a key dimension of management, and *The Search for Leadership* expresses a similar sentiment to that of Management Laboratory's '*Management 2.0*' project. As with management, leadership isn't in rude health and needs more than a wake-up call.

The same can be said of leadership development. Too often this seems content to improve individuals' performance at the margins but is unable to produce the step change required to make organisations better led. This comes as no surprise: a provider focus on individuals can never deliver a true organisational outcome. Lacking a pull that is based on the system's needs, learning is at best tactical, and the system will resist individuals' attempts at change.

Caulkin points out that little of what emerged from Half Moon Bay was new. 'The need for higher purpose, distributed direction and strategy-making, building of community and citizenship, increasing trust and driving out fear – have a familiar ring.' It was not surprising therefore that one participant claimed that the main effort should go into propagating the essence of what's already known, believing that implementation was required more than innovation. Good point. Besides the thought leaders, where are the action leaders who have access and clout?

Even implementation can suffer from a poverty of imagination, and a lack of courage, risk-taking, experimentation and openness to challenge. Witness the performance of the government and especially the so-called Delivery Unit operating out of the Prime Minister's office at Number 10 Downing Street, London. Critics accuse the Unit of relying on top-down exhortation and bullying, advocating crude targets coupled with financial incentives, believing in all-powerful strong leaders, pushing false public choice, denying managerial discretion, undoing the close-to-the-customer rule, a corrupting commercialisation of public guardians, and placing naive faith in big IT schemes – all ragged vestiges of the 20th century paradigm.

Progress means tackling armies of vested interests. As Donald Rumsfeld, ex-Secretary of the US Department of Defense, might have put it, they know what they know about leadership, and they know that they don't want to know what they know they don't know and don't know they don't know. On this point Rumsfeld was right. The other obstacle to a systemic approach to leadership is that people like a simple answer to the question 'Who is in charge?'. They want to know who to write to, who to blame, and who to promote, reward and fire. They find comfort in heroes and scapegoats.

For managers to lead and for organisations to have leadership requires an understanding, respect and working with the grain of the system. Several writers, Caulkin and Seddon among them, have been bravely and doggedly writing for years about the need to take a systems perspective on organisations, leadership and management, and getting hardly a hearing. There is the ever-present paradox – you have to work with the old to create the new. While recognising the forces of tradition that defend the familiar model of relying on individual leadership, the message in this book adds to that drive by proposing that a systemic model be applied. This book is a call for greater organisational literacy at the top of organisations based on a systems perspective of the role of leadership.

The system is in denial

Leadership interventions come about for several reasons. Sometimes a provider makes an offering to develop leaders. Managers may take action to obtain some form of leadership development for themselves. But mostly it's the system that identifies and targets people – individuals, classes of individuals and teams – that are deemed to be in need of, or able to benefit from, improvement, development, enhancement, counselling, coaching, feedback, etc. They are 'they', and don't include 'us'. 'They' and their performance are ring-fenced; that is, they are seen and responded to with a disregard for their context and what surrounds them, even though psychology teaches us that the 'individual and the environment are indivisible'.

Those responsible for the system – including government ministers – fail to understand the role the system is playing in people's performance, while it is the system that leads to their being identified as needing training and development. They also know little of the role the system will play in limiting desirable change.

If this were not enough, the intervention does not challenge or direct itself towards the system, but accepts its brief to work with those to whom it has been given access. An example: a prison governor hires developers to coach prisoners to raise their self-esteem, while being blind to how the prison system affects the prisoners. In business too, prevailing and constraining mental models about systems, leadership and various parties' roles holds everyone captive and longing for release.

This book has highlighted many other issues, needs and opportunities: Organisations tempering external supply-push pressure with their own demand-pull diagnosis. The scope for spotting and stopping waste and bridging spaces. The part played by chaos theory and organisation's shadow side, and the need to accept the non-rational nature of management and leadership. And the sad and destructive addiction to an extrinsic view of human behaviour - a dated model that persists with a structure of hierarchical controls, power differentials, targets, monitoring, incentives and punishments, in spite of the evidence that approaches based on intrinsic theories of behaviour are better at developing self-responsibility and proactivity.

It goes without saying that the factors described above hold serious implications for the role, learning and performance of those in leadership roles. It is equally clear that the implied change required is massive and needs to start at an early age. These factors are part of what surrounds managers and leadership interventions in organisations: these environmental factors include values, assumptions and mental models embedded in the culture of any organisation and the business world and society generally, and in the basic training, education and nurturing processes experienced by people in organisational life.

However we define 'system' – narrowly in an organisational context, or broadly in a societal context – the issues, solutions and progress keep bringing us back to our opening question: what are we surrounding people with? And the answer and the culprit? It really is the system, stupid! Look for it and you will see it.

Two steps forward, one step back – if we are lucky

Let's return to the book's beginning, both literally where I talked about searching inside the organisation if you want to find leadership, and also in terms of its origins in 2003. The initial idea of leadership as a resource spun off in multiple directions, all of them strands of systemic leadership. It therefore came as a shock to come across works much later that offered the same advice and used much of the same language. Especially shocking was that they vastly pre-dated my own work.

In *Why Leaders Can't Lead: The Unconscious Conspiracy Continues* (1989), Warren Bennis bemoans 'the idolatry of celebrity executives, the short-term bottom-line obsessions that blind managers to the true importance of human resources, the wilful distortion of reality to promote self-interests, and the unbridled greed of the 1980s' (yes, that long ago!). He claims that these societal developments contribute profoundly to the unconscious conspiracy against leadership.

James Krantz's *Lessons from the Field: An Essay on the Crisis of Leadership in Contemporary Organizations* (1990) makes painful criticisms of organisations and leadership that sound just like those we face today. The western economy is in collapse as bank chiefs behave in 'commander-in-chief' mode. Krantz proposed building 'systemic leadership capacity' as the answer. Yet he was writing in 1990. How can there have been so little learning since then?

The leadership challenge

When taking up their job, most managers who see themselves as having a clear leadership role gradually lose sight of their high hopes and aspirations for change and improvement. They fall victim to the pressures that come upon them. They find themselves reacting to demands, requests and circumstances. The managers become bureaucratised; their jobs are eroded by entropy. They forget why they were put there. The challenge to overcome this trap is mental. All managers should produce and then keep alive in their mind a plan for how to structure, prioritise and use time and resources for that part of the job that concerns their *leadership* role. They need to write answers to these questions on a piece of paper, keep it to hand, remind themselves, and reflect frequently on them:

- What am I trying to achieve with my leadership?
- What do I need to change around here?
- Who are my customers and what do they need from me?
- What are my leadership priorities?
- How will I manage the time I need to allocate to my leadership role?
- How will I enable others to use their leadership?
- What is the system doing to me and what am I doing to the system?
- How will I successfully account for my leadership?

The challenge for me and for you the readers is this:

Is *The Search for Leadership* destined to be just another of the hundreds of books published each year on the subject of leadership? Or can it ignite a much-needed systemic spark in our organisations?

If you want to pour water on the idea, all you need to do is nothing. If you want to blow oxygen onto the embers and start a fire, if you want to be part of a different leadership perspective, indeed if you want to take a lead, then do please contact me to continue the discussion.

William Tate
Jumps House, Churt, Surrey, UK
01252 792322
bill.tate@prometheus-consulting.com

APPENDIX ONE:

SYSTEMIC LEADERSHIP – AN OVERVIEW

The systemic leadership model constitutes a new paradigm for the improvement of leadership in an organisation. The systemic approach challenges the traditional paradigm focused on individual leader and leadership development. It can be defined as:

> *Improving the way an organisation is led, based on an understanding of the organisation as a system, focused on the interdependency between leadership and the organisation, concerning how leadership is applied, managed and developed.*

For appropriate leadership to flourish and bring benefits, the organisation's persona and needs have to be brought firmly into the frame. The systemic approach permits this by using organisation psychology and OD techniques, and by applying management development more strategically.

The book and its diagnostic toolkit shine a light on what goes on, and what needs to go on, in the organisation if appropriate leadership is to come to the fore and be applied. The approach helps managers to see and understand what they need to do with their leadership energies, ideas and skills to help the organisation. And it helps the organisation in turn to permit and assist leadership and enable it to flourish.

The uncomfortable truth about leadership in organisations – its identification, development and application – is that it is more challenging and complex than the popular development mindset and the army of developers would have us believe. It cannot be left to individual managers to try to work out the organisation's leadership needs, to remove the obstacles to leadership in their path, and to succeed alone as leaders. Nor can providers of development have the full picture, interest and responsibility, least of all for ensuring that leadership can be and is appropriately applied.

By using the systemic approach, organisations reclaim control of the full leadership agenda and take practical responsibility for making system-wide improvement, both in leadership capability and in using leadership to improve the organisation.

The quest reaches beyond the familiar focus of individual leadership to embrace 'leadership of, by and for the organisation'. The new model:

- addresses factors in the organisational 'system' that have a bearing on the practice and delivery of leadership, including barriers to leadership;

- targets the 'glue' that is needed to bind together the various system components (hierarchy, power, tenure, accountability, etc.) if the organisation is to manifest leadership and be well led;
- concentrates on the myriad of gaps and spaces in the system and in relationships in searching for enhanced organisational capability, as well as in individual managers' leadership competence;
- is concerned with outcomes (the resulting organisation improvement), outputs (applied leadership practice), and not just inputs (leader and leadership development);
- recognises that development of individual capability is just one of a number of levers available for improving the organisation's leadership;
- acknowledges that all the organisation's stakeholders have a legitimate interest in improved leadership.

Ultimately, the organisation's leadership is manifested through individuals. Within the systemic model these people provide personal leadership in a way that is mindful of the organisation's needs, and the organisation makes this possible. The development of such leadership draws upon what is currently happening in and to the organisation.

The essence of the approach

1. It begins with a clear aim; namely, working on the organisation as a system to enable appropriate leadership to flourish so that, in turn, the enterprise will be well led.

2. The organisation becomes clear about its particular need for leadership by its managers, and adopts a definition of leadership that distinguishes the activity from that of managing.

3. An honest analysis reveals the scope for improvement in the way the organisation works, and the way that leadership works. The organisation then uses this to pull a matched response into itself, and not be dependent on providers' supply push.

4. It embraces the novel perspective that leadership is a key resource that needs to be managed. Managing leadership requires pulling on a wide range of levers in the organisation that influence the delivery of appropriate and applied leadership.

5. The organisation is understood and managed as a system. This system is a powerful force and contributor that can either open or close doors to improved leadership. That system is part of managers' everyday environment, and it needs managing more than the individual managers if leadership is to flourish (like a fishtank is to fish).

6. Every system has its own shadow side. Many leadership issues, such as the use of power, need understanding, managing and improving whilst keeping the shadow in mind.

7. Improvement for the organisation comes ahead of development for the individual, and appropriately applying leadership comes ahead of increasing capability.

Everything else flows from this and is summarised below.

Leadership levels

Systemic leadership focuses on level 3 below, and uses this level to inform, drive and integrate leadership at the first two levels.

1. Individual managers
2. Managerial teams
3. The organisation

Strategies

- Spreading the power of leadership to achieve improvement and change ('distributed leadership') by involving practicing leaders at all levels in both diagnosing and making the changes needed.
- Leveraging the organisation's own distinctive systemic contribution to improving leadership.
- Clarifying what is happening externally and internally to the organisation that has a bearing on how the organisation and its leadership has to adapt.
- Anchoring development activity in the organisation's evolving context using OD methods.
- Considering all improvement activities, not just development programmes, including the targeting of organisation variables as well as people ones.
- Combining learning and doing to realise organisationally applied benefits.

Managing leadership

It is not enough to develop managers as leaders and leave them to work out what to apply their new leadership skills to. Treating and managing leadership as a key organisational resource means:

- clarifying and communicating the organisation's own needs for leadership;
- improving the leadership culture and relevant leadership-related systems, policies and procedures (alongside individual and team capability);
- identifying what are the organisation's enablers of leadership, and what are the obstacles and removing them;

- targeting for improvement action both leadership development and applied leadership practice;
- linking individual, collective, and whole-system leadership
- balancing and integrating supply- and demand-side perspectives and actions;
- aligning the organisation's structures, systems and processes to support leadership;
- taking a range of action along the employment spectrum;
- discovering the numerous gaps down which leadership and its potential falls and is wasted, and taking appropriate action;
- building relational competence between senior executives, hierarchical levels and departmental silos;
- putting appropriate mechanisms in place to ensure that executives are properly held to account specifically for their leadership on an ongoing basis.

What the systemic leadership model is good at

- Raising managers' awareness of what leadership means in their organisation, how the organisation and leadership need to change, and the part they can play in this.
- Changing managers' perceptions; for example, that:
  - the way the work works (a systems perspective) is often more significant than the way the people work
  - a manager's job is to improve the system and what surrounds people, more than to blame/improve the people.
- Saving money by not spending it on mass training to change people (who are only doing what the system expects of them and which can thwart their attempts at improvement).
- Distributing leadership by giving a large number of front-line managers the authority and means of helping to improve the way the organisation works and where and how it applies leadership.
- Building a state of discontent around aspects of the organisation's current functioning (either of leadership or requiring leadership), and galvanising energy to do something collectively about it.
- Identifying strategic leadership priorities.
- Identifying needed shifts in the leadership style, culture and climate.
- Considering what is in the organisation's environment and teasing out the implications for leadership to act or change the organisation or leadership itself.
- Allowing the organisation's norms to be held up for questioning.
- Enabling managers to discuss things that they would not normally find the time, permission or a safe environment to do.

- Revealing that the source of most organisation dysfunction is not a manager's personality or lack of skills, but a system shortcoming.
- Seeing the wider company picture and generating loyalty beyond managers' narrow technical specialisms and departmental silos.

HR processes relating to leadership

1. Defining leadership.
2. Specifying the organisation's leadership requirements.
3. Identifying managers with leadership qualities.
4. Recruiting leaders and leadership capability from outside.
5. Selecting managers to fill leadership vacancies.
6. Spotting the managers who will make good leaders.
7. Rewarding the managers with high leadership ability.
8. Developing leadership talent.
9. Developing leadership processes.
10. Placing and utilising leadership in the key jobs.
11. Appraising managers' leadership performance separately from their managing.
12. Promoting managers with leadership qualities.
13. Retaining managers with leadership talent.
14. Rotating managers proactively to reinvigorate and broaden their leadership.
15. Planning for the succession of leaders.
16. Removing obstacles in the path of managers and their leadership.
17. Plugging relationship gaps between executives, hierarchical levels and departments.
18. Managing and limiting the tenure of senior executives.
19. Moving managers who are poor leaders.
20. Retiring leaders who are past their sell-by date.
21. Facilitating the holding of executives to account for their leadership.
22. Rejuvenating the leadership culture.

Neglected and undiscussed aspects of leadership

- How to review the leadership process within an accountability structure.
- The organisation's handling of power, where there is either too much or too little.
- Managers' perceptions of their leadership role.

- Where leadership gaps occur and how leadership is wasted.
- The way the hierarchy functions, either to facilitate or to thwart managerial leadership.
- How the act of leading is performance managed separately from that of managing.
- What managers think the leadership psychological contract is.

Appendix Two:

The *Systemic Leadership Toolkit*

This is a practical toolkit used by organisation developers, facilitators and consultants as the basis for a high-level intervention in an organisation. Carried out with experienced managers, its purpose is to improve systemic leadership in organisations; i.e. the way leadership is applied to benefit the organisation as a whole and the business it serves.

The intervention begins with a substantial diagnostic phase undertaken in a workshop setting. Groups of practising managers speak from their experience, identifying opportunities for improvement in how the organisation works, and planning remedial action accordingly. The diagnosis covers the relevant organisational and leadership issues contained in this book.

Experience shows the risks of such interventions falling short of their transforming potential. For this reason, and based on practical use in interventions, the toolkit comes with a comprehensive guide offering advice on how each of the parties involved should conduct themselves for the intervention to have the greatest chance of being successful. The parties discussed include the chief executive, the top team, participating managers, internal Learning & Development/HR departments, MD and OD professionals and external consultants, facilitators and providers.

The toolkit is designed by William Tate and published by Triarchy Press.

Copies of the toolkit and further information can be obtained from:

www.triarchypress.com

William Tate
+44 (0)1252 792322
bill.tate@prometheus-consulting.com

Triarchy Press
+44 (0)1297 631456
info@triarchypress.com

Bibliography

Alimo-Metcalfe, B. and Alban-Metcalfe, J. (2008) *Engaging Leadership: Creating Organisations that Maximise the Potential of their People* (a 'Shaping the Future' report). London: Chartered Institute of Personnel and Development.

Alimo-Metcalfe, B., Ford, J., Harding, N. and Lawler, J. (2000) *Leadership Development in British Organisations – at the Beginning of the 21st Century* (research report). London: Careers Research Forum.

Angier, N. (2007) *The Canon: A Whirligig Tour of the Beautiful Basics of Science*. New York: Houghton Mifflin.

Bennett, N., Wise, C., Woods, P. and Harvey, J. A. (2003) *Distributed Leadership* (report). Nottingham: National College for School Leadership.

Bennis, W. (1989) *Why Leaders Can't Lead: The Unconscious Conspiracy Continues*. San Francisco: Jossey-Bass.

Bentley, T. (2008) *Systems at Work* (paper). Australia: The Space Between Pty Ltd.

Bentley, T. (2001) 'The emerging system: A gestalt approach to organisational interventions', *British Gestalt Journal*, Vol. 10, No. 1.

Birchmore, T. (2003) *Psychodynamics of Scapegoating, Persecution, Bullying* (paper). www.birchmore.org [accessed 11 March 2009].

Bolden, R. (2007) *Distributed Leadership*, a 'Discussion in Management' paper, 07/02. University of Exeter: Centre for Leadership Studies.

Bolden, R. and Gosling, J. (2006) 'Leadership competencies – time to change the tune?', *Leadership*, Vol. 2, No. 2. Sage.

Burke, W. W. (1972) 'The role of training in organization development', *Training and Development*, American Society for Training and Development, Vol. 26, No. 9.

Brecht, B. (1965) *The Messingkauf Diaries* [aka Dialogues]. London: Methuen.

Cavicchia, S. and Coffey, F. 'Gestalt in an Information Technology Organisation: A Case Study' in *The British Gestalt Journal*, 2005, Vol. 14, No. 2, pp 15-25.

Chapman, J. (2002) *System Failure*. London: Demos.

Cohen, M. D., March, J. G. and Olsen, J. P. (1972) 'A garbage can model of organizational choice'. *Administrative Science Quarterly, 17*(1).

De Pree, M. (1989) *Leadership is an Art*. London: Arrow Business Books.

(2007) 'Destructive leadership', *The Leadership Quarterly*, Vol. 18, Issue 3, June. Amsterdam: Elsevier.

Egan, G. (1994) *Working the Shadow Side: A Guide to Positive Behind-The-Scenes Management*. San Francisco: Jossey-Bass.

Egan, G. (1988) *Change Agent Skills 'A': Assessing and Designing Excellence*. San Diego: University Associates.

Fry, S. (1992) *Paperweight*. Quality Paperbacks Direct.

Gabriel, Y. (1996) 'The Hubris of Management', paper delivered at the Symposium 'Organizations 2000: Psychoanalytic Perspectives'. International Society for the Psychoanalytic Study of Organizations.

Gamblin, C. *et al* (2001) 'Essential leadership competencies', adapted from *Managing in the New Economy*. London: Centre for Tomorrow's Company.

Gemmill, G. (1986) 'The Dynamics of the Group Shadow in Intergroup Relations', Sage Journals: *Small Group Research*, Vol 17, No. 2.

Gillen, T. (2008) *Leadership or Management? The Differences* (member resource), May. London: Chartered Institute of Personnel and Development.

Gladwell, M. (2002) 'The Talent Myth', *New Yorker*, 22 July.

Goffee, R. and Jones, G. (2000) 'Why should anyone be led by you? What it takes to be an authentic leader'. *Harvard Business Review*, September-October.

Hayward, M. (2007) *Ego Check: Why Executive Hubris is Wrecking Companies and Careers and How to Avoid the Trap.* New York: Kaplan Publishing.

Heller, R. (2001) *Roads to Success.* London: Dorling Kindersley.

Iles, P. and Preece, D. (2006) 'Developing leaders or developing leadership?:The academy of chief executives' programme in the North of England', *Leadership*, Vol. 2, No. 3: Sage.

Jackson, D. (2004) *Distributed Leadership: spaces between the pebbles in a jar.* Nottingham: National College for School Leadership.

Jacobs, J. (1992) *Systems of Survival: A Dialogue on the Moral Foundations of Commerce and Politics.* New York: Random House.

Janis, I. J. (1972) *Victims of Groupthink.* Boston: Houghton Mifflin.

Jordan, J. (1980) *Passion: New Poems.* June M. Jordan Literary Estate Trust.

Jung, C. G. (1964) Part 1: 'Approaching the Unconscious', in Carl G. Jung *et al.*, *Man and his Symbols.* Doubleday Windfall.

Katz, D. and Khan, R. L. (1978) *The Social Psychology of Organizations.* New York: Wiley.

Kauffman, S. (1996) *At Home in the Universe: The Search for Laws of Self-Organization and Complexity.* New York: Oxford University Press.

Kearns, P. (1995): *Measuring Human Resources and the Impact on Bottom Line Improvement.* Hitchin: Technical Communications (Publishing) Ltd.

Kotter, J. (1990) *A Force for Change: How Leadership Differs from Management.* New York: Free Press.

Krantz, J. (1990) 'Lessons from the Field: An Essay on the Crisis of Leadership in Contemporary Organizations.' *The Journal of Applied Behavioral Science*, Vol. 26, No. 1, pp 49-64.

Lewin, K. (1951) *Field theory in social science: selected theoretical papers*, D. Cartright (ed.). New York: Harper & Row.

Lewin, R (1999) *Complexity: Life at the Edge of Chaos.* Chicago: The University of Chicago Press.

Lloyd-Jones, E. (2008) *The Forward March of Children's Justice Halted* (pamphlet). Axminster: Triarchy Press.

Luthans, F (1988) 'Successful vs. effective real managers'. *Academy of Management Executive*, 2(2).

Mangham, I. (1975) 'Organisation behaviour: Whatever made you think that organisation behaviour was to do with people?', *Industrial and Commercial Training*. MCB University Press.

McCrimmon, M. (2006) *Zaleznik and Kotter on Leadership*. www.leadersdirect.com [accessed 11 March 2009].

McCrimmon, M. (2007) 'Leader or Manager, Which Are You?'. *Business Management*, 12 December.

McCrimmon, M. (2008) 'What is Organization Development?'. *Human Resources Management*, 2 June.

Milgram, S. (1974) *Obedience to Authority: An Experimental View*. HarperCollins.

Mintzberg, H. (1999) 'Managing Quietly', *Leader to Leader*, No. 12, Spring. Jossey-Bass.

Mintzberg, H. (1987) 'The Strategy Concept I; Five P's for Strategy', *California Management Review*, Fall.

Pedler, M., Burgoyne, J. and Boydell, T. (2004) *A Manager's Guide to Leadership*. Maidenhead: McGraw-Hill Professional.

Powers, W. T. (1973) *Behavior: The Control of Perception*. Chicago: Aldine.

Rensberger, B. (1986) *How the World Works: A Guide to Science's Greatest Discoveries*. New York: William Morrow.

Salaman, G. (2004) 'Competences of managers, competences of leaders', in Storey, J. (ed.) (2004) *Leadership in Organizations: Current Issues and Key Trends*. London: Routledge.

Scott-Morgan, P. (1994) *The Unwritten Rules of the Game: Master Them, Shatter Them, and Break Through the Barriers to Organizational Change*. Maidenhead: McGraw-Hill Education.

Seddon, J. (2008) *Systems Thinking in the Public Sector*. Axminster: Triarchy Press.

Seddon, J. (2003) *Freedom from Command and Control*. Buckingham: Vanguard Education.

Senge, P. M. (1990) *The Fifth Discipline: The Art and Practice of the Learning Organization*. Century Business.

Shaw, P. (2002) *Changing Conversations in Organizations: A Complexity Approach to Change*. London: Routledge.

Sievers, B. (1999) 'The Organization Shadow', Orgdyne Global Village at www.orgdyne.ning.com [accessed 11 March 2009].

Skynner, R. and Cleese, J. (1984) *Families and How to Survive Them,* (in 'An afterthought on Paranoia and Politicians'). Oxford: Oxford University Press.

Stacey, R. D., Griffin, D. and Shaw, P. (2000) *Complexity and Management: Fad or Radical Challenge to Systems Thinking*. London: Routledge.

Stacey, R. D. (1996), *Complexity and Creativity in Organizations*: San Francisco: Berrett-Koehler.

Storey, J. (ed.) (2004) *Leadership in Organizations: Current Issues and Key Trends*. London: Routledge.

Tate, W. (2007) 'Organisational leadership wins', *CEO Today*, October. London: Sovereign Publications.

Tate, W. (2006) 'Looking inside the organisation for leadership', *Developing HR Strategy,* May. Kingston upon Thames: Croner Publications.

Tate, W. (2005) 'Training people for a better future', *Finance Today*, May. London: Sovereign Publications.

Tate, W. (2005) 'Working with the shadow side of organisations', *Developing HR Strategy*, May. Kingston upon Thames: Croner Publications.

Tate, W. (2004a) 'Linking development with business' (ch.) in Storey, J. (ed.) (2004) *Leadership in Organizations: Current Issues and Key Trends.* London: Routledge.

Tate, W. (2004b) *Communication in the shadows* (paper); delivered to Institute of Ethics conference, Lincoln University.

Tate, W. (2003a) *The Organisational Leadership Audit.* Axminster: Cambridge Strategy Publications.

Tate, W. (2003b) *The Organisation Shadow-Side Audit.* Axminster: Cambridge Strategy Publications.

Tate, W. (2003c) *The Business Innovation Audit.* Axminster: Cambridge Strategy Publications.

Tate, W. (2002) 'Leadership and Governance' in *The Corporate Social Responsibility Manual.* London: Spiro Press.

Tate, W. (2000) *Implications of futures studies for business, organisation, management and leadership.* Council for Excellence in Management and Leadership, Department of Trade and Industry.

Tate, W. (1999) *Demerging Organisations: A Best Practice Guide.* London: Financial Times Management.

Tate, W. (1997) 'Developing an integrative framework for corporate competence' (paper delivered at conference *Competence – a source of competitive advantage*). Leicester: The Centre for Labour Market Studies, University of Leicester.

Tate, W. (1995a) *Developing Corporate Competence: A High-Performance Agenda for Managing Organizations.* Aldershot: Gower Publishing.

Tate, W. (1995b) *Developing Managerial Competence: A Critical Guide to Methods and Materials.* Aldershot: Gower Publishing.

Turquet, P. (1974) 'Leadership: The individual and the Group' in Gibbard, G., Hartmann, R. and Mann, J. (eds.) *Analysis of Groups.* San Francisco: Jossey-Bass.

Vaughan, D. (1996) *The Challenger Launch Decision: Risky Technology, Culture, and Deviance at NASA.* Chicago: University of Chicago Press.

von Bertalanffy, L. (1968) *General Systems Theory: Foundations, Development, Applications.* New York: George Braziller.

Vroom, V. H. (1964) *Work and Motivation.* New York: Wiley.

Waterman, R. H. (1987) *The Renewal Factor.* New York: Bantam Books.

Whyte, W. H. (1952) 'Groupthink'. *Fortune* Magazine.

Xin-An Lu (2000) *"Public Secrets" as a Phenomenon in Organizational Communication: How Public Knowledge Fails to Become Organizational Action.* New York: iUniverse.

About the Author

WILLIAM TATE MA, FCIPD, MCMI, FRSA

William Tate is a consultant, writer, researcher, teacher and speaker in leadership, organisation development, the shadow side, change and learning, innovation and corporate social responsibility (CSR). He runs the independent consulting practice *Prometheus Consulting*. He is also a director of *Conduct Becoming*, a CSR consultancy.

A long career at British Airways included responsibility for management training and for human resource strategy and planning. He was part of a small team involved in the airline's privatisation and culture-change programme, where he worked alongside Professor W. Warner Burke of Columbia University, New York. He studied organisation psychology with Professor Gerard Egan in Chicago.

William is a prolific writer, having authored six earlier books and many magazine and journal articles, plus researching papers for The Chartered Institute of Personnel and Development, the Council for Excellence in Management and Leadership, and the Centre for Tomorrow's Company. He has taught Strategic HRM and Corporate Social Responsibility at London's City University Cass Business School on its Executive MBA Programme.

ABOUT THE PUBLISHER

Triarchy Press is an independent publishing house that looks at how organisations work and how to make them work better. We present challenging perspectives on organisations in short and pithy, but rigorously argued, books.

We have published a number of books by authors who come from a Systems Thinking background. These include: *The Three Ways Of Getting Things Done* by Gerard Fairtlough; *Management F-Laws* by Russell Ackoff, Herb Addison and Sally Bibb; *Systems Thinking in the Public Sector* by John Seddon and *Erasing Excellence* (published in the USA as *Liberating the Schoolhouse*) by Wellford Wilms.

Other titles in the area of leadership include *Ten Things To Do in a Conceptual Emergency* by Graham Leicester and Maureen O'Hara and *Leadership 2.0* by Jemima Gibbons (forthcoming).

Through our books, pamphlets and website we aim to stimulate ideas by encouraging real debate about organisations in partnership with people who work in them, research them or just like to think about them.

Please tell us what you think about the ideas in this book. Join the discussion at:

www.triarchypress.com/telluswhatyouthink

If you feel inspired to write - or have already written - an article, a pamphlet or a book on any aspect of organisational theory or practice, we'd like to hear from you. Submit a proposal at:

www.triarchypress.com/writeforus

For more information about Triarchy Press, or to order any of our publications, please visit our website or drop us a line:

www.triarchypress.com
info@triarchypress.com

GLOSSARY

Accountability	A governance process by which managers may be held to account for the discharge of their responsibilities.
Adaptive capacity	The capacity of a social-ecological system to adapt to its changing environment without losing options for the future.
Arational (compare with irrational)	Non-rational. Neutral, not necessarily negatively 'irrational'.
Basic Assumption Dependency (Wilfred Bion's Theory)	Dependency is one of three group states in which members of a group share a basic assumption that the group is sustained by a leader on whom it depends for having its nourishment, material, spiritual and protection needs met, with corresponding disempowering consequences for members.
Business (compare with organisation)	Essentially outwardly focused and profit driven. Business factors are concerned with why the company exists and how it survives; e.g. brands, customers, prices, markets.
Business model	Answers the question: 'How will this company make money out of what it is doing?'.
Chaos theory (also see Complexity Theory/Science)	Allied with Complexity Theory/Science. Explains how complex and unpredictable results can and will occur in systems that are sensitive to their initial conditions. Explains how very simple things can generate complex outcomes that could not be predicted by looking at the parts by themselves.
Commercial Syndrome	One of two types of 'survival system' in society (the other being 'guardian syndrome'). Based on trading, precepts include 'compete', 'use enterprise' and 'be efficient'.
Complexity Theory/Science	The scientific study of complex systems. Concerned with self-organizing phenomena and the effect of one subsystem behaviour on another.
Climate (compare with culture)	How it feels around here at the moment. A psychological state as perceived by individuals and teams at a group, departmental or whole organisation level.
Culture (compare with climate)	How things are round here: a mix of the organisation's values, norms and collective behaviours.

Dark side (compare with shadow side)	Undesirable aspects of the shadow side (in organisations, and also in individuals) which holders, as well as those who are impacted by the holder's personality or behaviour, do not view in a favourable light and might seek to hide, to cast into their unconscious shadow or project onto others in order to protect their self-image.
Demand-side issues (compare with supply-side issues)	Interests, issues and needs prompted by awareness of, and concern about, the client organisation, that enables it to 'pull' the solutions and services it needs and wants, rather than be beholden to provider/supplier interests.
Dispersed leadership	(See 'Distributed leadership'.)
Distributed leadership	Where leadership responsibility and action on behalf of the organisation is widely dispersed and shared through the hierarchy by interaction. The opposite of an organisation's command-and-control style of functioning, where leadership is reserved for a small cadre of senior members of the hierarchy.
Edge of Chaos	A point between excessive stability and anarchy where an organisation remains manageable while ready for change.
Entropy	The process of naturally occurring and increasing disorder, disintegration, disorganisation, decline, degeneration, disease and decay.
Ethos	The set of fundamental values held by a group or organisation. Characterises the tone or culture of an organisation.
Environment	Those things which surround the manager or unit in question, which may be an individual (e.g. supervision), department (e.g. targets), organisation (e.g. labour market), or business (e.g. competition) which, in an 'open system' (q.v.) need to be factored in when understanding, analysing or considering the manager's or unit's performance.
Fishtank and fish	A metaphor for an organisation as a receptacle for its employees (fish), which considers the tank as a source for all those things that the organisational system surrounds people with, such as culture, policies, rules, etc., and other 'effluent' contributed by those with responsibility for the fishtank as well as by the tank's inhabitants, which result in the tank's contamination, making it difficult, energy-sapping and unsafe to navigate.

Fundamental Attribution Error	The tendency for people to over-emphasise personality-based explanations for behaviours, while under-emphasising the role and power of situational influences.
General Systems Theory	Postulates that traditional closed system thinking cannot explain the types of systems that are found about us in our world. Emphasises holism over reductionism and organism over mechanism.
Guardian Syndrome	One of two types of 'survival system' in society (the other being 'commerical syndrome'). Precepts include 'shun trading', 'be loyal', 'adhere to tradition' and 'treasure honour'.
Going/working upstream	A metaphor for thinking more strategically and preventatively about possible action that can be taken to address problems associated with people (e.g. addressing causes of bullying, and not just helping victims).
Governance	Is concerned with accountability and responsibilities; it describes how the organisation is directed and controlled. Relates to decisions that define expectations, grant power, or verify performance. Is either a separate process or a specific part of management or leadership processes.
Groupthink	A mode of thinking that people engage in when they are deeply involved in a cohesive in-group, when the members' strivings for unanimity override their motivation to realistically appraise alternative courses of action.
Holding to account	A management process by which managers, or managerial teams, may be called before a superior or a panel or forum and asked to account for their action, inaction or performance.
Held (to be or to have been) accountable	A manager or management team, deemed (beforehand) to be, or to have been deemed (afterwards) to be responsible for a particular activity or outcome, especially when things have gone wrong.
Irrational (compare with arational)	Negatively or anti-rational.
Leader development (compare with leadership development	A variety of means and processes designed to enable learning, skill, behaviour and/or attitudinal growth to occur to build capability; most commonly focused on individuals in some form of management development activity.
Leadership (compare with management)	A role undertaken some of the time by managers concerned with improvement and change in order for an aspect of the organisation to be become fitter.

Leadership development (compare with leader development and with leadership improvement)	Used by many synonymously with (individual) leader development. May alternatively be used to focus on developing the process of leadership, which may introduce into the equation other individuals and their relationships.
Leadership improvement (compare with leadership development)	A wider concept than leadership development, taking into account non-people variables in the organisational system, which may include changes which do not necessarily entail training, education or learning experience, activity or take place in such venues (e.g. restructuring the system for holding executives to account).
Management	Concerned with delivering today's agenda within the existing paradigm.
Manager /management development (compare with organisation development)	A variety of activities and ways of intervening in organisations where the focus is generally on individual managers (including teams of managers) with the aim of improving their capability and the(ir) process of managing, irrespective of whether the organisation (and its own variables such as structure, culture, values, processes) is also being directly targeted for improvement).
Milieu	All those things in an employee's environment; i.e. those things that an organisation surrounds its people with, in which they have to survive, be able to see, feel nourished, etc. (e.g. culture, climate, rules, relationships, targets, bureaucracy, etc.).
Open system	State of a system, in which it continuously interacts with its external environment and is capable of self-maintenance on the basis of throughput of resources from that environment.
Organisation (compare with business)	The organisation is the set of internal arrangements at the service of the business. These internal arrangements enable a soundly conceived business to succeed; e.g. skills, culture, rules, leadership.
Organisation(al) capacity (compare with organisation(al) capability)	A measure of what the organisation has the potential to do based on its resources and how roles, responsibilities and authority are allocated and marshalled. (May be spoken of jointly with capability.)
Organisation(al) capability (compare with organisation(al) capacity)	A measure of what the organisation has the potential to do based on its competence and that of its managers and employees and their collective effort and relationships. (May be spoken of jointly with capacity.)

Organisation(al) development (OD) (compare with management development)	A variety of activities and ways of intervening in organisations where the focus is on the 'soft' elements of the internal aspects and dynamics of the organisation as an entity (rather than individuals and their skills) with the aim of improving the way the organisation works, its effectiveness, efficiency, culture, climate and wellbeing.
Organisational leadership (compare with systemic leadership)	A way of viewing overall leadership in, of, by and for an organisation that combines the leadership contribution of people and non-people resources and systems.
Organisation model	Answers the question: 'What is the best way of organising ourselves to serve the business objectives?'.
Paradigm	A thought pattern, philosophical or theoretical framework.
Perceptual Control Theory	A model of how a human being must be internally organised to accomplish the controlling process.
Shadow network	The web of informal relationships and communication flows inside an organisation, and across organisation boundaries, that fall outside the official structure of the organisation and its planned roles, relationships and processes.
Shadow side (compare with dark side)	The informal, unofficial, non-rational aspects of an organisation and its character, dynamics and communication.
Shadow system	How the various aspects of an organisation's shadow side can be understood and managed as a system.
Stakeholder	All those parties who have an interest in a business's operations, either impacting them or being impacted by them. Principally customers, employees, investors, supplies and society. Many others, including media, regulators, institutes, etc.
Supply-side issues (compare with demand-side issues)	Interests, issues and needs prompted by awareness of, and concern about, the suppliers/providers of products, services, solutions, programmes that can be 'pushed' onto clients.
System	A dynamic and complex whole, interacting as a functional unit. The system is a community situated within an environment. Energy, material and information flow along the different elements that compose the system.

Systemic leadership	1. Manifestation of organisation-wide leadership as an effective and integrated system, serving the business and all its stakeholders. 2. An improvement and management model that treats the organisation as a whole system, including the environment that surrounds individual leaders. 3. The focus given to the way that managers contribute their individual leadership abilities to achieve systemic leadership for the organisation. 4. Also used synonymously with organisational leadership.
Systems perspective	A way of conceiving of an issue or of an organisation and aspects of how it works that is based on how the various parts fit and work together as a whole system.
Systems thinking	A management discipline or framework that is based on the belief that the component parts of a system can best be understood in the context of relationships with each other and with other systems, rather than in isolation.

INDEX

Index

Index

Index

Praise for *The Search for Leadership*:

Leading change has become the mantra of the moment, and Tate's book is a timely and highly significant contribution towards our thinking about the interactions between an organisation and leadership, and how each influences the other in an open systems model. His work is thoughtful, clear and highly practical. *Professor W. Warner Burke, Edward Lee Thorndike Professor of Psychology and Education, Teachers College, Columbia University, New York City*

In his fascinating new book Bill Tate offers a fresh perspective for thinking and talking about leadership in organisations, looking beyond individual leadership development to the systemic development of leadership, equipping organisations as systems to use leadership to continuously change and adapt. Full of practical tips and insights, this is a 'must read' book for any leadership or organisational development practitioner who wants to make a difference to business success. *Linda Holbeche, Director of Research and Policy, Chartered Institute of Personnel and Development*

William Tate has written a comprehensive assessment of the leadership debate and, in a congested arena, found space for a different way of understanding leadership from which new applications can be developed. He asks the critical question 'How does the system work to deliver leadership and ... take advantage of it?' After a testing review of the conventional approaches to leadership, in the second half of the book he tests his proposition by assessing his systemic approach against key criteria. The book deals with an unclear subject with great clarity and contains many practical measures for the practitioner in addition to a thorough analysis of the subject of leadership. *Keith Cameron, HR Director, Marks & Spencer (2004-2008)*

This is a refreshing, insightful and above all, useful book on leadership in organisational contexts. It is a pleasure to read and it offers a practical road map for understanding and improving organisations and the way they are led. *John Storey, Professor of Management, The Open University Business School*

Our work in the Management Lab at London Business School calls for nothing less than wholesale reinvention of how to run companies. Bill's latest book makes a valuable, timely and highly practical contribution to that debate. The travails in the financial sector show how urgent and deep the need is. His forthright, informed and practical style shows organisations how to assess their system's leadership needs and how to go about getting them met using a systemic perspective. The financial crisis in Britain's and western economy brings into sharp relief how badly broken are our models of management and leadership. Bill's bold model shows how a systemic approach sheds light in some dark corners that are badly in need of illumination and improvement. *Julian Birkinshaw, Professor of Strategic and International Management, London Business School*

Praise for *The Search for Leadership:*

Organisations spend a fortune developing leaders, most focusing on the individual rather than the organisation. Without addressing leadership as a fundamental part of the organisation the organisation will never progress. Bill Tate proposes that the organisation must address leadership as a corporate responsibility. Organisations that value leadership flourish, but to achieve this all the various levels of management must embrace leadership, with systems and processes that support the ethos. *Dr Richard Cullen, former Director of Training and Development, Metropolitan Police Service*

Seeing leadership from the organisational rather than the individual dimension makes obvious sense - you can train individual swimmers to perfection but put them in a swamp and the dynamic changes completely. In this book, Bill Tate rightly re-focuses the lens onto the organisation itself in a series of simple, clear and relevant examples. As someone who has used the diagnostic Organisational Leadership Audit, I believe this offers insights that simply cannot be achieved in other ways; you might have gut feelings, but do you have the evidence? The first step is, however, for the leadership to look at itself and realise what its organisation needs. This book is that first step. *Jon Lamonte, Air Vice-Marshal, Royal Air Force*

Bill's insights into systems leadership enable developers to move beyond short-term operational needs and pressures. The book provides the language and rational argument that will enable the kind of strategic conversations with your executive to transform the way that leadership is developed in organisations. Let's stop polishing the fish and tackle the dirty tank instead! *Karen McKenzie-Irvine, VP Learning & Development, Metronet Rail*

Bill Tate has produced a book to challenge both orthodox thinking on leadership, and shift the focus to the organisation. He cleverly mixes generic concepts with case studies and real experience, in a blend of the commercial and public sectors. There is also a neat diagnostic tool to ensure engagement with the approach articulated. This book is a valuable addition to the corpus of leadership doctrine. *Robin Field-Smith, Her Majesty's Inspector of Constabulary*

Much has been written about personal leadership, but until now very little about leadership's organisational purpose. William Tate offers a journey of discovery, looking through the other end of the telescope and focusing on what leadership should really be about – engaging directly with the organisation's needs. Tate's book de-mystifies the complexity and theory of leadership in a practical and systematic way, enabling the reader to appreciate the strong inter-dependency between the leadership process and organisations looking for wholesale improvement. This ground-breaking work should be read by all who are interested in improving the way their organisation works and how it is led. *Richard Crouch, Head of Human Resources and Organisational Development, Somerset County Council*

Printed in the United Kingdom by
Lightning Source UK Ltd., Milton Keynes
142592UK00001B/63/P